COLORADO

SUMMIT Hikes
For Everyone

Dave Muller

The Colorado Mountain Club Press
Golden, Colorado

Published by The Colorado Mountain Club Press. Founded in 1912, the Colorado Mountain Club is the largest outdoor recreation, education and conservation organization in the Rocky Mountains. Look for our books at your favorite book seller or contact us at:
    710 10th Street, Suite 200, Golden, CO 80401,
    Phone: (303) 996-2743, Email address: *cmcpress@cmc.org*,
    Website: *http://www.cmc.org/cmc*

Managing Editor for CMC Press: Terry Root.
Graphics Design and Maps: Terry Root and Steve Meyers.
Proofing: Linda Grey.
All photographs in this book by Dave Muller, except as credited.
Front cover photo: Tyler Stableford ©.
Back cover photo: courtesy of The Colorado Mountain Club.
Title page photo: Torreys Peak by Nelson Chenkin.
Text copyright 2003: Dave Muller.

Colorado Summit Hikes For Everyone
by Dave Muller
Library of Congress Control Number: 2003112178
ISBN # 0-9724413-3-6

(Material from this book has been published previously under the title *Colorado Mountain Hikes For Everyone,* by Dave Muller, Quality Press: Denver, Colorado, 1998.)

We gratefully acknowledge the financial support of the people of Colorado through the Scientific and Cultural Facilities District of greater metropolitan Denver, for our publishing activities.

The
Colorado
Mountain
Club's

CMC CLASSICS *series*

of guidebooks explores the very best of the Colorado Rockies as only the CMC can. With nearly a century of experience, leading 2,000 outings a year into the backcountry, we've earned the title *experts in the Rockies.* Discover new wonders, hike or ski a classic route, scale a famous fourteener — we'll lead you there with these authoritative guides. Income from sales helps to support our mission of conservation and outdoor education.

Classics
This symbol indicates hikes that have become **CMC Classics** — favorites of the Colorado Mountain Club, enjoyed year-after-year. We recommend these hikes because of their outstanding scenic or wilderness qualities — or because they are just, plain fun!

Classics
Colorado's best from the experts in the Rockies

Meet The Author

Author Dave Muller has been hiking in the Colorado mountains for 30 years and finds that being in the mountains promotes renewal and reflection. Since 1988, he has written a popular "Hike of the Week" and "Cross-Country Ski and Snowshoe of the Week" column for the *Denver Post.* He has also authored two other Colorado guidebooks: *Colorado Lake Hikes For Everyone* and *The Colorado Year Round Outdoor Guide* (available 2003), both published by the Colorado Mountain Club Press. A psychiatrist, Dave lives with his wife, Jackie, in Denver.

Thanks From The Author

The assistance and encouragement of many persons were necessary for the completion of this hiking guide. My parents, Irish-American Margaret and Swiss-German Albert, nurtured me in many ways and encouraged walking. My wife, Jackie, has provided excellent home support and accompanied me on some of these hikes. My children have been special partners in my mountain explorations. My two eldest sons, Paul, who started it all by daring me to climb Pikes Peak with him, and Tom, who has made many a summit possible, deserve special mention. Mairi Hamilton Clark assisted with enthusiasm by typing the text. I am also grateful to my many hiking companions especially Tony Bianchi, Mary Brewer, S. Macon Cowles, Larry Currier, D.J. Inman, Jim Mahoney, Andrew Muller, Matthew Muller, Sara Muller, Jim Sherman and Harve Smith. Above all, I thank the Lord of the Universe who provides us with such wonderful playgrounds.

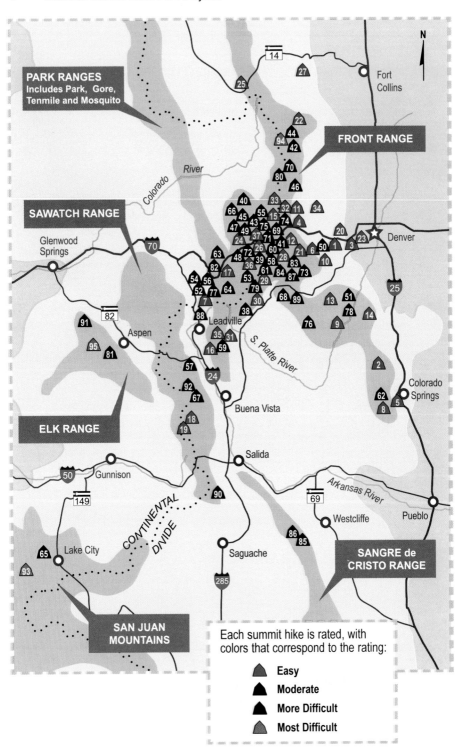

TABLE OF CONTENTS

Hiking Colorado's Summits 9
How To Use This Guide 13
Wilderness Responsibilities 19
Safety On The Hike 20

THE HIKES	SPECIAL FEATURES (see page 16-17)	PAGE
1 Genesee Mountain		24
2 Ormes Peak		26
3 Mount Falcon		28
4 Fox Mountain		30
5 Mount Cutler		32
6 Squaw Mountain		34
7 Chalk Mountain		36
8 St. Peters Dome		38
9 Cheesman Mountain		40
10 The Brother		42
11 Fairburn Mountain		44
12 Alps Mountain		46
13 Baldy Peak		48
14 Devils Head		50
15 Colorado Mines Peak		52
16 South Peak		54
17 Royal Mountain		56
18 Emma Burr Mountain		58
19 Fitzpatrick Peak		60
20 Mt. Zion and Lookout Mtn.		62
21 Chief Mountain		64
22 Lily Mountain		66
23 Green Mountain		68
24 Coon Hill		70
25 Diamond Peaks		72
26 Mount Sniktau		74
27 West White Pine Mountain		76
28 Geneva Mountain		78

THE HIKES	SPECIAL FEATURES *(see page 16-17)*	PAGE
29 Glacier Peak		80
30 Mount Volz		82
31 Round Hill		84
32 Kingston Peak		86
33 Mount Epworth		88
34 Tremont Mountain		90
35 Mount Sheridan		92
36 Revenue Mountain		94
37 Woods Mountain		96
38 Little Baldy Mountain		98
39 Kelso Mountain		100
40 Bottle Peak		102
41 Griffith Mountain		104
42 Horsetooth Peak		106
43 Red Mountain		108
44 Estes Cone		110
45 Vasquez Peak		112
46 Caribou Peak		114
47 Mount Trelease		116
48 Grizzly Peak		118
49 Mount Bethel		120
50 Bergen Peak		122
51 Raleigh Peak		124
52 Resolution Mountain		126
53 Bald Mountain		128
54 Hornsilver Mountain		130
55 Twin Cones		132
56 Jaque Peak		134
57 Quail Mountain		136
58 Mt. Wilcox and Otter Mtn.		138
59 Horseshoe Mountain		140
60 Sugarloaf Peak		142
61 Whale Peak		144
62 Mt. Manitou and Rocky Mountain		146
63 Buffalo Mountain		148

THE HIKES	SPECIAL FEATURES *(see page 16-17)*	PAGE
64 Peak 8	📷 🍃	150
65 Matterhorn Peak	📷 🌼 🌀 ⛰	152
66 Bills Peak	📷 ⛰	154
67 Birthday Peak	📷 🌼 ⛰	156
68 North Twin Cone Pk. and Mt. Blaine	📷 🍃 🌼 🚲 🏃	158
69 Republican Mountain	📷 🔭 🚲	160
70 Paiute Peak	📷 🌼 ⛰ 💲	162
71 Ganley Mtn. and Pendleton Mtn.	📷 🌼	164
72 Grays Peak and Torreys Peak	📷 🌼 🔭 🏔	166
73 Rosedale Peak	📷 🌀 ⛰	168
74 Breckinridge Peak	📷 🌼 ⛰ 🏔	170
75 Engelmann Peak and Robeson Peak	📷	172
76 Bison Peak	📷 🔭 🍃 🌀 ⛰	174
77 Corbett Peak	📷 🌼 🏔	176
78 Long Scraggy Peak	📷	178
79 Mount Guyot	📷 🌼 🌀	180
80 Satanta Peak and Mount Neva	📷 🌼 ⛰	182
81 Mount Buckskin	📷 🌼 🍃 🌀 ⛰	184
82 Uneva Peak	📷 🌼 ⛰	186
83 Bandit Peak	📷 🔭 ⛰	188
84 Kataka Mountain	📷 🍃 ⛰	190
85 Comanche Peak	📷 🌀 ⛰	192
86 Venable Peak	📷 🌀 ⛰	194
87 Mount Logan	📷 🔭 ⛰	196
88 Buckeye Peak and Mount Zion	📷 🌼 🔭 🚲 🏃	198
89 South Twin Cone Peak	📷 🍃	200
90 Antora Peak	📷 🔭 🏔 🏔	202
91 Mount Sopris and West Mt. Sopris	📷 🌼 🌀	204
92 Iowa Peak	📷 🌼 ⛰	206
93 Engineer Mountain	📷 🚲 🏃	208
94 Pagoda Mountain	📷	210
95 Capitol Peak	📷 🍃 ⛰	212

Resource Guide 215

Scrambling on Capitol Peak (Terry Root)

HIKING COLORADO'S SUMMITS

Colorado's Rocky Mountains form a spectacular roof, capping the western United States. With 54 peaks over 14,000-feet high, over 1,500 others that extend above timberline and nearly 4,000 individual summits in all, Colorado offers an alpine playground with some of the best hiking and climbing opportunities in the world. Excellent access to this mountain paradise is courtesy of a maze of developed roads and trails that reach the most scenic areas. Yet, Colorado's mountains still contain wild and pristine places that will thrill any backcountry user.

This guide describes 105 summit hikes that explore some of the best that the Colorado Rockies has to offer. Many have either not appeared before in other guides, or have lacked certain details or emphasis which the author considers important. With the tremendous interest in hiking and climbing summits in Colorado, special care has been made to avoid some peaks that are overly popular. Instead, you will get to know for yourself many lessor-known and uncrowded gems, hopefully experiencing the same sense of discovery as the author. These routes are intended for a wide variety of hikers with different skill and experience levels. The beginning hiker, the newcomer to Colorado, families with children, those with certain physical limitations and even the advanced hiker will all find routes of interest in this guidebook.

None of the hikes require special technical ability or equipment. The routes cover peaks ranging from 6,000 feet to over 14,000 feet in height and are situated throughout the vast topography of the Colorado mountains. Users of this guide, who reach even just a sampling of the varied summits, will nonetheless come away with a deep appreciation of the splendor and majesty of the Colorado Rockies.

Mountain Geography

While the Colorado mountains have been divided into dozens of individual ranges, it is useful and common to speak of six main geographic sections or groups, listed from east to west: the *Front Range*, the *Sangre de Cristo Mountains*, the *Park Range* (including familiar sub-units of the Park, Gore, Tenmile and Mosquito Ranges), the *Sawatch Range*, the *Elk Mountains* and the *San Juan Mountains* . Most of these groups run in a general north-south direction, with exceptions being the Elk Mountains which trend west and east and the expansive jumble of the San Juan Mountains. The *Continental Divide* winds through these ranges

Fast moving, late afternoon thunderstorms are typical in the summer. (Terry Root)

for nearly 700 miles, creating headwaters for many of the nation's major river systems and effectively dividing the state and its communities into the "Western Slope" and the "Eastern Slope." Looking at the map on page 4, please notice that this guide contains summit hikes in all of the six major ranges and on both "slopes" of the Divide.

Mountain Climate and Weather

Classics

23

spring

72

summer

68

autumn

Within the huge elevation gradient that exists in the mountains of Colorado, climate is relative to location. A warm, sunny day in the foothills may present near winter-like conditions on the high peaks. Even in one location, mountain weather can be unpredictable, with large temperature swings throughout the day, or as Coloradans are wont to say, "If you don't like the weather, wait ten minutes."

None of the summit hikes in this guide are described as winter outings. We can make some general observations about what you might expect from the remaining three seasons. In **spring**, the high peaks are still gripped with snow, with most hiking opportunities occurring on the foothill peaks, especially those with southern exposures. March through May can be comfortably warm, but often can be windy as well. Sudden, spring storms can dump fresh snow on the mountains, closing off access to even the lowest peaks in the foothills, for a few days. The arrival of **summer** brings low humidity, sunny mornings, stormy afternoons and clear nights to the Colorado high country. From July through August, warm (and even hot) conditions prevail, offering access to even the highest summits in this guide. It is critical get an early start on your hike, as severe local thunderstorms typically rack the mountains on most afternoons. While brief and fast moving, these storms contain high winds, rain or hail and dangerous lightning. **Autumn**, though heartbreakingly short in the high country, can be the best time of all to experience many of the summit hikes in this book. Days are crystal clear, with less chance of late-day storms; while nights are quite crisp. The quaking aspen turn ablaze and the tundra is carpeted with rich, fall colors. During this less-crowded time of year, the mountain world seems to pause and reflect, before the first snow falls in early October. Soon the storms arrive in earnest, closing off the high peaks for another year; but many of the foothill summits in this guide can be enjoyed for several more weeks.

Mountain Geology

The present-day Rockies began to take shape about 70 million years ago, during a massive uplift called the *Laramide orogeny*. After a long period of erosion reduced these ancestral Rockies to mostly rubble, a second period of mountain building began about 26 million years ago, pushing the peaks close to their present height. An intense period of glaciation over several thousand years, ending only recently in geologic time, helped shape and scour the landscape to the forms that we see today.

Classics

79

cirque

46

lake

85

fault-block

73

mineral

7

mining

Pikes Peak granite on Bison Peak. (Terry Root)

The several processes involved in creating the Rockies have resulted in many rock types to be found on the summit hikes in this guide, including examples of the three main classifications: *igneous*, *sedimentary* and *metamorphic*. Hiking up these summits, you will also discover interesting landforms and features that result from both the recent and ancient geologic past: for example, glacial cirques, alpine lakes, fault-block ranges and unusual minerals, including the gold and silver bearing deposits that fed Colorado's great mining era.

Mountain Lifezones

Classics

10
foothill

44
sub-alpine

29
alpine

The Colorado summits described in this book range in altitude from foothill peaks, shoved up against the Plains at 6,800 feet, to the highest peaks in the Rockies at over 14,000 feet, providing the summit hiker with a remarkable variety of habitats to experience and enjoy. Three *lifezones* are represented on these summits, each with characteristic plants and animals.

The **Foothills** begin at the edge of the Plains' grasslands and range to an elevation of about 9,000 feet. Summits here typically have fine, open stands of ponderosa pine on their south-facing slopes, with dense forests of Douglas fir on their northern exposures. A thick, riparian forest flourishes along rivers and streams, supporting numerous bird species. Beaver, porcupine, skunk and fox are common, with herds of mule deer and elk as winter migrants. The hiker on a foothill summit will be eye-to-eye with red-tailed hawks, climbing thermals from more than a thousand below.

The **Subalpine**, between altitudes of 9,000 to 11,000 feet, is a rich and varied environment with dominant forests of Englemann spruce and subalpine fir. The dark, shady spruce-fir forests support more solitary-like animals such as black bear, mountain lion, lynx and wolverine. In higher forests, ancient and wind-blasted bristlecone pine and limber pine replace the spruce-fir forest near timberline. Burned-over areas soon become clothed with fast-growing aspen or lodgepole pine. Aspen groves are very rich in life with abundant bird species, as well as mule deer and elk. The understory is open enough to harbor showy displays of summer wildflowers. Summit hikers, pausing for lunch on one of these subalpine peaks, will likely soon meet the gray jay, or *camp robber*.

At about 11,000 feet, the cold and wind begin to preclude upright trees, producing stunted versions, shaped by those elements of the high **Alpine**. Above that, the trees give way to the tundra which holds a wide variety of habitats, including nearly impenetrable willow stands, rocky and gravelly areas with scattered cushion plants, fell fields of boulders, snowbeds with meltwater bogs beneath, and lush meadows of tussock grasses. Hugging the ground are hardy alpine wildflowers, sharing this harsh landscape with interesting animal species, among them marmot, pika and white-tailed ptarmigan. Lucky summit hikers in the alpine may spot a magnificent bighorn sheep ram, silhouetted along a high ridge, or mountain goats patrolling the ledges of a steep cliff face.

Bighorn sheep (Dave Stewart)

HOW TO USE THIS GUIDE

Each summit hike is rated as *easy*, *moderate*, *more difficult* and *most difficult,* with background colors that correspond to the rating (see below). Ratings are based on distance, elevation gain, and special challenges of the route. The hikes are presented in ascending degree of difficulty. When two peaks are listed for one hike, the rating applies to the difficulty in reaching both summits combined. Note that these ratings are highly subjective, and what may be easy for a seasoned hiker, may be difficult for another. Start with a few easier summit hikes. After a few hikes, you should be able to get an idea of what level is right for you.

 EASY

 MORE DIFFICULT

 MODERATE

 MOST DIFFICULT

Information Box

Each hike description begins with an *information box* that displays important key facts about the outing. Use this information to quickly tell whether this hike is right for you and your abilities.

The **Hike Distance** shown is the mileage each way between the trailhead and the summit; in other words, the "one way" distance. Double this number to determine the round-trip distance for that outing. When there is a loop hike, with different ascent and descent routes, the two respective distances are given. If there is a hike with multiple destinations, then distances are given "point-to-point." In these latter cases then, just add all the distances for the total hiking distance.

The time required for each hike, the **Hiking Time**, is divided into ascent and descent times and, when applicable, time necessary between two summits. These times were achieved by the author (a middle-aged, non-smoking "peakbagger" in good condition) and include brief, but not significant, breaks of a few minutes. Obviously, your times may be more or less, depending on your conditioning, your hiking habits or the condition of the trail. You should use these times simply as a yardstick. After a few hikes, you should be able to determine whether to add or subtract any time for future planning.

Starting Elevation and **Elevation Gain** are self explanatory. However, the latter is especially important in assessing the energy required for a summit hike. Sometimes, extra elevation gain is noted. This can occur if some elevation gain is lost, due to traveling through a dip or saddle, that must be re-gained; or if there is elevation gain required on a descent.

On the trail beneath Capitol Peak (David Hite)

The **Trail** listing takes note of how much of the hike, if any, is traveled on a trail. A trail is reassuring to most hikers, although some enjoy the greater feeling of adventure from off-trail travel. When there is bushwacking involved in the hike, this is noted, often with a modifier such as "tundra and talus" or "some hand work or scrambling." Please note, that with the single exception of the last outing in this guide, there are no routes that involve extended rock scrambling.

The knowledge and use of map and compass, as well as attention to features of the terrain, are necessary skills for any of the hiking trips in this book, but are especially critical for bushwacking. If you own a GPS receiver, you will want to establish several "waypoints" from the trailhead to the summit. These can be invaluable in navigating your return. Remember, dozens of people get lost in the Colorado Rockies each year. Don't be one of them.

The optimal time of the year for that hike is indicated by **Season**. On average, this is when the route is most likely to be free of snow. However, there is no such thing as an "average" year in the Rockies. Some winters are more severe and long-lasting than others. Routes on south-facing slopes, in years with less than average snowfall, will often open up several weeks earlier than listed. Conversely, north-facing routes may stay snow-covered well into summer, after a particularily severe winter. The first significant snowfall can occur as early as September, or as late as November, in the high country. The hiking season in Colorado is generally from early June through early October; but many of the peaks described in this guide, especially those at lower elevations, may be accessible over a longer period.

You will want to check with the management agency for the **Jurisdiction** that contains your hike, in order to learn about the condition of your intended trail. Closures are not uncommon due to weather, fire or maintenance issues. You will find a list of management agencies, and their addresses, in the *Resource Guide* in the back of this book. Please take special notice when your intended hike enters a jurisdiction where special regulations are in force, such as a federally designated Wilderness Area.

Several types of relevant **Maps** are listed. The *USGS 7½'* series, usually called "topos" by users, are the most detailed. They are excellent for interpreting natural features, but may not reflect the most recent man-created features, such as roads or trails. The *County* maps listed are also issued by the United States Geological Survey, in cooperation with local agencies. These are produced in sets covering each county and are similar to topos, but at larger scale. *USFS* maps are issued by the Forest Service within each jurisdiction. These are more useful for showing general features, such as access roads and facilities, than for use in the field. Maps offered by *Trails Illustrated* are commercially produced, and now cover virtually all of Colorado. They offer topographic features, good detail and are weather-proof and tear-resistant. Finally, we list maps that are sometimes available for local parks, usually in kiosks right at the trailhead. (Also, it is worth mentioning that there are several software packages now available for consumers that allow home printing of maps at various output qualities.)

Directions to the Trailhead

Trailheads are described from some close-by point of reference, such as a town, major highway or interchange. Obviously, the best way to get to somewhere is determined by where you start. Often, two different routes may be listed (for instance, from the north or from the south) but you may find another route more convenient. To the left of the description is a box, which graphically shows at a glance, the condition of the access road to that trailhead. While there are very few hikes in this book that need a vehicle with four-wheel drive for access, there are several accesses on semi-rough, dirt roads that may become impassible to regular passenger cars during certain times, or be difficult in spots for low-clearance vehicles. Once again, check with the managment agency for that jurisdiction, if you have questions about road conditions.

RATING THE ACCESS ROADS: These symbols indicate the normal condition of the access road.

 The trailhead can be reached by a normal passenger car. The road is paved or well-graded dirt or gravel

 The road is rough and ungraded. The trailhead can usually be reached by a normal passenger car with adequate clearance. (Poor road conditions at certain times of the year or after severe weather may limit access or require high-clearance or even four-wheel drive.)

 The trailhead can ONLY be reached by a four-wheel drive vehicle with high clearance.

The Hike Descriptions

The text presents detailed descriptions for each hike. To minimize the chance for becoming lost or confused, special effort has been taken to give clear, unambiguous information about the route, without a lot of extraneous information. (But you will find a lot of useful, secondary information in the *FYI* boxes.) Emphasis is on distances, compass directions and landmarks. In most cases, the word "trail" signifies a foot, bicycle or stock route, maintained by a management agency. In several cases, the word also applies to unmaintained "game" trails and to primitive roads. "Bushwack" means to walk through forest, field or underbrush without benefit of trail. "Off-trail" is similar in meaning, but in this guide, applies to walking cross-country in open areas, such as above treeline. "Tundra" refers to the grassy landscape above treeline at higher elevations. "Scree" is a collection of small rocks and gravel on a mountainside, as opposed to "talus" which is a mass of rocks, ranging from fist-size to small boulders. A "couloir" refers to a narrow ravine on a steep mountainside. Finally, a "saddle" is a low point or pass between two summits or highpoints.

The final paragraph of the hike descriptions sometimes indicates optional possiblities for creating a loop trip or for continuing the hike to other close-by summits. Obviously, distances and elevation gain will typically increase from those indicated in the *information box* for that hike, if you choose one of these options.

Hikes With Special Features or Outstanding Qualities

To the left of the hike description are symbols that convey additional information about special features or outstanding qualities of each hike. Many of these summit hikes are particularily ideal for special activities, such as wildlife or wildflower viewing, for families or persons with disabilities, or for hanging out with your canine companion. We also use symbols here to alert you when a hike shares a portion of the well-known Colorado Trail or the Continental Divide Trail, or if the hike enters a federally designated Wilderness Area, where special use regulations may apply. Some of these summits are even great for mountain bicyclists, looking for a challenging ride, or for trail runners. You will find a complete **Legend** describing all the symbols used for identifying special hikes on the facing page. The special characteristics of each hike are also listed in the *Table of Contents* on pages 4 through 7.

Classics

Some of these summit hikes have become **CMC Classics** — favorites of the Colorado Mountain Club, that are enjoyed year-after-year. We highly recommend these hikes because of their outstanding scenic or wilderness qualities — or because they are just, plain fun! But remember, the most rewarding *classics* are the ones that you discover yourself.

Scenic Hikes: Of course, any trip to a Colorado summit is a scenic adventure. But with this symbol, we indicate truly outstanding examples. It may be a wonderful summit panorama, or a view of famous fourteeners or a chance to marvel along the way at examples from Colorado's storied, gold/silver rush history. You'll want to have your camera ready on these hikes.

Family Hikes: This symbol indicates a good hike for families with small children, for hikers with limited mobility, or for seniors who are looking for a less-strenuous hike. These summit hikes are short, with modest elevation gain, and on well-maintained trails. All of them are in the "Green" section (portion of the book with easier hikes.)

Wildlife Hikes: Here we indicate hikes where you have a good chance of viewing some of our spectacular Rocky Mountain wildlife. Wildlife viewing is possible on any hike in this book; but in the text for these hikes, we indicate some unique or, better-than-average opportunites. You can increase you chances of viewing animals on any hike by being out early or late in the day.

Wildflower Hikes: The Colorado Rockies are justifiably famous for spectacular displays of summer wildflowers. Many of the hikes in this book are excellent for viewing plants in all three, encountered lifezones. But the hikes indicated here are especially wonderful, with many species represented in large numbers. Peak times are early May (foothills) to early July (high peaks.)

Doggie Hikes: This symbol shows hikes that you may enjoy sharing with your canine companion. Few of the hikes in this book restrict dogs; but we have tried to choose outings where dogs typically are welcome and common. Dogs have varying abilities, just like people. We have picked hikes that have good trails, suitable for most dogs. Remember to keep your dog leashed and under control.

Trail Running: Trail running in the mountains is a growing sport, particularily around the urban centers of the Front Range. We have picked out a handful of good ones that are recommended by enthusiasts. Since most people are not ultra-marathoners or long-distance runners, we have chosen short to moderate runs, on good trails, with modest gradients.

Geology/Geography Hikes: The Colorado Rockies have been shaped by complex forces over millions of years. Any hike in this book has a fascinating story to tell in its rocks and landforms. We have only picked a handful of hikes that have something truly interesting about them.

Fall Hikes: Autumn in the high country is a magic time, as aspen leaves change to golden hues and the tundra becomes a soft carpet of muted reds. We indicate hikes here that will delight your senses and consume rolls of film! The fall season is short — from early September to early October — with peak times varying from year to year, according to weather.

Bike Trips: Mountain bicycling is enormously popular in Colorado. Some of the summit hikes in this guide are suitable for bike rides. Riders should be experienced with riding on single tracks with steep grades. Remember that bikes aren't allowed in designated Wilderness Areas.

Fee Areas: This symbol alerts you when a hike enters a managed area where fees are charged for day use. This is becoming more common, especially with so-called "demonstration projects" in certain National Forest areas. State and National Parks also typically have entrance fees.

Wilderness Area: This symbol indicates that a portion of this hike is in a federally designated Wilderness Area where special regulations typically apply. See page 19 for more information.

Colorado Trail: The familiar *Colorado Trail* symbol is used to indicate a hike that shares a segment of the popular 468-mile trail between Denver and Durango.

Continental Divide Trail: This symbol means that a portion of the hike is along the *Continental Divide National Scenic Trail*. Note that this trail is not always right on the Divide, but often follows existing trails that parallel the Divide. The Colorado portion of this trail is about 750 miles long.

FYI

"For Your Information" boxes appears beneath the hike description for each summit hike. Each *FYI* box contain lots of useful and interesting stuff on everything from local history and natural history, to tips on spotting wildlife and "fun facts" — all adding to your hiking experience. There is more to enjoying these hikes than just getting to the top. Take the time to learn and explore something about each place, and you will find that each of these hikes visits a unique and distinctive corner of the Colorado Rockies.

Trail Map and Elevation Profile

Each summit hike includes a **trail map** and **elevation profile**. While the effort has been made to make these maps as useful and informative as possible, you will want to bring along more detailed maps, such as listed in the *information box* for each hike. The maps in this guide are tinted with the colors shown below, indicating the approximate elevation above sea level. Contour intervals are 500 feet apart and range from a low of 6,500 feet to over 14,000 feet. *Elevation profiles*, for hikes with more than 1000' elevation gain and more than one mile distance, show the one-way, ups and downs between the trailhead and the summit. These are useful for judging the relative steepness for sections of the trail or route.

MAP LEGEND   SYMBOLS   ELEVATION TINTS

USING PEAK FINDER

One of the great pleasures of standing atop a Colorado summit is in identifying for yourself and friends the many peaks around you. **Peak Finder** can help. It shows the approximate position of neighboring peaks by compass direction, relative to the summit you are on. Your summit is located by GPS coordinates, expressed as *latitude* and *longitude*, in the center of the Peak Finder circle.

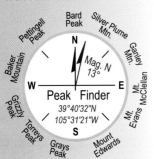

Symbol	Meaning
▲	summit
– – – – –	trail
· · · · ·	route (off-trail)
– · – · – ·	alternate route
– – – – –	other trails
P	trailhead
?	information board
WC	restroom
70	US highway
20	CO highway
) (	pass or saddle
13,164'	spot elevation

Elevation tints:
14,000'
13,500'
13,000'
12,500'
12,000'
11,500'
11,000'
10,500'
10,000'
9,500'
9,000'
8,500'
8,000'
7,500'
7,000'
6,500'

WILDERNESS RESPONSIBILITIES

The hikes in this guide traverse a number of publicly managed land units, including several National Forests, one National Park, Colorado State Park lands and several parks under local control by counties or cities. Please be cognizant of the fact that private land often abuts these units. Respect any private property and "no trespassing" postings. Remember also that federal law protects cultural and historic sites on public lands, such as old cabins, mines and Indian sites. These historic, cultural assets are important to us all as a society, and are not meant to be scavenged for personal gain.

Forest Service occupancy regulations are primarily designed to limit wear and tear in fragile wilderness areas. However, even non-wilderness areas need to be treated lightly to preserve resources for future generations. Strive to leave no trace of your passing and follow the principles of **Leave No Trace**.

The Leave No Trace message promotes and inspires responsible outdoor recreation through education, research, and partnerships. Managed as a non-profit educational organization, authorized by the Forest Service, LNT is about enjoying places like the Colorado Rockies, while traveling and camping with care.

Before starting your hike, check with the Forest Service for the current forest fire danger, which can sometimes be extreme, and for any restrictions on campfires. A list of contact addresses for Forest Service offices, and the offices of other publicly managed lands, is provided on page 217.

LEAVE NO TRACE

The seven LNT Principles of outdoor ethics form the framework of LNT's message:
1. *Plan Ahead and Prepare*
2. *Travel and Camp on Durable Surfaces*
3. *Dispose of Waste Properly*
4. *Leave What You Find*
5. *Minimize Campfire Impacts*
6. *Respect Wildlife*
7. *Be Considerate of Other Visitors*

See pg. 216 for contact information for LNT.

WILDERNESS AREAS

In this guide, we alert you to hikes that enter any federally designated Wilderness Area. The Wilderness Act of 1964 prohibits logging, mining, permanent structures, commercial enterprises, and motorized/mechanical transport in these protected areas. Minimize impact on these pristine and spectacular places by following these rules:

Collegiate Peak WA trailhead
(Aaron Locander)

1. Camp at least 200 feet from lakes and streams. 2. Use a stove rather than building a fire. 3. Bury human waste six inches deep and 200 feet from water sources. Pack out toilet paper. 5. All dogs must be leashed (or are prohibited in some areas). 6. Pack out your trash. 7. Mountain biking is prohibited.

SAFETY ON THE HIKE

Although the Colorado Rockies generally are one of the safest mountain environments in North America, any book of hiking routes cannot free the user from the need for good judgement. There are dangers in the backcountry that every hiker needs to be aware of. Each year, serious injuries and deaths occur in the Colorado backcountry — despite most accidents being preventable. Even a minor fall on rock can be injurious and weather conditions can change rapidly, transforming an easy route into a difficult one.

Abandoned Mines

The Colorado mountains are littered with long-abandoned mine shafts and old workings. Some of the charm of the hikes in this guide is due to these fascinating, historic sites. In addition to being inherently unstable, mines may still harbor poisonous gasses or caustic materials. Old buildings and workings often lean precariously, ready to collapse at a touch. Take photos, marvel at the tenacity of the old pioneers, but stay out!

Altitude Sickness

Hiking up summits in this guide will take you to altitudes ranging from a modest 6,000 feet, to a headache inducing 14,000 feet. Every hiker will react differently to the effects of altitude. *Acute Mountain Sickness* (AMS), a mild form of altitude sickness, is caused by a lack of oxygen when traveling to higher elevations. This usually occurs in individuals exposed to an altitude over 7,000 feet (2,100 m), who have not had a chance to acclimate to the altitude before engaging in physical activities. The symptoms of AMS include, but are not limited to, headache, nausea, vomiting and shortness of breath. Drinking plenty of fluids and ascending at a reasonable rate will help to offset the potential of being afflicted with AMS. If you do get AMS, the best advice is to descend immediately to a lower altitude.

Avalanche Awareness

Avalanches are, for the most part, a winter phenomenon which will not be a consideration on most of the hikes in this book. However, avalanches do still occur in late spring and early summer on the high peaks. Avoid walking out on cornices or climbing up steep couloirs that might break and run on a warm afternoon. Take an *Avalanche Awareness* course, offered by several Colorado recreational organizations, including the Colorado Mountain Club, to learn how to judge danger in the snowpack.

Hypothermia

Hypothermia occurs when the internal core body temperature drops to dangerous levels after exposure to cold and wetness. With the quick changing weather patterns typical of high mountains, this is a real danger in Colorado, even in summer. Symptoms are slurred speech, irrational behavior, drowsiness and intense shivering. Keep warm and dry, carry spare clothing, and respond quickly to rain and wind by donning appropriate clothing (see the *Recommended Equipment List* on page 23.) Treat a victim by replacing wet clothing with dry, by providing warm drinks and high-energy foods, and by huddling for shared body warmth.

Lightning

Deadly lightning is always a threat when thunderstorms are present. Afternoon thunderstorms are fairly common during the summer in Colorado, especially on the high peaks. These storms are quick moving and brief, but can be very violent. Lightning normally strikes the highest features in the vicinity — that could be YOU, if you are on a summit or a high ridge. Head down from any highpoint immediately when you see a thunderstorm starting to materialize. If caught in a place threatened by a strike, crouch down in a depression, with a pack or article of clothing to insulate you from potential ground currents, and discard any metal objects, such as an ice axe.

Rock Fall

Scree and talus fields can potentially pose a danger to hikers from rock falls. This is actually one of the most common accidents, especially occurring in narrow gullies and couloirs. Even just a fist-size rock can strike with amazing velocity, seriously injuring a climber. Spread out laterally in a couloir to prevent one person from being in "the line of fire" of another. Test handholds and footholds in scrambling situations and wear a helmet specifically designed for climbing.

Sun Exposure

At higher altitudes, ultraviolet rays (UVRs) are approximately 50 to 60 percent stronger than at sea level. Therefore, sunburn can occur more quickly and severely at altitude, especially in snowy terrain where the sunlight is reflected back up by the snow. UVRs can also penetrate cloud cover — so that even on cool, overcast days, you can be at risk. Apply sunscreen to all exposed skin areas, one hour prior to sun exposure. This gives the sunscreen time to penetrate the deeper skin layers. Sunscreen which is rated SPF 30 is the suggested standard for extended outdoor exposure. Look for sunscreens that block both UVA and UVB rays. Don't forget to protect your eyes with sunglasses that are rated to block both types of UVRs. Dark lenses with side shields are quite appropriate.

Water

Treat any water taken from unprotected sources before you drink it, and practice proper hygiene. You are at risk from *Giardia* contamination anytime you drink from untreated water sources in the Colorado backcountry. Giardia is a microscopic organism which, once it has inhabited the digestive system, can cause severe diarrhea. Giardia is mainly spread by the activity of animals in the watershed area of the water supply, or by the introduction of sewage into the water supply.

Giardia has become so common, even in wilderness areas, that water should always be treated chemically with pills which are specifically designed for water purification, by filtering the water with an approved water filter, or by boiling untreated water for several minutes before using.

Wildlife Encounters

While most hikers don't perceive wildlife as a threat to them, serious encounters with aggressive animals are on the rise in Colorado. Most problems center around food. Don't feed wildlife, and be sure to hang your food out of reach when in the backcountry. Any large animal should be treated cautiously, but bears and mountain lions are the main concern. Hiking at dawn or dusk may increase your chances of meeting a bear or mountain lion. Use extra caution in places where hearing or visibility is limited: in brushy areas, near streams, where trails round a bend or on windy days. Avoid hiking alone and keep small children close and in sight. Fortunately, both bears and mountain lions are reclusive creatures that still largely have a healthy fear of humans in unpopulated areas.

Staying Found

Be prepared for the backcountry with a good map, a compass and orienteering skills. It is not advised to hike alone; but if you do so, make sure to leave plans with someone — including information about your trailhead, your destination and your date of return.

Self-rescue should be the first consideration in the case of illness or an accident on a hike. If it is deemed necessary to seek outside help, someone should stay with the injured person; or failing that, then leave warm clothing, food and water behind. Purchase a *Colorado Outdoor Recreation Search and Rescue Card*, offered by the state of Colorado and available at outdoor retailers or sporting goods stores. This protects the bearer against being held responsible for the cost of search and rescue in Colorado.

Clothing and Equipment

When preparing for a hike, always start with the *Ten Essentials* as your foundation. Boots should be light but sturdy (no tennis shoes). Backpackers will want heavier, stiffer boots for good support. For clothing, modern synthetics, like polypropylene and pile, are light, insulate well and dry quickly. But traditional wool clothing is still effective, even when damp.

Avoid cotton entirely, as it loses all insulating ability when wet. Effective, good-quality clothing and other gear will often determine the difference between a safe, enjoyable day in the mountains and an unpleasant, or even potentially disastrous, experience.

Finally, consider joining an organization that offers classes and training in hiking, climbing, and general outdoor skills. You will find the names of several in the *Resource Guide* on page 216, including several based in Colorado.

Trailhead near Bison Peak
(Aaron Locander)

RECOMMENDED EQUIPMENT LIST

The 10 Essentials

Food
Water
Emergency shelter
Extra clothing
First aid kit
Flashlight
Map and compass
Matches/fire starter
Pocket knife
Sunglasses/sunscreen

For Day Hiking

❑ Day-pack:1500 to 3000 cubic inches
❑ Insulating layer: poly tops and bottoms
❑ Shirt or sweater: poly or wool
❑ Pants: poly or wool
❑ Parka shell: waterproof, windproof
❑ Pants shell: waterproof, windproof
❑ Hat
❑ Gloves: poly or wool
❑ Extra socks
Optional Gear: ice axe (for snow travel),
helmet (for rock scrambling)

For Multi-Day Hiking Trips

❑ Backpack: 3500 cubic in. or more
❑ Pack cover: waterproof
❑ Sleeping bag
❑ Sleeping pad
❑ Extra clothing
❑ Stove and fuel
❑ Cooking gear
❑ Eating utensils
❑ Food and food bags
❑ Tent or bivy sack
❑ Groundcloth: waterproof
❑ Personal toiletries
❑ Camp shoes
❑ Headlamp
❑ Repair kit and sewing kit

❑ Water filter and/or iodine tablets
❑ Plastic trowel: for catholes
❑ Plastic bags: for garbage
❑ Rope or cord

Optional Gear:
Pillow
Camera gear and film
Reading material and/or journal
Fishing gear
Binoculars
Camp chair
Radio and cell phone
Walking stick(s) or pole(s)

1 GENESEE MOUNTAIN 8,284 Feet

Combine an easy hike, suitable for kids, with a picnic at this popular Denver Mountain Park.

Distance: 0.3 miles each way
Hiking Time: Up in 12 minutes, down in 8 minutes
Starting Elevation: 7,980 feet
Elevation Gain: 304 feet
Trail: Partial, plus some easy off-trail hiking
Season: Early April to early November
Jurisdiction: Denver Mountain Park
Maps: *USGS 7 ½'* — Evergreen, *County* — Jefferson # 1, *Trails Illustrated* — #100

Directions to the Trailhead

From I-70 at Exit #254, 20 miles west of Denver, cross south over the highway. Turn right after a few hundred yards onto Genesee Trail Road (which winds for 2.5 miles to the road end, just below the summit.) Drive 1.1 miles from I-70 up this road, and park in the clear area on your right (west).

The Hike

Follow a trail leading up and northwest, past picnic tables, and cross the road which has continued a winding ascent from where you parked. Continue up in a west-northwesterly direction to a large flagpole on the top. Trees obscure some of the views to the north and west. Return to the east-southeast, on the same route as you ascended. Be on the lookout for beautiful, cup-shaped *pasqueflowers* that commonly dot these slopes in early spring.

Buffalo at Genesee Park

FYI

This hike lies within an area designated as a Denver Mountain Park, part of one of the largest urban park systems in the country. Begun in 1912 with the acquisition of Genesee, the system now has 31 named properties on 14,000 acres of mountains and foothills.

A group of buffalo graze in a large enclosure on the north flank of Genesee Mountain. The herd was started with seven animals that were shipped by rail from Yellowstone at around the time of the First World War. Both buffalo and an elk herd can be viewed year-round by the public.

A local group of the Daughters of the American Revolution has placed a new flag on the summit flagpole on every Flag Day since 1911.

(Right) A hiker descends through open slopes of ponderosa pine on Genesee Mountain. (Terry Root)

(Below) Pasqueflowers are common on this hillside in April. (Eric Wiseman)

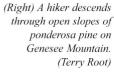

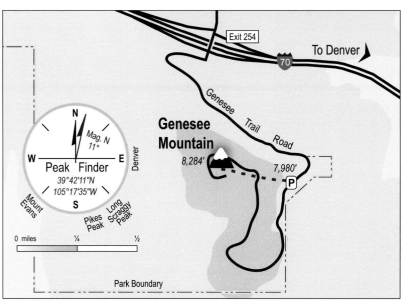

2 ORMES PEAK 9,727 Feet

A stunning view of Pikes Peak can be enjoyed from the summit for your modest effort.

Distance: 0.3 miles each way
Hiking Time: Up in 22 minutes, down in 8 minutes
Starting Elevation: 9,320 feet
Elevation Gain: 407 feet
Trail: Intermittent and faint
Season: Early May to late October
Jurisdiction: Pike National Forest
Maps: *USGS 7 ½'* — Cascade and Woodland Park,
County — El Paso #1, *USFS* — Pike National Forest, *Trails Illustrated* — #137

Directions to the Trailhead

From Colorado Springs, drive northwest from I-25 on US-24 for 17.8 miles to the town of Woodland Park. At Baldwin Street, where a sign welcomes the visitor to Woodland Park, turn right (northwest). Baldwin becomes a street called Rampart Range Road (and also Teller County Road 22.) Take this street for 2.95 miles from US-24, to an intersection with Loy Creek Road. Turn right on Loy Creek Road and ascend the canyon for 1.5 miles to a four-way intersection. Turn right (south) onto the *real* Rampart Range Road, which is unpaved. Go southwest on the Rampart Range Road for 6.1 miles to a turnoff to the east, which is Road 303. Follow this road east for 0.95 miles to another fork. Take the right fork which is Road 302. Take this road east for 1.35 miles and park off the road on the left (north).

From the south, access is via the Rampart Range Road which begins in the southwest corner of the Garden of the Gods, 0.1 miles east of Balanced Rock. To reach the turnoff onto Road 303, drive north on Rampart Range Road for 15.15 miles. The last mile or so (on Road 302) can be deeply rutted, so a vehicle with adequate clearance is recommended.

The Hike

Proceed up and due north through the sparse trees. A faint trail is intermittent to the top, but the hike is easily done without any trail. The unmarked summit lies at the northwestern edge of a relatively flat area. The view of Pikes Peak from here is extraordinary. Return by the ascent route.

FYI

This mountain is named after Manley Ormes, the father of Robert M. Ormes who was the original editor of the frequently revised *Guide to the Colorado Mountains*, in continuous publication for half-a-century. The elder Ormes mapped some of the area and helped found the Saturday Knights, a group that hiked every Saturday in the Pikes Peak area.

Ormes Peak has a wonderful,
close-up view of Pikes Peak.
(Eric Wiseman)

A view of Ormes Peak
from the south.
(Eric Wiseman)

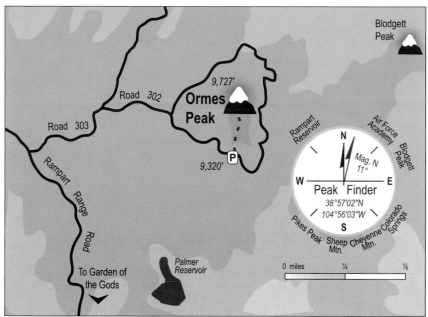

3 MOUNT FALCON 7,851 Feet

An interesting tour of one man's dream of a summer White House for the President.

Distance: 0.66 miles each way
Hiking Time: Up in 20 minutes, down in 15 minutes
Starting Elevation: 7,780 feet
Elevation Gain: 231 feet (includes 80 feet extra each way)
Trail: All the way
Season: Early April to late November
Jurisdiction: Jefferson County Open Sapce Park
Maps: *USGS 7 ½'* — Morrison, *County* — Jefferson #1,
Trails Illustrated — #100, Mount Falcon Park Map (Jefferson County Open Space)

Directions to the Trailhead

Either drive south from CO-74 at Kittredge on the Meyers Gulch Road for 2.9 miles, or drive north from US-285 on the Parmalee Gulch Road for 2.75 miles. (The Parmalee Gulch Road goes north from US-285 in Turkey Creek Canyon, east of Conifer and west of the Evergreen cutoff. This road becomes the Meyers Gulch Road before it reaches CO-74). Turn east on Picutis Road and make a quick left turn onto Comanche Road. After 0.1 miles, make a right onto Oh Kay Road and after another 0.1 miles, turn right onto Picutis Road. After 0.45 more miles, turn left onto Nambe Road and drive 1.3 miles further to road end at the Mount Falcon Park parking area.

The Hike

The well-marked trailhead is evident at the southeastern corner of the parking area. Continue southeast past picnic tables and toilet facilities for 0.3 miles to a fork. Turn right and continue to the south on the Tower Trail, which also leads to the Eagles Eye Shelter. In another 0.1 mile on the Tower Trail, there is another fork. Keep right and stay on the Tower Trail, ascend some stone steps, and in 0.26 more miles, the summit and overlying, wooden lookout tower are reached. The most direct descent route is to backtrack on the route just described. However, if you wish to take a longer loop trail back to your vehicle, and perhaps explore the park futher, there are several possible trails on the Mount Falcon Park map.

Classics

FYI

Mount Falcon was named by John Brisben Walker, a successful entrepreneur who died in 1931 at the age of 84. Walker had a Doctor of Philosophy degree from Georgetown University in Washington, D.C. He brought *Cosmopolitan* magazine into prominence and established nearby Red Rocks Park. He hoped to build a mansion for himself, as well as a summer White House for the President near the top of Mount Falcon. The home's ruins are located 0.5 mile north of the summit and the summer White House ruins are 1.0 mile northeast of the summit tower. Both can be reached easily by trail.

The ruins of "Walker's castle" are a short side trip.

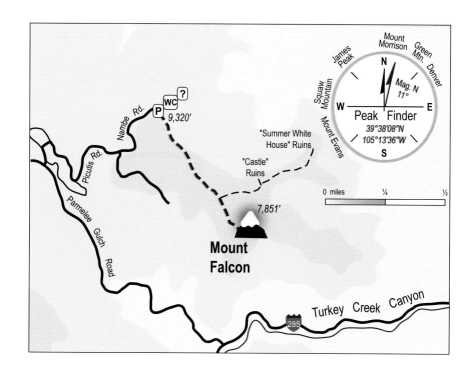

4 FOX MOUNTAIN 10,921 Feet

This aerie-like summit has great views of summer snowboarders shredding down nearby St. Marys Glacier.

Distance: 0.65 miles each way
Hiking Time: Up in 25 minutes, down in 15 minutes
Starting Elevation: 10,470 feet
Elevation Gain: 451 feet
Trail: To St. Marys Lake, off-trail beyond the lake
Season: Late May to early October
Jurisdiction: Arapaho National Forest
Maps: USGS 7 ½' — Empire, County — Clear Creek,
USFS — Arapaho National Forest, Trails Illustrated — #103

Directions to the Trailhead

Drive west of Idaho Springs on I-70 for about two miles and turn off on Exit #238. Go north on Fall River Road (which is designated Road 275) for 9.7 miles to a right-turning curve off the paved road. Turn left at this curve and drive north-northwest on a dirt road, with Silver Lake on your right (east), for 0.2 miles to a four-way intersection. Park off the road. Regular cars can come this far.

The Hike

From the four-way intersection, proceed south up an old mining road for about ten minutes to a bend in the road toward the north. Follow a trail which passes to the west, on the north side of the creek. In another seven minutes, you will arrive at St. Marys Lake. From the eastern margin of the lake, leave the trail and bushwhack east, up over mostly talus, to the

Summer snowboarder (CMC archive)

Classics

FYI

St. Marys Glacier is located above the north end of St. Marys Lake. It is actually an icefield, rather than a true glacier, and sits at the bottom of a natural funnel. During the winter, snow blows down from the Continental Divide and is swept into this narrow valley, collecting into an area approximately ten acres wide. In most years, this snow never completely melts. However in 2002, after three years of severe drought in the area, the "glacier" nearly disappeared, revealing an assortment of long-lost, oddball items, from broken skis, to an engine block, to a recliner!

With a *nearly* permanent snowfield so easily accessible, St. Marys Glacier is very popular with summer skiers and snowboarders. Organizations, like the Colorado Mountain Club, regularly conduct classes here that train in mountaineering skills.

A hiker and his dog scramble up the last few feet to the top of Fox Mountain.
(Linda Grey)

top of Fox Mountain. Some easy hand work is necessary near the summit, which consists of three rocky knobs on a rocky mesa. Descend via the ascent route.

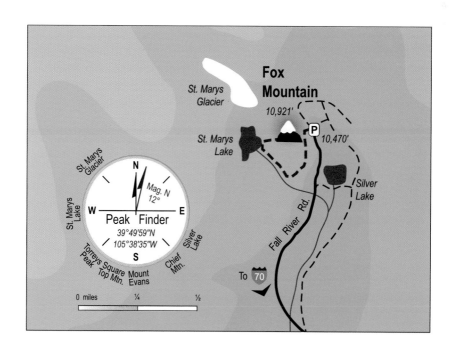

5 MOUNT CUTLER 7,200 Feet

Close-in to town, this low elevation hike is snow and ice free for much of the year.

Distance: 1.0 mile each way
Hiking Time: Up in 23 minutes, down in 20 minutes
Starting Elevation: 6,785 feet
Elevation Gain: 427 feet (includes 31 feet extra each way)
Trail: All the way
Season: Early April through late November
Jurisdiction: North Cheyenne Cañon Park (Colorado Springs)
Maps: USGS 7 ½' — Manitou Springs, *County* — El Paso #1, USFS — Pike National Forest, *Trails Illustrated* — #137, North Cheyenne Cañon Park Map (Colorado Springs Park and Recreation Department)

Directions to the Trailhead

At the southern part of Colorado Springs, drive south from I-25 via Exit #140B onto South Tejon Street for 0.4 miles. Then turn right on Cheyenne Boulevard and proceed southwest for 2.5 miles to an intersection with Evans Avenue, close-to the entrance to Seven Falls (fee area) and a sign marking the beginning of North Cheyenne Canyon. Drive up the scenic, paved North Cheyenne Canyon Road for 1.5 more miles to a parking area on the left (south) side of the road and a Mount Cutler trail sign. Park here.

The Hike

Follow the clear trail, up and southeast, as it curls to the unmarked, tree-covered top of Mount Cutler. En route to the top, there are good overlooks of Seven Falls to the south. Descend as you came up.

FYI

This mountain is named after Henry Cutler, a Massachusetts man who gave large amounts of money to Colorado College in its early years.

The hiking area lies within North Cheyenne Cañon Park, part of the city of Colorado Springs park system. Close-in to the city with easy access, nearly 70,000 visitors a year enjoy the towering evergreens, interesting rock formations and scenic waterfalls of this 1,000-foot deep gorge, which cuts through ancient Pikes Peak granite. Several other trails and picnic areas can also be found within the 1,600 acre park. This particular hike will usually be free of snow and ice between April and November.

Cheyenne Mountain from the summit of Mount Cutler.

Fairyslipper orchid, found in shady,
damp crannies along the trail.
(Eric Wiseman)

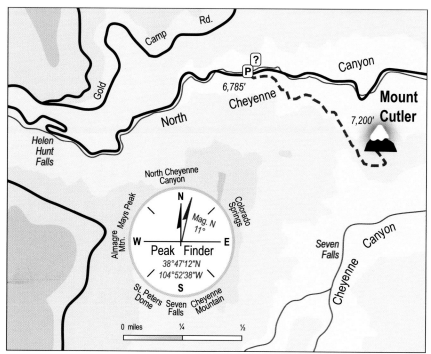

6 SQUAW MOUNTAIN 11,486 Feet

On the summit is one of the best remaining examples of an old-style fire lookout tower.

Distance: 0.6 miles each way
Hiking Time: Up in 27 minutes, down in 21 minutes
Starting Elevation: 10,960 feet
Elevation Gain: 526 feet
Trail: All the way
Season: Mid May to mid October
Jurisdiction: Arapaho National Forest
Maps: *USGS 7 ½'* — Idaho Springs and Squaw Pass;
County — Clear Creek; *USFS* — Arapaho National Forest; *Trails Illustrated* — #100

Directions to the Trailhead

Drive south on CO-74 from Exit 252 of I-70. After 3.3 miles, turn west on CO-103 (the Squaw Pass Road) for 12.0 miles. Turn left (southeast) on a dirt road. Drive mostly east and up on this road, until a barrier blocks further vehicular traffic after 0.9 miles from CO-103. Park off the road.

The Hike

Proceed northeast on the road past the barrier. The road makes several curves as it ascends. Take the right fork in the road near the top and hike directly toward the lookout tower. A good trail begins at a wooden pole, at the edge of a turnaround area at road end. Take the trail northeast, and then east, for the last 300 feet to the summit lookout tower. Descend by the same route.

To within 300 feet of the summit

FYI

Squaw Mountain, with its bare area on the north flank, can usually be clearly seen from Denver. The summit is easily accessible and affords excellent vistas from its historic lookout tower.

The first lookout on the site was put up in the 1920s by the city of Denver. In 1940, the present, more premanent, structure was built of wood and stone by the Civilian Conservation Corps. It was still in service until the late 1980s, then was restored recently by the Forest Service and placed on the National Historic Lookout Register.

It is being considered for re-staffing again to help in fire detection because of the tremendous growth of expensive homes, just outside the National Forest. Unfortunately, the site is also being sought for further expansion of the existing radio and TV antenna facilities.

A hiker and her canine companion approach the lookout tower on the summit of Squaw Mountain. (Terry Root)

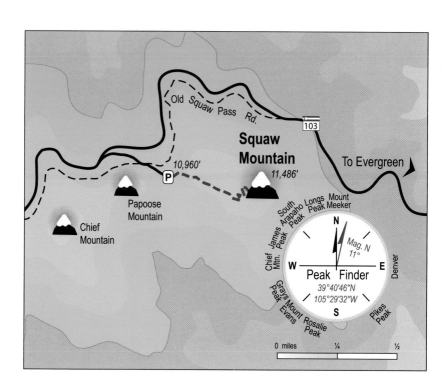

7 CHALK MOUNTAIN 12,017 Feet

Enjoy exceptional views of a famous peak and an equally incredible hole that was once a mountain.

Distance: 0.8 miles each way
Hiking Time: Up in 30 minutes, down in 22 minutes
Starting Elevation: 11,316 feet (Fremont Pass)
Elevation Gain: 701 feet
Trail: Initial 0.25 mile, faint trail beyond
Season: Late May to mid October
Jurisdiction: San Isabel National Forest
Maps: *USGS 7 ½'* — Climax; *County* — Lake;
USFS — San Isabel National Forest; *Trails Illustrated* — #109

Directions to the Trailhead

Drive to Fremont Pass on CO-91 at the Climax mining area, between Leadville and Copper Mountain. Park on the west side of the pass.

The Hike

Proceed west, and then north, on a dirt road for a hundred yards. Fork left and ascend more steeply. After a quarter mile from the trailhead, leave the road and follow an overgrown trail up to the west. At 0.75 mile from the trailhead, you will reach a ridge, and fifty yards farther, a rock pile on the flat summit. From here, you enjoy some exceptional vistas, including views of a famous mountain and of an incredible hole that was once a mountain. To the west is famous Mount of the Holy Cross. Visit Chalk Mountain in early summer when the snowy cross is still in fine form. To the east is the Climax Mine with its gigantic open pit. Return by the ascent route.

FYI

In 1936, a ski area with a double rope tow was begun on Chalk Mountain and continued for a few years. The Chalk Mountain summit lies on the Continental Divide.

Fremont Pass is named after the explorer, General John C. Fremont. The massive Climax Mine spills over hundreds of acres on the opposite side of the pass. During its hey-day, it was the world's leading producer of *molybdenum* which was used as a hardening agent in steel.

In the 1880s, miners searching for gold were puzzled by the strange, greasy metal. But after its unique properties were discovered in the early 20th century, the property was developed into a huge complex that employed thousands, transformed the valley and reduced much of Bartlet Mountain to mine tailings. The mine closed in 1986 but you can view an interpretative display about the mine, a few yards from the trailhead.

Bartlett Mountain has nearly been mined away by the Climax operation.

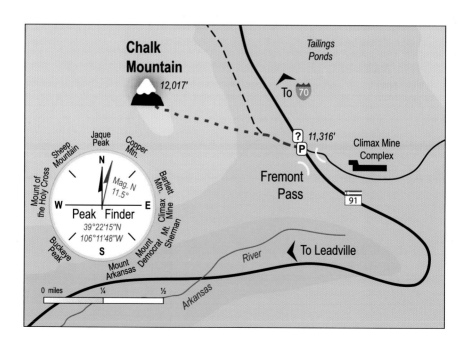

8 ST. PETERS DOME 9,690 Feet

This hike from the scenic and historic Old Stage Road is in the heart of Pikes Peak country.

Distance: 0.8 miles each way
Hiking Time: Up in 28 minutes, down in 21 minutes
Starting Elevation: 9,278 feet
Elevation Gain: 612 feet (includes 65 extra feet each way)
Trail: Most of the way, vague around the top
Season: Early May to early November
Jurisdiction: Pike National Forest
Maps: *USGS 7 ½'* — Mount Big Chief; *County* — El Paso #3; *USFS* — Pike National Forest; *Trails Illustrated* — #137

Directions to the Trailhead

From I-25, in southern Colorado Springs, drive south on Nevada Avenue (which becomes CO-115) for 1.8 miles and turn right on Cheyenne Mountain Boulevard. Follow this road around a circle and past various intersections for 2.4 miles to the intersection with the Cheyenne Mountain Zoo Road. Continue straight onto the Old Stage Road for 6.8 miles to an intersection with the Gold Camp Road. Go left for another 0.9 miles on the Gold Camp Road and park on the right, near a metal trail sign and a side road leading to the right. Regular cars can reach this point.

The Hike

From the parking area, with its great view north to Colorado Springs, hike north-northwest, following the trail as it curves to the right and enters the trees. After 0.5 miles from the trailhead, go left (south) at a fork. (The right fork takes you up difficult terrain to the lower, north summit.) Follow this left fork around rocky cliffs, before curving up and to the right for the final segment to the top. There is no trail for the final fifty yards.

Easily ascend the rocks to a flat, unmarked summit. Enjoy the view and retrace your ascent route back to the trailhead.

FYI

This used to be a popular hike, with wooden stairs for the final ascent to the summit. Some of the wood from these steps can still be found near the top. The final part of this hike requires some caution, since the route gets obscure near the top. The rocky summit projection to the south is designated St. Peters Dome. This hike also involves the lovely and historic Old Stage Road which connects Colorado Springs with Cripple Creek. An old railroad bed for transporting Cripple Creek gold at the turn of the last century, Theodore Roosevelt described its beauty as *". . . bankrupting the English language."*

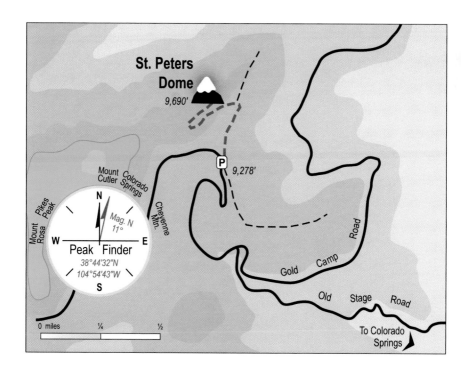

Colorado Springs spreads out beneath the rocky summit.

St. Peters Dome
9,690'

9,278'

Mount Cutler
Colorado Springs
Cheyenne Mtn.
Pikes Peak
Mount Rosa

N
Mag. N
11°
W — **E**
Peak Finder
38°44'32"N
104°54'43"W
S

Gold Camp Road
Old Stage Road

To Colorado Springs

0 miles   ¼   ½

9 CHEESMAN MOUNTAIN 7,933 Feet

O bserve the after
effects of the
largest wildfire in
Colorado history on
this summit jaunt.

Distance: 0.8 miles each way
Hiking Time: Up in 34 minutes, down in 26 minutes
Starting Elevation: 7,180 feet
Elevation Gain: 853 feet (includes 100 feet extra each way)
Trail: None, all bushwacking with some easy scrambling
Season: Late April to early November
Jurisdiction: Pike National Forest
Maps: *USGS 7 ½'* — Chessman Lake; *County* — Jefferson #2; *USFS* — Pike National Forest; *Trails Illustrated* — #105 & 135

Directions to the Trailhead

From US-285 at Pine Junction, drive south on Jefferson County Road 126 through Buffalo Creek for a total of 22.5 miles. Turn right onto a dirt road, passing up and west for 2.1 miles to a fork. (The right fork goes to Lost Valley Ranch in 7.0 miles, and the left goes to Cheesman Reservoir in 0.72 miles.) Park near this fork. Observe any posted parking directives due to the 2002 Hayman Fire.

The Hike

Hike up, and east, to a rather steep false summit and a ridge which leads to the top. Some easy use of hands may be needed in reaching this ridge. Once on the ridge, continue northeast, skirting another false summit on its south side, to the true summit — a huge boulder, unclimbable, except with technical assistance. Some wires extend downward from its top, but these do not appear safe. Two USGS markers are present on the eastern edge of a rocky mesa, adjacent to the summit boulder. Return by your ascent route.

FYI

Named after Walter S. Cheesman, a Denver businessman from around the turn of the century, this peak can be reached even into November. The reservoir to the south also carries the same name and was formed by construction of the dam between 1900 and 1905.

On June 8, 2002, this area was engulfed by the largest wildfire in Colorado's history. The human-caused Hayman Fire charred over 135,000 acres, burned 133 residences, and took nearly six weeks and hundreds of firefighters to control. Chessman Mountain was heavily burned over in places. While the area has now reopened, you should consult the informational signs posted by the Forest Service on access roads about temporary closures or other directives. Be especially careful because of potential tree falls. As rehabilitation progresses, it will be interesting to observe as life and the forest return.

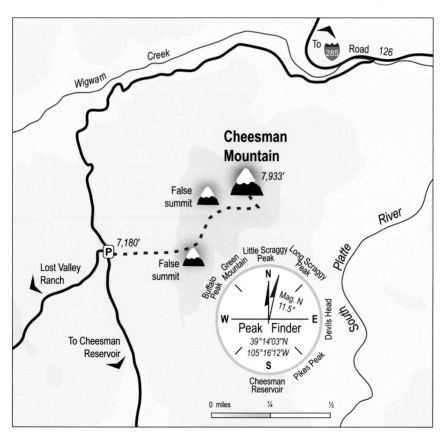

The summit boulder presents a technical problem.

10 THE BROTHER 7,810 Feet

From atop this perch in summer, hawks can often be spotted soaring on thermals.

Distance: 0.7 miles on ascent, 1.5 miles on descent (loop)
Hiking Time: Up in 21 minutes, down in 38 minutes
Starting Elevation: 7,480 feet
Elevation Gain: 465 feet (includes 135 extra feet)
Trail: All the way
Season: Early April to late November
Jurisdiction: Jefferson County Open Space
Maps: *USGS 7 ½'* — Evergreen; *County* — Jefferson #1; *Trails Illustrated* — #100; Alderfer-Three Sisters Park Map

Directions to the Trailhead

At the center of the town of Evergreen, from the intersection of CO-74 and Jefferson County Road 73, drive south-southwest for 0.6 miles on Jefferson County Road 73. Then turn right onto Buffalo Park Road and drive on this paved road for 1.3 miles. Park on the right at the trailhead parking area.

The Hike

Start up the trail, to the left of the signboard, traveling north-northwest. Within fifty yards, continue straight (north-northeast) at a four-way intersection on the Sisters Trail. After another 120 yards, turn left onto the Ponderosa Trail and begin your clockwise loop. Ascend 0.3 miles to a ridge and turn right onto the Brothers Lookout Trail, rising in 0.2 miles to the rocky summit and a benchmark. Enjoy the great views, before returning to the last fork at the ridge.

To continue the loop, descend seventy-five yards to the right and take the right fork onto the Sisters Trail, circling back 1.0 mile to where your loop began. En route to this point, stay on the Sisters Trail and avoid the Hidden Fawn Trail. From the loop onset point, descend south for 0.2 miles back to the trailhead.

Turkey vulture

FYI

*These trails are popular with both hikers and mountain bikers.
Two riders pause at the information sign at the trailhead.
(Terry Root)*

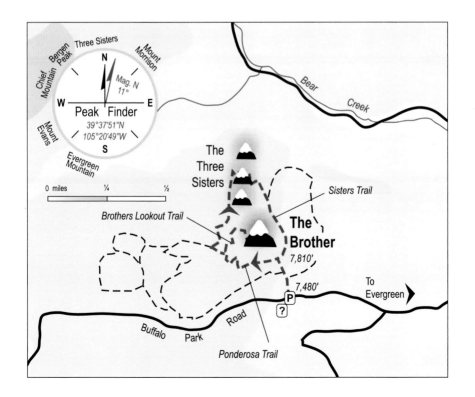

11 FAIRBURN MOUNTAIN 10,390 Feet

Your route finding skills will come into play on this summit in a historic mining district.

Distance: 1.1 miles each way
Hiking Time: Up in 45 minutes, down in 35 minutes
Starting Elevation: 9,310 feet
Elevation Gain: 1,130 feet (includes 25 feet extra each way)
Trail: None, bushwack all the way
Season: Mid May to mid October
Jurisdiction: Arapaho National Forest
Maps: *USGS 7 ½'* — Central City; *County* — Gilpin; *USFS* — Arapaho National Forest; *Trails Illustrated* — #103

Directions to the Trailhead

This hike begins at the Cold Springs Campground, north of Black Hawk, off of CO-119 (the Peak-To-Peak Highway.) The campground entrance is 0.1 miles southwest of the intersection of CO-119 and CO-46, or 5.2 miles north of the intersection of CO-119 and CO-279 at Black Hawk. Drive northwest into the campground for 0.8 miles and park near where a creek, flowing from the north, crosses the campground's dirt road.

The Hike

Proceed north, keeping the creek to your left. Quickly, you reach a large clearing with excellent views to the south and southwest of the Mount Evans massif. Continue upward to the north and traverse a false summit, en route to a small rock cairn at the tree-covered summit. The views are partial and to the west. Descend to the south, approximating your ascent route.

FYI

This hike will provide good practice with map and compass, since there is no trail. Your route is due north but don't forget to factor in the declination — in this case, magnetic north is about 11.5 degress east of true north. Try this one from May until October to avoid snow underfoot.

Fairburn Mountain lies just north of "the richest square mile on earth," as some early chroniclers dubbed Gregory Gulch. The colorful towns of Central City and Black Hawk in the gulch are experiencing a renaissance of sorts, since the beginning of limited stakes gambling in 1991. But despite the new-found riches, you may notice on the drive to this trailhead that Black Hawk hardly resembles the historic mining and milling town that it once was. Vegas-like casinos and gambling tourists have largely taken the place of Victorian false-fronts and history buffs.

The tree-covered summit of Fairburn Mountain, as viewed from the southeast.
(Eric Wiseman)

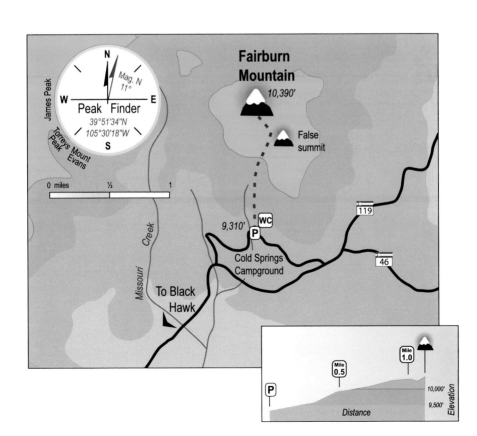

12 ALPS MOUNTAIN 10,560 Feet

This is a hike through history with relics from Colorado's gold rush days along the way.

Distance: 0.45 miles each way
Hiking Time: Up in 30 minutes, down in 26 minutes
Starting Elevation: 9,940 feet
Elevation Gain: 620 feet
Trail: Initial 0.3 miles, bushwack beyond
Season: Early June to early October
Jurisdiction: Arapaho National Forest
Maps: *USGS 7 ½'* — Idaho Springs, *County* — Clear Creek, *USFS* — Arapaho National Forest, *Trails Illustrated* — #104

Directions to the Trailhead

From I-70 in Idaho Springs, drive southwest on CO-103 for a half mile. Turn right onto unpaved Spring Gulch Road and ascend 4.3 miles to a four-way intersection and park. En route to this point, drive parallel to the small creek on your left. Keep right at mile 1.6, left at mile 1.75, straight at mile 2.1 and again at mile 2.5, left at mile 2.6, right at mile 3.0 and again at mile 3.9, left at mile 4.0 and again left at mile 4.1. Regular cars can reach this trailhead.

The Hike

Proceed southeast up the road on your left. The road curves south and, in a quarter mile, you will arrive at a restored, old cabin. Take the left fork above the cabin and continue southwest and west. Thirty yards past the cabin, take a left fork to the west-southwest, just before some mine remnants. The trail ends in a loop within forty yards. Then bushwhack southwest past some diggings, with an abandoned cabin on your left. Ascend west on a faint trail and then curve southwest to reach the unmarked, rocky summit at the west end of an irregular ridge. The views from the top are partially obscured by trees. Return as you ascended.

FYI

From the summit of Alps Mountain, the terrain drops steeply down into the canyon of Chicago Creek. It was along the banks of this stream, near present-day Idaho Springs, that George Jackson discovered placer gold in January of 1859. The ensuing rush pushed miners into the surrounding hills, searching for the load. As a result, the area of this hike is honeycombed with old mines and their roads.

This is a good outing for beginners or for early season conditioning. The route should be free of snow at least between June and October.

Alps Mountain drops steeply on its east into the canyon of Chicago Creek.

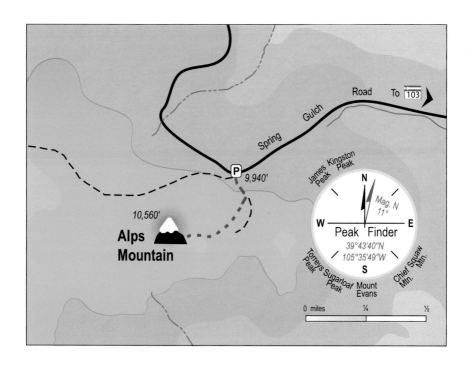

13 BALDY PEAK 7,872 Feet

Curious outcrops and interesting geology are the hallmarks of this portion of the Pike National Forest.

Distance: 2.3 miles each way
Hiking Time: Up in 72 minutes, down in 54 minutes
Starting Elevation: 6,650 feet
Elevation Gain: 1,222 feet
Trail: Initial 1.5 miles, then bushwacking with easy scrambling
Season: Late April to early November
Jurisdiction: Pike National Forest
Maps: USGS 7 ½' — Green Mountain and Pine; *County* — Jefferson #2; *USFS* — Pike NF; *Trails Illustrated* — #105

Directions to the Trailhead

From Pine Junction on US-285, drive south on Jefferson County Road 126 for 9.8 miles. Turn right onto Buffalo Creek Road at a stop sign (Road 543). Follow this narrow road, which soon becomes dirt, for 1.6 miles to a road closure. Park off the side of the road.

The Hike

Effected by the Buffalo Creek fire, this road is now closed to vehicles beyond this point. Hike southwest along the road for 1.5 miles. As Baldy Peak becomes visible as a rocky point to the west-northwest, follow an old mining road, leading west from the road at a metal gate. Cross the creek and follow the old road. At a fork, keep left and eventually leave the road, proceeding toward the left (southwest) side of Baldy Peak. Ascend in a clockwise direction. The final ascent moves toward the northeast from the southwest. There is an easily negotiated route to the summit, with a few hand holds necessary near

FYI

This makes a good early or late season hike, with some enjoyable, easy rock hiking over the last few hundred yards to the summit. The rock you are scrambling on is the very granular Pikes Peak granite, common throughout the area. Dozens of peaks and prominent outcrops around here exhibit a curious pattern of sheer, south-facing cliffs and forested north slopes. Thousands of years of near-daily, freeze/thaw cycles on the southern exposures, has broken the rock and produced dramatic cliffs, with nearby Cathedral Spires as a classic example. But on the shady north slopes, snow lies deep all winter without melting, allowing a richer soil cover to built up.

The devastation in the area from the fire is shocking but already there are fascinating signs of life coming back to the forest.

The Pike National Forest commemorates Zebulon M. Pike, an army officer, who explored various parts of the United States and was killed in the War of 1812 at the age of 34.

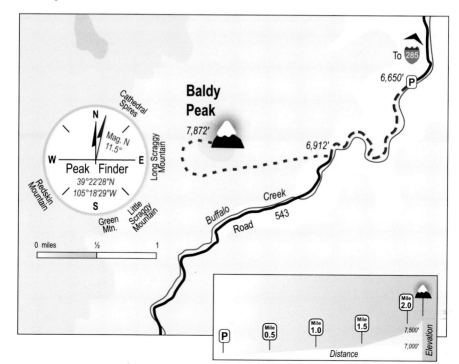

The Buffalo Creek fire in 1996 scorched the eastern half of Baldy Peak, shown here from the southeast. (Terry Root)

the top, marked by an USGS marker and a small pile of rocks. There are no trees to obscure the excellent panorama in every direction. Descend as you came up.

Baldy Peak
7,872'

To 285
6,650' P

6,912'

Cathedral Spires
Long Scraggy Mountain
Little Scraggy Mountain
Green Mtn.
Redskin Mountain

Mag. N 11.5°
Peak Finder
39°22'28"N
105°18'29"W

N
W   E
S

Buffalo Creek Road 543

0 miles   ½   1

P   Mile 0.5   Mile 1.0   Mile 1.5   Mile 2.0

7,500'
7,000'

Distance   *Elevation*

14 DEVILS HEAD 9,748 Feet

A magnificent 360 degree view is your reward from one of Colorado's last working fire lookouts.

Distance: 1.9 miles each way
Hiking Time: Up in 53 minutes, down in 48 minutes
Starting Elevation: 8,780 feet
Elevation Gain: 1,080 feet (includes an extra 112 feet)
Trail: All the way
Season: Early May to mid November
Jurisdiction: Pike National Forest
Maps: *USGS 7 ½'* — Devils Head; *County* — Douglas #1; *USFS* — Pike National Forest; *Trails Illustrated* — #135

Directions to the Trailhead

From Sedalia on US-85 (south of Denver and northwest of Castle Rock), drive west on CO-67 for 10.0 miles to a four-way intersection. Turn left (south) here onto the Rampart Range Road (unpaved, but drivable by regular cars.) Stay on this main road as it continues south for 9.0 miles to a fork and a sign. Park here. (The right fork continues 31 miles to Woodland Park.)

The Hike

Walk east up the left fork and reach the trailhead sign in a half mile. En route to this point, keep right at two forks and avoid the campground. Ascend southeast from the trailhead sign. After a mile reach a signed fork. (The left trail leads 0.4 miles to the Zinn Memorial Overlook of Pikes Peak. A plaque at the overlook honors Commander Ralph Theodore Zinn, a 1922 graduate of the U.S. Naval Academy.)

Classics   To reach Devils Head, take the right fork and quickly reach a cabin and a clearing, below the lookout tower. Ascend the stairway up the last 200 feet to the top, and the excellent 360-degree view. Be careful on the steps, when you retrace the ascent route back to the trailhead.

FYI

This hike will usually be possible from May until November. Several informational signs and benches lie along this excellent trail.

Devils Head was originally called Platte Mountain until 1923. From certain viewpoints, the devil's head can be seen, formed by rugged rock outcrops. The formation can readily be seen from Denver, prominent on the southwest skyline.

The tower and cabin at the top were built by the U.S. Forest Service in 1907 and replaced in 1951 by the Army Corps of Engineers. The tower is the last operating fire lookout along Colorado's Front Range. It is open to the public but certain restrictions apply. Please observe the posted signs. In particular, do not climb the strairs when lightning is present.

The Devils Head lookout tower.
(Donna Kelley)

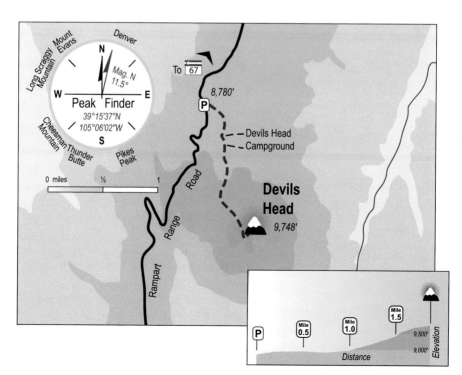

15 COLORADO MINES PEAK 12,493 Feet

*T*his is a perfect early summer hike along the crest of the Continental Divide.

Distance: 1.3 miles each way
Hiking Time: Up in 55 minutes, down in 38 minutes
Starting Elevation: 11,315 feet (Berthoud Pass)
Elevation Gain: 1,178 feet
Trail: All the way on a dirt road
Season: Early June to early October
Jurisdiction: Arapaho National Forest
Maps: *USGS 7 ½'* — Berthoud Pass, *County* — Clear Creek, *USFS* — Arapaho National Forest, *Trails Illustrated* — #103

Directions to the Trailhead

Drive on US-40 north from Empire, or drive south from Winter Park, to the top of Berthoud Pass. Park in the area on the east side of the pass, by the former restaurant and ski lodge.

The Hike

Proceed southeast up a well-maintained road, beginning south of the lodge. Follow this service road, winding up through the ski area, to the top of Colorado Mines Peak. Several buildings are located on top, including a large telecommunications structure. Return to Berthoud Pass via the ascent route.

For extra credit, a ridge walk northeast along the Continental Divide will reach the top of Mount Flora in 37 minutes. Mount Eva, after a false summit, is 49 minutes more. Return to the saddle between Colorado Mines Peak and Mount Flora. The Continental Divide Trail descends west from there, contouring around the hill to rejoin the ski service road at about treeline.

FYI

Berthoud Pass is named after Edward Louis Berthoud, who was born in Geneva, Switzerland. Berthoud was an explorer, a faculty member at the Colorado School of Mines and at one time, President of the Colorado Central Railroad.

Colorado Mines Peak lies astride the Continental Divide and on the boundary between Clear Creek and Grand Counties. It was named by Neal Harr, a student at the Colorado School of Mines, in 1954.

In 2002, the ski lifts began to come down on the historic Berthoud

Pass Ski Area. One of the earliest established areas in Colorado, it was a favorite for generations but began to come upon hard times with the rise of much larger, corporate-run areas. Guided skiing will continue, using snow cats for access to the pass areas famous powder. If you hike this peak in June, you'll undoubtedly see a few diehards, carrying their gear up the road to carve a few more turns before the slopes melt out.

The Forest Service is studying future uses for the ski lodge, including use as a summer visitor center.

Communications equipment bristles on the summit , as seen in this view from the north.

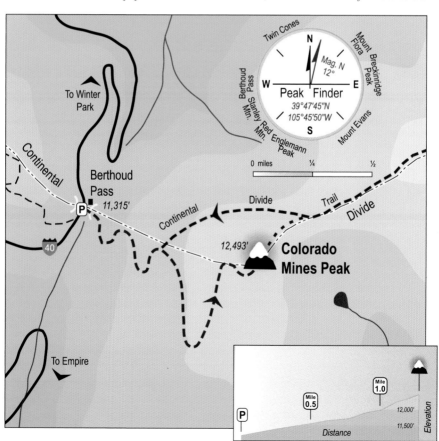

16 SOUTH PEAK 12,892 Feet

S tart this hike from an historic toll road and enjoy fantastic views of South Park.

Distance: 1.4 miles each way
Hiking Time: Up in 60 minutes, down in 40 minutes
Starting Elevation: 11,921 feet (Weston Pass)
Elevation Gain: 1,091 feet
Trail: Initial 0.35 miles, easy tundra and talus walking beyond
Season: Early June to early October
Jurisdiction: San Isabel National Forest
Maps: *USGS 7 ½'* — Mount Sherman and South Peak;
County — Lake; *USFS* — San Isabel National Forest; *Trails Illustrated* — #110

Directions to the Trailhead

Drive to Weston Pass, connecting US-285 on the east with US-24 on the west. Either drive 16.2 miles west from US-285 (11.2 miles south of Fairplay) or drive 11.1 miles east from US-24 (6.5 miles south of Leadville). Despite a few rough spots, this pass can be readily traversed in a regular car. Park at the summit of the pass.

The Hike

Proceed about 200 yards west on the main Weston Pass road to an old mining road, on your left, which leads southwest. Follow the old road until it ends at some abandoned cabins. South Peak is visible directly ahead to the southwest, with white, rocky slopes leading to its summit. Cross the tundra, and then some easy talus, to a large rock cairn at the summit. There is a small radio tower nearby. Take the same route down to your car.

FYI

Weston Pass was first an Indian trail and then a stage and wagon road, connecting South Park with Leadville. On the east side of the pass lay the town of Weston which once contained several restaurants and bars, serving traffic to the busy mining activities in California Gulch.

There is some confusion over who the town and pass were named after, as two prominent citizens named "Weston" settled in the area at about the same time. Phuo M. Weston arrived in South Park in 1861 and owned various properties along the old toll road. Algernon S. Weston showed up at about the same time and also acquired a ranch along the road.

As you travel the largely empty expanse of this road today, it's hard to imagine that in its heyday, the Weston Pass Toll Road was perhaps the busiest thoroughfare in Colorado. On September 4, 1879, 225 wagon teams were counted as they crossed the summit of the pass. Within two years though, the train route was completed to Leadville from Buena Vista and traffic dried up.

Beyond the miners' cabins is a tundra walk to the gentle summit.

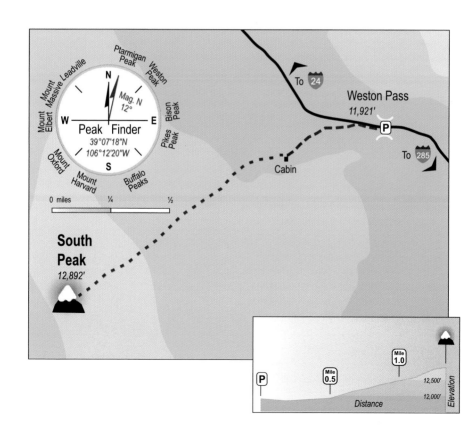

17 ROYAL MOUNTAIN 10,502 Feet

This peak, which forms the northern terminus of the Tenmile Range, features a fine overlook of Lake Dillon.

Distance: 2.0 miles each way
Hiking Time: Up in 56 minutes, down in 38 minutes
Starting Elevation: 9,095 feet
Elevation Gain: 1,477 feet (includes 35 feet extra each way)
Trail: All the way
Season: Early June to early October
Jurisdiction: Arapaho National Forest
Maps: USGS 7 ½' — Frisco; *County* — Summit #2;
USFS — Arapaho National Forest; *Trails Illustrated* — #108

Directions to the Trailhead

Drive to Main Street in Frisco. The trailhead lies on the south side of the street, 0.28 miles east of I-70 or 0.8 miles west of CO-9. A sign states *"Vail Pass — Ten Mile Canyon — National Recreational Trail."* Park around this sign.

The Hike

From the parking area, walk southeast and cross Tenmile Creek on a bridge. This is the only flowing water on this hike. Go left onto the paved bikepath. After three-tenths of a mile, leave the path and enter the trees on a trail to your right, at a sign. Ascend south-southeast and soon pass through the remnants of Masontown. Follow the sign to Mount Royal and continue up and south by the right trail fork. The steep trail then reaches a fork after 1.7 miles from the trailhead. Go right (northwest) at this fork. (The other trail leads up Peak One.) After two hundred yards, you reach an overlook of Tenmile Canyon and I-70. Go to the right at the rockpile and follow the ridge northward to reach the highpoint. The views from here are partially obstructed by trees. If you want a better overlook, continue down on a faint trail to the north-northeast for another quarter mile to a rocky knob. Be sure to return by your ascent route, since there are steep dropoffs to the east and north.

FYI

The trail to Royal Mountain passes through the ghost town of Masontown which was settled in the 1860s by a group from the town of the same name in Pennsylvania. The founders apparently didn't know much about avalanches, because they built it in a prominent avalanche path. One hundred years later, artificial Lake Dillon was established.

The first part of this hike is on a popular, paved bike and foot path which extends from Vail, to Copper Mountain, to Frisco and on to Breckenridge.

Lake Dillon and the Front Range form the backdrop to the east.

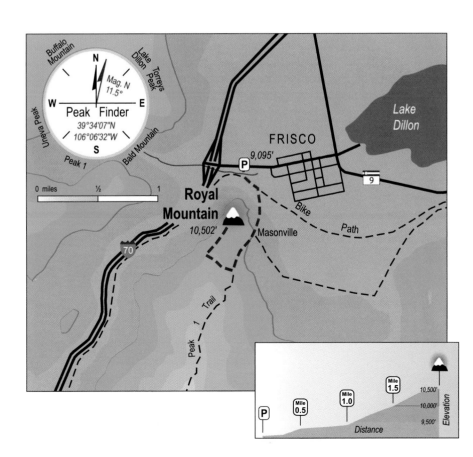

18 EMMA BURR MOUNTAIN 13,538 Feet

*H*ere's an all-above-treeline hike with constantly unfolding vistas and summer wildflowers.

Distance: 2.2 miles each way
Hiking Time: Up in 56 minutes, down in 34 minutes
Starting Elevation: 12,154 feet (Tincup Pass)
Elevation Gain: 1,384 feet
Trail: Initial few hundred yards, tundra walk beyond
Season: Early June to early October
Jurisdiction: Gunnison and San Isabel National Forests
Maps: *USGS 7 ½'* — Cumberland Pass; *County* — Gunnison #5 and Chafee #2; *USFS* — Gunnison NF and San Isabel NF; *Trails Illustrated* — #130

Directions to the Trailhead

From the east

From the west

Drive to Tincup Pass. From the east, drive south for 5.7 miles from the US-24 and US-285 intersection (2.8 miles south of Buena Vista.) Then turn west onto Chaffee County Road 162. Continue west on this road for a total of 16.2 miles to the historic town of Saint Elmo. Turn right in the center of town, cross a bridge and turn immediately left onto Chaffee County Road 267. This road continues for 6.3 miles up to Tincup Pass. If the snow is gone, some passenger cars can make the pass from the east.

From the west, Tincup Pass is reached via Cumberland Pass or Taylor Park to the town of Tincup. It is 6.7 miles east, and then south, from Tincup to Tincup Pass. Four-wheel drive is necessary for the final three miles to the pass from Mirror Lake. Park off the road, near the sign at Tincup Pass. If your car is unable to reach the pass, add the extra distance to that given for the hike as described from Tincup Pass.

The Hike

Crossed at Tincup Pass

Proceed on a blocked road, which leads up and east from the roadway at Tincup Pass. When this road ends after a few hundred yards, angle left (northeast), up over tundra, to a saddle. At the saddle, hike north up the ridge, skirt left around a false summit, then drop briefly into another saddle. Continue north to a cairn on the grassy highpoint. Go down as you ascended.

 FYI

No one seems to know how this mountain got its name. It is one of only about a dozen in Colorado that honor the fairer sex. It lies on the Continental Divide, on the boundaries between Chaffee and Gunnison Counties and also between the San Isabel and the Gunnison National Forests. The hike is completely above timberline with constantly unfolding vistas and tundra flowers.

The town and pass both acquired their names because an early prospector reputedly carried his gold dust out in a cup.

The summit is to the far left in this view from southwest of Tincup Pass.

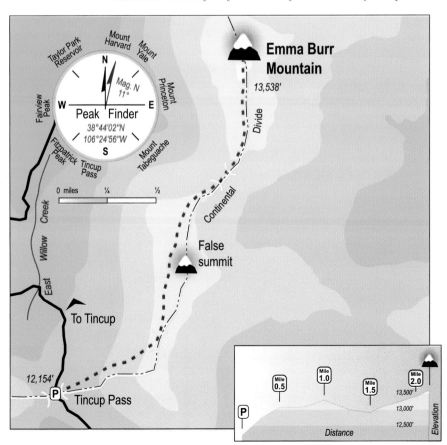

19 FITZPATRICK PEAK 13,112 Feet

Fine views of the Sawatch Range are yours on this hike from historic Tincup Pass.

Distance: 1.35 miles each way
Hiking Time: Up in 57 minutes, down in 40 minutes
Starting Elevation: 12,154 feet (Tincup Pass)
Elevation Gain: 1,258 feet (includes 150 feet lost at beginning)
Trail: To the saddle, talus and tundra beyond
Season: Early June to early October
Jurisdiction: Gunnison and San Isabel National Forests
Maps: *USGS 7 ½'* — Cumberland Pass; *County* — Gunnison #5 and Chafee #2; *USFS* — Gunnison NF and San Isabel NF; *Trails Illustrated* — #130

Directions to the Trailhead

From the east

From the west

Drive to Tincup Pass. From the east, drive south for 5.7 miles from the US-24 and US-285 intersection (2.8 miles south of Buena Vista.) Then turn west onto Chaffee County Road 162. Continue west on this road for a total of 16.2 miles to the historic town of Saint Elmo. Turn right in the center of town, cross a bridge and turn immediately left onto Chaffee County Road 267. This road continues for 6.3 miles up to Tincup Pass. If the snow is gone, some passenger cars can make the pass from the east.

From the west, Tincup Pass is reached via Cumberland Pass or Taylor Park to the town of Tincup. It is 6.7 miles east, and then south, from Tincup to Tincup Pass. Four-wheel drive is necessary for the final three miles to the pass from Mirror Lake. Park off the road near the sign at Tincup Pass. If your car is unable to reach the pass, add the extra distance to that given for the hike as described from Tincup Pass.

The Hike

CDT is crossed at Tincup Pass

Drop down about 150 feet to the southwest and keep to the left of the talus. Fitzpatrick Peak is the prominent mountain visible to the southwest. Find a sometimes faint trail and head for the saddle to the right of the peak. En route you pass along a shelf, leading to a large cairn at the saddle. The trail continues west and down to Napoleon Pass, but leave the trail at the saddle and go directly south up the ridge to a cairn at the top. The best route down is as you ascended. (For a side trip to Napoleon Pass, and possibly Napoleon Mountain, descend the ridge, going north partway to the saddle. Then turn west and either, continue west on the trail from the saddle, or head more directly west to unmarked Napoleon Pass, which connects Tincup with the south side of the Cumberland Pass Road.)

FYI

Tincup Pass has been a route from the east to the town of Tincup since the 1800s. It was first a burro trail and later a toll road. Continuing improvements have made this road more passable in recent years. The road and pass are part of the Continental Divide Trail (Segment 26.)

Fitzpatrick Peak, as seen from Tincup Pass.

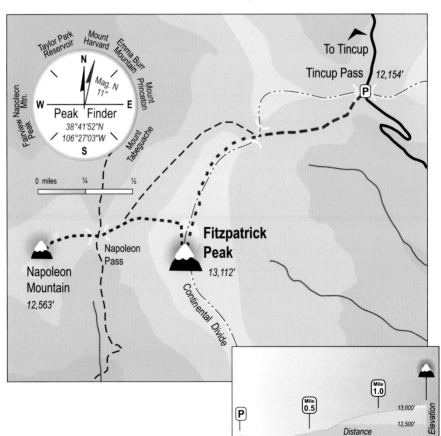

20 MOUNT ZION 7,059 Feet & LOOKOUT MOUNTAIN 7,560 Feet

*T*wo trails lead to two summits, and other attractions, in this delightful Jefferson County Open Space park.

Distance: Mount Zion: 0.6 miles each way
Lookout Mountain: 1.3 miles each way
Hiking Time: Mount Zion: Up in 21 minutes, down in 18 minutes
Lookout Mtn.: Up in 38 minutes, down in 25 minutes
Starting Elevation: 6,900 feet (Windy Saddle) for each
Elevation Gain: Mount Zion: 459 feet (inc. 150 ft. extra each way)
Lookout Mountain: 660 feet
Trail: All the way to each summit
Season: Early April to Late November
Jurisdiction: Windy Saddle Park (Jefferson County Open Space)
Maps: *USGS 7 ½' —* Morrison; *County —* Jefferson #1;
Trails Illustrated — #100; Windy Saddle Park Map

Directions to the Trailhead

From 1.0 mile south on US-6 from the intersection with CO-58 in Golden, turn and go southwest on 19th Street (the Lariat Loop Road), through two pillars, for 3.5 miles to a parking area and a sign for the Beaver Brook Trail. Park here, on the west side of the road at Windy Saddle.

The Hike

For Mount Zion, proceed due north up the ridge on a rough dirt road from the parking area. A Jefferson County Open Space trail sign is present at the beginning. After twelve minutes of steep going, you reach the high point of the ridge, but this is not officially designated as the Mount Zion summit. Continue north on the ridge, losing about 150 feet, before you ascend an unmarked, rocky knob which is considered the summit. It will take you about nine minutes to get here from the high point. (You may wish to continue eight minutes farther north, and a bit lower on the ridge, to a metal pole in the rock, and the end of the faint trail.) Return via the same ridge to the trailhead.

Another nice hike, which can be combined with the Mount Zion ascent, is up Lookout Mountain. From the parking area, take the Beaver Brook Trail west

FYI

Mount Zion has a large letter "M" on its east flank, which can be seen for a considerable distance. Students from the Colorado School of Mines whitewash it each spring. Lookout Mountain, like Mount Zion, is one of several peaks so-named in Colorado. Its summit can be reached by driving up the Lariat Loop Road, beyond Windy Saddle. There are museums, restaurants and homes around the summit mesa. The most interesting spot is the gravesite of frontier scout and showman, Buffalo Bill Cody. The panoramic view takes in the entire Denver metropolitan area, an especially stunning sight at night.

from the trail sign. After 0.3 miles, the Lookout Mountain Trail forks south, up through the trees. In 38 minutes from the parking area, you reach the summit mesa of Lookout Mountain and Colorow Road. Just across the road is the *Lookout Mountain Conference and Nature Center* which has exhibits and two loop trails. The center's building at 7,560 feet is the highpoint for Lookout Mountain. A trail passes along the west side of the center and eventually connects with the Apex Trail. The *Buffalo Bill Museum* is another nearby mountain top point-of-interest, on the east end of the mesa. To descend, take the same trail on which you ascended.

A hiker descends the Mount Zion Trail.
(Terry Root)

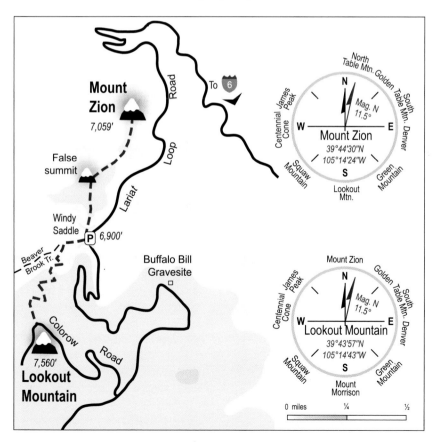

21 CHIEF MOUNTAIN 11,709 Feet

*T*his close-to-
Denver hike is a
good choice as an
introduction to
Colorado's alpine.

Distance: 1.5 miles each way
Hiking Time: Up in 45 minutes, down in 39 minutes
Starting Elevation: 10,680 feet
Elevation Gain: 1,129 feet (includes 50 feet extra each way)
Trail: All the way
Season: Late May to late October
Jurisdiction: Arapaho National Forest
Maps: *USGS 7 ½'* — Idaho Springs, *County* — Clear Creek,
USFS — Arapaho National Forest, *Trails Illustrated* — #104

Directions to the Trailhead

Drive south on CO-74 from Exit 252 of I-70. After 3.3 miles, turn west on CO-103 (the Squaw Pass Road) for 12.4 miles (3.8 miles from Squaw Pass). There is a well-graded parking area off the road on the right (with ski lift machinery just below.) Look for a wooden pole and a trail, going initially southeast, on the left (south) side of the road. Just above the trailhead, on the south side of the road, is a cement marker with "*# 290*" on it. Park in the clear area, on the north side of the road.

The Hike

Classics

Cross to the south side of the road and proceed southeast by trail. Enter the trees and cross a dirt road (the old Squaw Pass Road) after 0.4 miles. Continue up and southeast. After another 0.3 miles, the trail curves south at a cairn. (At this point, you are at a saddle with Papoose Mountain, an easy bushwhack up to the northeast.)

Continue on the good trail through a couple of switchbacks until past timberline. Then finally reach the rocky summit in a clockwise direction. A benchmark and a Colorado Mountain Club register cylinder lie at the high point. Enjoy the scenery, especially the fine views of nearby Mount Evans, and return by your ascent route.

FYI

This readily accessible peak offers wonderful vistas of mountains and plains at, and near, the top. It forms a mountain family with Squaw Mountain (*see Summit Hike #6*) and Papoose Mountain in the middle, despite regular letters to the Denver newspapers suggesting more politically correct names.

While Squaw Mountain bristles with man-made structures, Chief Mountain has more of a wild and natural feel to it. Closeness to Denver, and a well-graded trail, make Chief Mountain a good choice to introduce out-of-town hiking guests to their first taste of the Colorado alpine.

Chief Mountain, as viewed from the east. The trail passes up through this thick forest, emerging onto the tundra over the last few hundred feet. (Terry Root)

Hikers pass the cement marker near the start of this popular trail. (Terry Root)

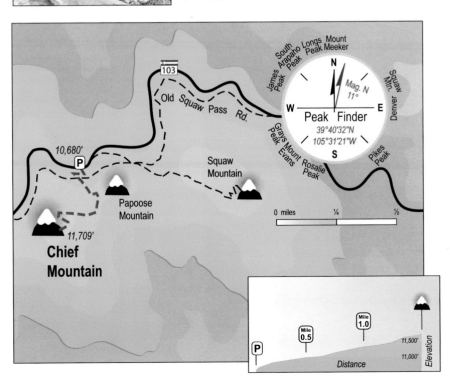

22 LILY MOUNTAIN 9,786 Feet

The impressive east face of Longs Peak is in view from this summit, near Rocky Mountain National Park.

Distance: 2.2 miles each way
Hiking Time: Up in 55 minutes, down in 53 minutes
Starting Elevation: 8,780 feet
Elevation Gain: 1,336 feet (includes 165 extra feet each way)
Trail: All the way, plus a little hand work near the top
Season: Early May to early November
Jurisdiction: Roosevelt National Forest
Maps: *USGS 7 ½' —* Longs Peak; *County —* Larimer #3;
 USFS — Roosevelt National Forest; *Trails Illustrated —* #200

Directions to the Trailhead

Either drive on CO-7 27.7 miles northwest from Lyons from the junction with US-36, or drive 6.0 miles south from Estes Park from the junction with US-36. A yellow call box and a trail sign lie off the west side of the road. Park close to this point, off of the road, and be careful due to the fast moving traffic.

The Hike

Begin north from the trail sign. Pass a trail register and continue northwest for 1.1 miles, until the trail curves up and to the left. Avoid faint side trails. Over the final 50 yards, ascend directly south-southwest at a faint fork. Follow cairns steeply to the flat, unmarked summit. Some easy hand work may be needed. If you reach a ridge saddle, you have gone too far. (In which case, the highpoint will lie to the northwest.)

FYI

This hike lies just outside of Rocky Mountain National Park. The vista from the summit is impressive, especially the view of Longs Peak. Lily Lake lies to the south and is not encountered on this route, nor is any running water. But this lake (located a couple of miles away on the highway) is a good after-hike place to stop and have a picnic. There is a Rocky Mountain National Park information center with rest rooms and interpretative displays on the opposite side of the highway.

Lily Mountain is nearly completely covered with a thick forest of lodgepole pine. These pines typically are the result of a past wildfire, since they require heat for their cones to split open. Dense, mature forest of lodgepole, such as on Lily Mountain, are the least diverse of Colorado's forests, with rows of seemingly same-age, same-species trees that tend to exclude other plant species and limit the variety of species of animals.

Lily Mountain reflected in the waters of nearby Lily Lake.
(Brent J. Murphy)

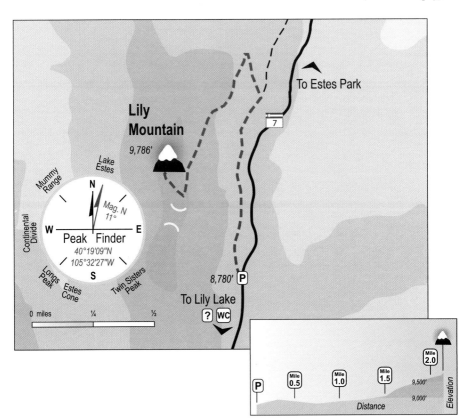

23 GREEN MOUNTAIN 6,855 Feet

The prairie meets the Rocky Mountains at this urban park oasis near Denver.

Distance: 2.25 miles each way
Hiking Time: Up in 60 minutes, down in 45 minutes
Starting Elevation: 6,060 feet
Elevation Gain: 895 feet (includes 50 feet extra each way)
Trail: All the way
Season: Nearly year-round
Jurisdiction: Hayden Green Mountain Park (City of Lakewood)
Maps: *USGS 7 ½'* — Morrison; *County* — Jefferson #1; *Trails Illustrated* — #100

Directions to the Trailhead

The trailhead lies at a parking area on the north side of West Alameda Parkway, east of West Utah Avenue, in the city of Lakewood. This site is 1.75 miles southwest of Union Boulevard, coming from the east on West Alameda Parkway, or 0.8 miles east of West Jewell on West Alameda Parkway.

The Hike

Proceed north-northeast, following the trail as it curves gradually to the northwest, and then to the west. When you reach a radio tower in about 35 minutes, keep left and hike northwest on the summit mesa. Lose a little elevation. Near the highpoint, leave the trail and go left over grassland for about 50 yards to three rock piles at the summit.

Western meadowlark along the trail. (Terry Root)

FYI

Classics

This is the shorter of two Green Mountains in Jefferson County and the first named foothill as you leave Denver, going west. Green Mountain is one of the excellent recreational areas of the City of Lakewood, a unique blend of the prairie and the Rocky Mountains in an urban setting. With 2400 acres, the park is very popular with hikers, trail runners, mountain bikers and equestrians. There is even a place for paragliding at the north end of the mesa.

While Green Mountain appears as a fairly non-descript, nearly treeless, rounded hill, it has some interesting geology. *Green Mountain conglomerate* — essentially a pile of gravel — makes up the mesa. This gravel was laid down as the adjacent Rockies rose and began to erode. Later, the valley to the west, which today contains C-470, eroded away to isolate the more resistant mesa from the foothills.

This hike can be enjoyed nearly year-round, except right after a snow storm. The best time is perhaps late May, when prairie wildflowers and *yucca* bloom on the hillsides, and meadowlarks sing their liquid song from every *mullein* stalk.

Bicyclist climbs the trail with the radio tower in the distance. (Linda Grey)

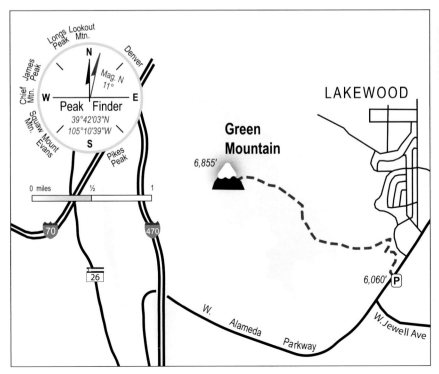

24 COON HILL 12,757 Feet

A hike to this tundra-covered summit affords views of the famous tunnel through the Divide.

Distance: 1.3 miles each way
Hiking Time: Up in 66 minutes, down in 42 minutes
Starting Elevation: 11,140 feet
Elevation Gain: 1,637 feet (includes 10 feet extra each way)
Trail: Initial 0.3 miles, steep tundra walking beyond
Season: Early June to early October
Jurisdiction: Arapaho NF, Ptarmigan Peak Wilderness
Maps: *USGS 7 ½'* — Loveland Pass; *County* — Summit #1 and Grand #4; *USFS* — Arapaho National Forest; *Trails Illustrated* — #104

Directions to the Trailhead

Via I-70, drive to the west end of the Eisenhower-Johnson Memorial Tunnel. From the parking area on the north side of the highway, drive east on the paved road which passes to the left of an administrative building for 0.2 miles, until the road is blocked. Park here, on the side of the road.

The Hike

Begin east, on the dirt road, and turn left (north) within one hundred feet. Continue 0.2 miles up this road and reach a small cement building, between two lanes of the road. Coon Hill will be visible as the high point to the west-northwest. Leave the road and proceed west across the creek, up over grassy slopes and some rocks to the saddle, on the right side of a rocky subpeak. Then ascend the ridge to the right (north), along the boundary of the Ptarmigan Peak Wilderness, and reach a register cylinder, a cairn and a benchmark at the summit.

On your descent to the east, avoid the steep rocky areas and stay on tundra wherever possible.

FYI

Coon Hill, with its southern, rocky subpeak, is prominent to the northeast as one approaches the Eisenhower-Edwin C. Johnson Memorial Tunnel from the west. It is the highest named peak in the Williams River Mountain Range, a short spur-range that extends west off the Continental Divide. The Eisenhower-Edwin C. Johnson Memorial Tunnel is named after the 34th president of the United States and after a former Governor of Colorado, who also served 18 years in the United States Senate. The first bore of the tunnel opened in 1973, and the second bore in 1979. It courses through a flank of Mount Trelease for a length of 8,941 feet.

The dirt road, followed briefly at the start of this hike, is actually a service road, built over the Divide for the tunnel project to carry men and materials to both ends of the job site.

Hikers descend the tundra-covered east slopes of Coon Hill. (Terry Root)

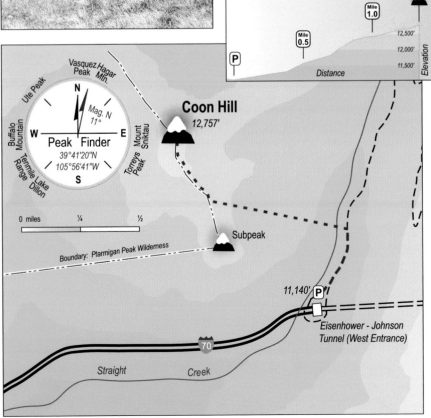

25 DIAMOND PEAKS 11,852 Feet

Enjoy summer wildflowers on a hike to this summit in the northernmost portion of the Front Range.

Distance: 1.4 miles on ascent, 1.1 miles on descent
Hiking Time: Up in 66 minutes, down in 33 minutes
Starting Elevation: 10,276 feet (Cameron Pass)
Elevation Gain: 1,576 feet
Trail: Initial first half until basin, open tundra walking beyond
Season: Early June to early October
Jurisdiction: Roosevelt NF, Colorado State Forest
Maps: *USGS 7 ½'* — Clark Peak; *County* — Larimer #3;
USFS — Roosevelt National Forest; *Trails Illustrated* — #112

Directions to the Trailhead

Drive on CO-14 to Cameron Pass. From the east the pass is 59.3 miles from the edge of Fort Collins, at the point where US-287 and CO-14 intersect. From the west, Cameron Pass is about 33.5 miles east of Walden on CO-14. Park in the designated area, by a picnic ground on the west side of the pass.

The Hike

Head west-southwest from your car, up into the trees and find the trail. You will reach a creek, which you should keep on your right. Stay on the trail and ascend alongside the creek. The trail fades as you reach an open basin at the foot of the peaks. The highest peak will be visible to the northwest. Your target has a distinct hump near its summit. Proceed to the ridge on the south side of the summit and then ascend over tundra to the top, marked by an USGS marker, a cairn, a metal pole and several pieces of wood and wire. To descend, hike directly down (southeast) from the summit to the trail that you left in the basin.

FYI

This group of peaks is located about 30 miles south of the Wyoming state line. The details given describe the route to the highest of these peaks. They are to be distinguished from Diamond Peak, 8,668 feet high, which lies to the northeast, much closer to Wyoming, but also in Larimer County. Cameron Pass was discovered by General R.A. Cameron who also founded the city of Fort Collins.

This Northermost portion of the Front Range is known both as the Rawah (an Indian word for "wilderness") Range and as the Medicine Bow Mountains. Structurally, they continue south of Cameron Pass and the highway, but with another name change, the beautiful Never Summer Range, which is likewise a translation from an Arapaho name. The Rawahs are celebrated for summer wildflowers.

The summit from south along the ridge.

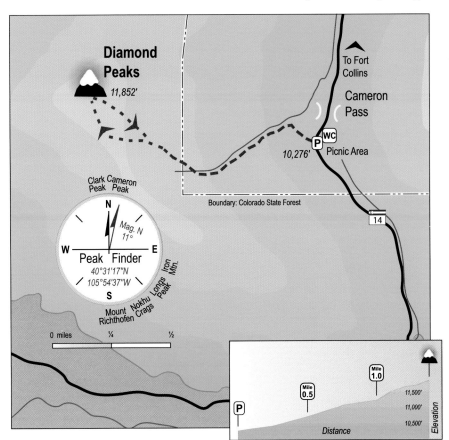

Diamond Peaks
11,852'

To Fort Collins

Cameron Pass

WC
P 10,276' Picnic Area

Boundary: Colorado State Forest

14

Clark Peak   Cameron Peak

Mag. N 11°

N
W — Peak Finder — E
40°31'17"N
105°54'37"W
S

Iron Mtn.

Longs Peak

Mount Richthofen   Nokhu Crags

0 miles   ¼   ½

Mile 1.0

Mile 0.5

P

11,500'
11,000'
10,500'

Distance   Elevation

26 MOUNT SNIKTAU 13,234 Feet

This easily recognized landmark above I-70 is a great early-season conditioner.

Distance: 1.5 miles each way
Hiking Time: Up in 71 minutes, down in 52 minutes
Starting Elevation: 11,990 feet (Loveland Pass)
Elevation Gain: 1,244 feet
Trail: All the way
Season: Early June to early October
Jurisdiction: Arapaho National Forest
Maps: *USGS 7 ½'* — Grays Peak and Loveland Pass;
County — Clear Creek; *USFS* — Arapaho National Forest; *Trails Illustrated* — #104

Directions to the Trailhead

Drive to Loveland Pass either from the north via I-70 and US-6 or from the south via US-6 from Lake Dillon and the Keystone resort area. Park in the paved area near the Loveland Pass sign, on the east side of the highway.

The Hike

Take the initially, clear trail going east, and then northeast, up the ridge. The trail becomes fainter in the tundra further up, but the route is always obvious. The trail passes four cairn-marked knobs en route to the fifth and highest cairn on the Mount Sniktau summit. The descent route is identical.

FYI

Sniktau was a pen name used by E.H.N. Patterson, a Clear Creek County journalist of the mid 1800s. Originally from Virginia, he edited the *Georgetown Courier* and was associated with the writer, Edgar Alien Poe.

Mount Sniktau can be seen prominently from I-70, as one drives west from Silver Plume, toward Loveland Pass. While Loveland Pass is on the Continental Divide, Mount Sniktau is on a short spur extending north off the main crest. The pass is popular with late season skiers and snowboarders looking for that last turn before the snow disappears. June hikers will likely share the trail with a few of them.

This hike has a high, easily accessible starting point, a very unambiguous route and is completely above timberline. Due to its ease of access, Mount Sniktau is a fine peak for early season conditioning, or to take out-of-town hikers up for their first taste of a Colorado peak. Occasionally, you can spot mountain goats on the eastern slopes, near the summit.

*The ridge walk along the Divide from Loveland Pass is very popular.
Mount Sniktau is shown in the background. (Eric Wiseman)*

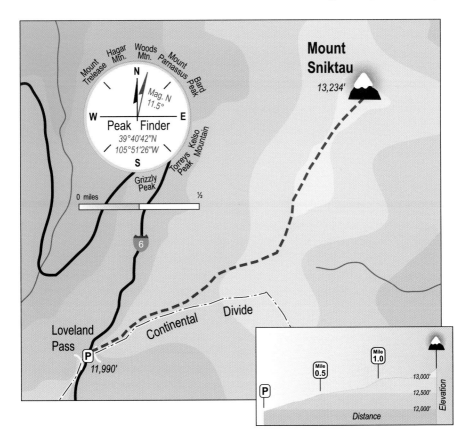

27 WEST WHITE PINE MOUNTAIN 10,305 Feet

A trip through the beautiful Buckhorn Valley begins this hike to a double summit.

Distance: 2.6 miles each way
Hiking Time: Up in 76 minutes, down in 54 minutes
Starting Elevation: 8,288 feet
Elevation Gain: 2,017 feet
Trail: All the way on an old mining road
Season: Early May to late October
Jurisdiction: Roosevelt National Forest
Maps: USGS 7 ½' — Crystal Mountain; County — Larimer #4; USFS — Roosevelt National Forest; Trails Illustrated — #101

Directions to the Trailhead

Drive 6.7 miles west on US-34 from its intersection with US-287 in Loveland. Turn right (north) and continue 5.4 miles to Masonville, where the road continues as a "T". Take the left turn, and after 3.7 miles from Masonville, the road becomes unpaved. Drive 3.5 miles more to a fork. Take the left fork for 11.9 more miles along Buckhorn Creek to the Buckhorn Ranger Station, on your left. (The total distance from the intersection in Loveland to the Buckhorn Ranger Station is 31.2 miles.) Just past the Ranger Station, on your right, is Road 100 going north. When open, this road leads to the summit of West White Pine Mountain but four-wheel drive is required. Park about 0.2 miles north of the Ranger Station, just off Road 100, near the site of the road barrier.

Another route to the trailhead is from Fort Collins via Rist Canyon to Stove Prairie. Drive south from Stove Prairie 3.8 miles and then make a sharp right turn at an intersection, proceeding 11.9 miles to the Buckhorn Ranger Station. Regular cars should be able to reach the trailhead by either route, from Loveland or Fort Collins.

The Hike

Follow the road up and north, as it passes through many aspen trees and a meadow. After 1.8 miles, you reach a saddle between West and East White Pine Mountains. A USGS marker lies just north of the road. Follow the road, as it turns up and west from the saddle. In 0.8 miles from the saddle, the road brings you to the top of West White Pine Mountain, which is covered by ruins of

FYI

This hike provides an opportunity to experience the lovely Buckhorn Valley. Buckhorn Creek flows by Masonville into the Big Thompson River, west of Loveland. Masonville was named after James R. Mason who was born in Kentucky in 1849 and overcame great poverty to become a successful farmer and cattle rancher in the area.

an old lookout structure. Four cement pillars and a makeshift bench mark the summit. Trees block some of the views, but it is open to the southwest and west. Follow the road back to your car.

(If you want to reach the lower, East White Pine summit as well, bushwhack up and east from the saddle. This will require about 22 minutes up and 16 minutes back down to the saddle and 608 feet of extra elevation gain. The east summit lies amid some rock formations, which are easily negotiated. Do not descend southwest from the summit to save time, lest you pass south of a 9130-foot subpeak and miss Road 100 completely.)

A bull elk is spotted among the aspen along Road 100. (Eric Wiseman)

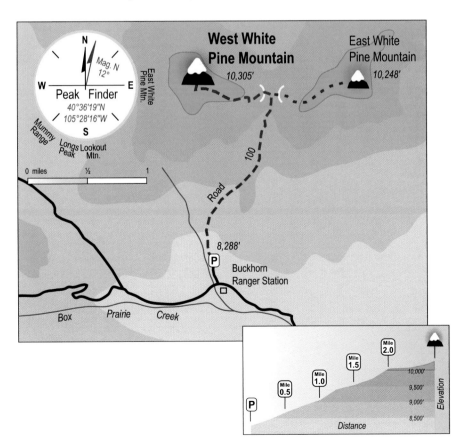

28 GENEVA MOUNTAIN 12,335 Feet

This tundra stroll affords excellent views of nearby Mount Bierstadt, as well as the famous Sawtooth Ridge.

Distance: 3.5 miles each way
Hiking Time: Up in 88 minutes, down in 86 minutes
Starting Elevation: 11,669 feet
Elevation Gain: 1636 feet (includes 485 feet extra each way)
Trail: First half, tundra walking beyond
Season: Early June to early October
Jurisdiction: Pike NF, Mount Evans Wilderness Area
Maps: USGS 7 ½' — Mount Evans; *County* — Park #2; *USFS* — Pike National Forest; *Trails Illustrated* — #104

Directions to the Trailhead

Drive to Guanella Pass, either heading north from the town of Grant at US-285 for 13.0 miles or south from Georgetown off of I-70 at Exit 238 for 10.0 miles. Park at the pass in the designated area by a information sign on the east side of the road. Regular cars can traverse Guanella Pass from either the north or south access route.

The Hike

Begin hiking south-southeast on the trail from the Guanella Pass parking area. In five minutes, take the left fork and continue on Trail #603. Within ten more minutes, you will see Geneva Mountain and two subpeaks to its right. Continue on an old road for about 30 minutes from the trailhead, then leave the road and ascend southeast, mostly over tundra. Skirt the first subpeak to the left (east) and cross directly over the second subpeak to reach the top of Geneva Mountain, with its small rock pile and register jar.

FYI

Ptarmigan (Terry Root)

This Geneva Mountain is not to be confused with Geneva Peak, north of Webster Pass and farther southwest in Park County. Guanella Pass was named after Byron Guanella, a Clear Creek County Commissioner who promoted work on the pass. The 23-mile road is a desginated Scenic Byway, embroiled in a controversial proposal to pave it.

This hike is all above timberline and therefore affords extensive vistas over its entire length. You are likely to spot hikers scaling the nearby fourteener, Mount Bierstadt, as well as get a look at its rugged Sawtooth Ridge. You are advised to arrive early, as the parking lot for this popular area fills up quickly in the summer. The area is critical to wildlife also. The thick stands of willows in the bottomland between Geneva Mountain and Mount Bierstadt attract large numbers of ptarmigan in the winter, seeking food and shelter. And elk favor the area for dropping their calves in the spring.

The rugged Sawtooth Ridge between Mount Bierstadt (right) and Mount Evans (center) is in view as you enter the Mount Evans Wilderness. (Terry Root)

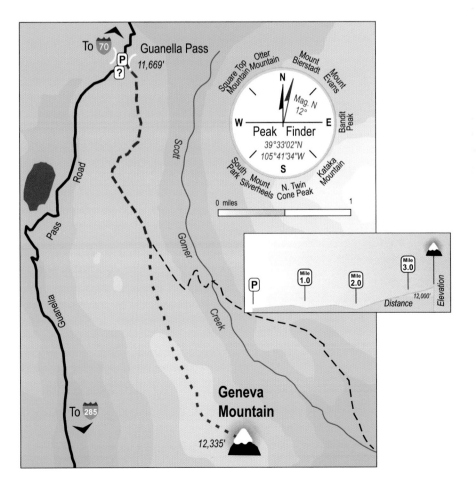

29 GLACIER PEAK 12,853 Feet

The famous Colorado Trail intersects your route on this summit hike along the Continental Divide.

Distance: 2.9 miles each way
Hiking Time: Up in 77 minutes, down in 65 minutes
Starting Elevation: 11,585 feet (Georgia Pass)
Elevation Gain: 1,668 feet (includes 200 feet extra each way)
Trail: All the way until just below the summit
Season: Early June to early October
Jurisdiction: Pike National Forest
Maps: *USGS 7 ½' —* Boreas Pass; *County —* Park #1; *USFS —* Pike National Forest, *Trails Illustrated —* #109

Directions to the Trailhead

From the east

From the west

At the town of Jefferson in South Park, drive northwest from US-285 on the National Forest access road (marked "Michigan Creek Road".) Avoid the right fork at mile 2.0. Turn right at mile 2.9 onto Road 54. Keep to the main road, reaching Georgia Pass at mile 11.9. Park off the road. In most years, cars with good clearance can make it all the way to the pass, but sometimes visitors will be forced to stop and hike the final mile or so. If that is the case, then add an extra mile each way to the distance listed above. Access from the opposite end at CO-9, north of Breckenridge, is via a difficult four-wheel drive road.

The Hike

To within 0.25 mile of top

Route crosses the CT

Begin on foot up the old, rough road to the north. In less than 0.5 mile, cross the Colorado Trail and continue up the road to a four-way intersection. Continue north-northeast on the road, now closed to vehicles. Pass over two subpeaks on Glacier Ridge and reach a ridge at mile 2.8. Leave the road here and ascend right (east-southeast) over tundra for another 0.1 mile to a rock pile and USGS benchmark at the top of Glacier Peak. A subpeak lies to the east, as does Whale Peak, another 1.5 miles along the Divide. The easiest return from Glacier Peak descends directly south to the road and then back along the ascent route.

FYI

The town of Jefferson was once a gold mining camp, and later, a railroad shipping station. The railroad tracks were removed in the 1930s. The town, Jefferson Lake, Jefferson Creek and Jefferson Hill were all named to honor President Thomas Jefferson.

The route, entirely above treeline, mostly follows the Continental Divide Trail and provides lovely vistas. It also crosses Segment 6 of the 468-mile Colorado Trail, one of the most popular long-distance trails in the country. The CT winds its way through the heart of the Rockies between Denver and Durango, crossing eight mountain ranges en route. Segment 6, between Kenosha Pass and Breckenridge, is the longest at 32 miles.

En route along the Continental Divide to Glacier Peak.

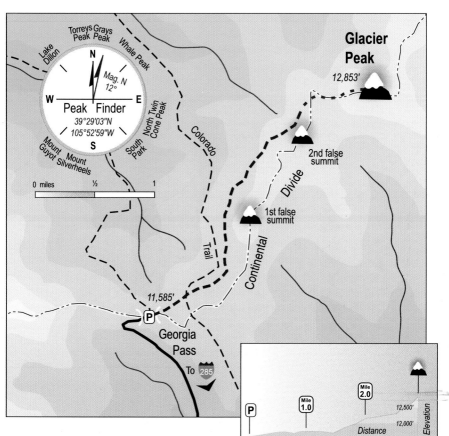

30 MOUNT VOLZ 12,589 Feet

Fall is the best time of year to enjoy gorgeous stands of colorful aspen on the drive to this trialhead.

Distance: 1.75 miles each way
Hiking Time: Up in 79 minutes, down in 58 minutes
Starting Elevation: 10,900 feet
Elevation Gain: 1,789 feet
Trail: Initial 0.9 miles, tundra and talus beyond
Season: Early June to early October
Jurisdiction: Pike National Forest
Maps: *USGS 7 ½'* — Boreas Pass; *County* — Park #1; *USFS* — Pike National Forest; *Trails Illustrated* — #109

Directions to the Trailhead

From 10.0 miles north of Fairplay on US-285, drive north on the Boreas Pass Road (Park County Road 33) through the town of Como for a total of 8.2 miles. A longer access from the north is by way of Breckenridge on the Boreas Pass Road, until 3.1 miles south of Boreas Pass. At a bend in the road and a creek crossing, park off the road near a blocked-off side road which leads up and to the east. Regular cars can usually negotiate the entire 21.5 mile Boreas Pass Road.

The Hike

Go east on the old road, soon curving south, then crossing the creek and rising to the east and timberline. As the road ends, continue due north over talus to a saddle, with Mount Volz to your left and a small rocky knob to your right. Proceed west up the talus ridge to a large summit cairn, a rock shelter and a USGS marker within a circle of rocks. Return as you ascended.

FYI

Access to this peak from the east is blocked by the Volz Ranch. To reach this summit, follow the directions carefully, since there are several unnamed high points in the area. Mount Volz can be seen from the trailhead to the east-northeast, and throughout the hike.

Named after the God of the North Wind, Boreas Pass was an important crossing between Breckenridge and South Park. The Denver South Park and Pacific operated a narrow gauge line along the present county road until the 1930s. After your hike, stop in Como to take a peak at the old round house, one of only a few still remaining from that period.

While this hike is pleasant at any time of the summer, it is especially fine in the fall, with gorgeous displays of aspen throughout South Park and along the pass road.

Mount Volz is always in sight on this hike. (Terry Root)

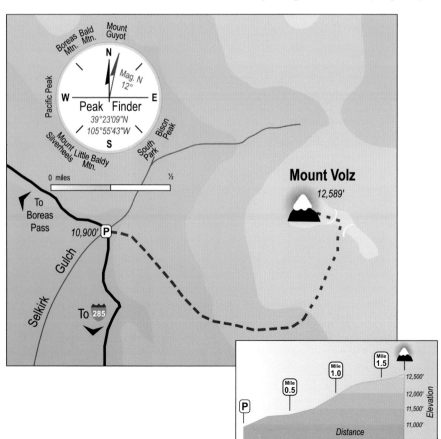

31 ROUND HILL 11,243 Feet

An interesting tour of historic Fairplay can be combined with this hike in beautiful South Park.

Distance: 3.2 miles each way
Hiking Time: Up in 80 minutes, down in 70 minutes
Starting Elevation: 10,080 feet
Elevation Gain: 1,163 feet
Trail: All the way until 300 feet from the top
Season: Late May to late October
Jurisdiction: Pike National Forest
Maps: *USGS 7 ½'* — Fariplay West; *County* — Park #1; *USFS* — Pike National Forest; *Trails Illustrated* — #110

Directions to the Trailhead

Drive south on US-285 from the intersection of CO-9 at Fairplay for 4.75 miles. Turn west onto Park County Road 5, which is the more northerly route to Weston Pass from the east. After 1.7 miles on this road, a side road leads to the right at a sign *"Breakneck Pass Road — Private Property next 1.5 miles. Stay on Main Road."* Follow this road, passable to regular cars, for at least 1.65 miles to a sign stating that you are entering the Pike National Forest. Park off the road at this point.

The Hike

To within 100 yards of the summit

Proceed on the old mining road, designated #175, as it leads west, and then southwest, in 1.8 miles to Breakneck Pass. At the pass, which is well-forested, take a mining road which leads southeast (left) off the main road. Follow this road as it gradually ascends to just east of the summit. Leave the road and hike about 100 yards west to the unmarked, tree-covered summit. Return by the same route. (About 50 yards west of Breakneck Pass there is a four-way intersection. Road 175 goes east and west, with the western road passing into Sheep Park. Road 426 goes north, dead-ending along Sheep Ridge, and south to join the Weston Pass Road.)

FYI

Despite the name, Breakneck Pass can easily be reached by four-wheel drive or mountain bike. Stands of aspen are common along the road, making this a good fall hike.

Settled in 1859, Fairplay was originally called South Park City and once had a population as high as 8,000. It was renamed as a retort to the gold strike at Tarryall which locals called "Grab-all." After your hike, if interested in the history of the old west and western mining, visit the *South Park City Museum* in Fairplay. 34 buildings have been moved here and restored and a narrow gauge train stands at the depot. It's all at the corner of 4th and Front Street.

The road up to Breakneck
Pass is lined with aspen,
making this a fine fall hike.
(Eric Wiseman)

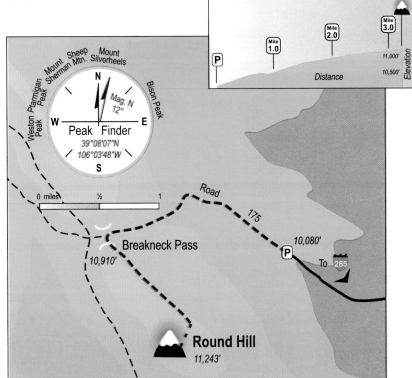

32 KINGSTON PEAK 12,147 Feet

*E*asy access makes Kingston Peak a fine early evening hike during the long days of summer.

Distance: 1.9 miles each way
Hiking Time: Up in 82 minutes, down in 58 minutes
Starting Elevation: 10,470 feet
Elevation Gain: 1,677 feet
Trail: To St. Marys Lake, off-trail beyond the lake
Season: Early June to early October
Jurisdiction: Arapaho National Forest
Maps: *USGS 7 ½'* — Empire; *County* — Clear Creek; *USFS* — Arapaho National Forest, *Trails Illustrated* — #103

Directions to the Trailhead

Drive west of Idaho Springs on I-70 for about two miles and turn off at Exit #238. Go north on Fall River Road (which is designated Road 275) for 9.7 miles to a right turning curve off the paved road. Turn left at this curve and drive north-northwest on a dirt road, with Silver Lake on your right (east), for 0.2 miles to a four-way intersection. Park off the road. Regular cars can come this far.

The Hike

From the four-way intersection, proceed south up an old mining road at the foot of Fox Mountain for about ten minutes to a bend in the road toward the north. Follow a trail, which passes to the west from the road on the north side of the creek. In another seven minutes, this trail will bring you to the east side of Saint Marys Lake. Continue on the trail, past the north end of the lake, to the area of Saint Marys Glacier, where the trail ends. Hike west and up, either around or through the icefield, for 0.75 miles. (The best route to avoid the snow and ice is to keep well to the right of the glacier.) At the top of the glacier, turn north for another 0.6 miles over tundra to a summit cairn with two poles. Descend via your ascent route.

> ## FYI
>
> Kingston Peak forms part of the boundary between the Roosevelt and Arapaho National Forests and between Gilpin and Clear Creek Counties. The best time for this hike is late August or early September when St. Marys Glacier is most easily traversed or bypassed. Kingston is also a popular evening hike in the summer, due to its easy access.
>
> St. Marys Glacier isn't really a true "glacier," but rather, a semi-permanent snowfield. Use care while on it, as several accidents per year typically occur here, including occasional injuries from uncontrolled slides into exposed rocks at the base.

By late summer, the "glacier" has shrunk to half the size of a few months earlier. The route goes up the right side of the gulley, then on to the open tundra slopes of Kingston Peak.
(Terry Root)

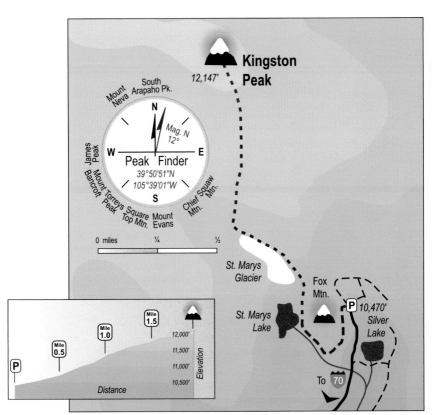

33 MOUNT EPWORTH 11,843 Feet

Follow the historic path of one of the highest operating railroads in the world on your ascent of Mount Epworth.

Distance: 3.25 miles each way
Hiking Time: Up in 83 minutes, down in 72 minutes
Starting Elevation: 11,080 feet
Elevation Gain: 1,263 feet (Includes 250 feet extra each way)
Trail: Initial 3.0miles, talus and tundra beyond
Season: Mid June to mid October
Jurisdiction: Arapaho National Forest
Maps: USGS 7 ½' — East Portal; County — Grand #4;
USFS — Arapaho National Forest, Trails Illustrated — #103

Directions to the Trailhead

Either drive on US-40 11.8 miles north from Berthoud Pass or drive 1.75 miles south from Vasquez Road in Winter Park. Turn northwest onto the Rollins Pass (Corona Pass) Road. Follow the road for a total of 11.0 miles to an abandoned railroad trestle on your left, at what is known as Riflesight Notch. Regular cars can make it this far, if there is no obstructing snow. Park here off the road.

En route to this trailhead on the Corona Pass Road, keep right at 3.7 miles, continue straight (southeast) at a five-way intersection at mile 3.8, keep right on the main road at mile 4.55, keep southeast on the main road at a four-way intersection at mile 6.6, keep right at mile 8.6 and again at mile 8.85. In optimal conditions, regular vehicles may be able to reach Corona Pass and shorten this hike considerably.

The Hike

To within 0.4 mile of the summit

Continue on foot up the road, winding east and north for 2.5 miles, to a point five minutes past a sign on your left with the number 17. Two lakes and Mount Epworth will be to the west (on your left). Near the level of the more northerly, Pumphouse Lake, an old mining road leaves the main road and descends to the north (left). After about four minutes on this road, take a left fork and soon leave this road, passing to the northwest of the lake and ascending the north ridge of Mount Epworth. Proceed upward and south, over tundra and talus, to a modest cairn at the summit. Descend by your ascent route, since the loop descent to the southwest from the top loses too much altitude and distance.

FYI

John Quincy Adams Rollins built a toll road over what once was called Boulder Pass, then Rollins Pass and later, Corona Pass. One of the highest operating railroads in the world also operated over this route from 1904 until the rails were tore up in 1937.

Epworth is the English village where John and Charles Wesley were born. The *Epworth League*, a national Methodist organization, named this mountain on July 8, 1905.

Mount Epworth, with a view west toward the Winter Park Ski Area.
(Terry Root)

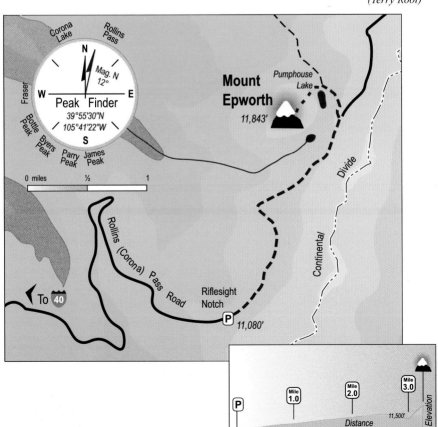

34 TREMONT MOUNTAIN 10,388 Feet

A tremendous view of over 100 miles of the Continental Divide can be enjoyed from this rocky summit.

Distance: 1.0 mile each way
Hiking Time: Up in 90 minutes, down in 60 minutes
Starting Elevation: 8,860 feet
Elevation Gain: 1,528 feet
Trail: Initial 0.25 mile, bushwack beyond with some scrambling
Season: Early May to early November
Jurisdiction: Golden Gate Canyon State Park
Maps: *USGS 7 ½'* — Black Hawk; *County* — Gilpin, *Trails Illustrated* — #100; Golden Gate Canyon State Park Map

Directions to the Trailhead

Drive to Golden Gate Canyon State Park, northwest of Golden and northeast of Black Hawk. From CO-93, 1.0 mile north of Golden, turn west onto Golden Gate Canyon Road (Jefferson County Road 70.) At mile 13.0, there is an intersection where Jefferson County Road 70 becomes CO-46. Stop at the visitor center there, on your right, to pay the park day-use fee at the self-service kiosk. Continue west on CO-46 for another 1.1 miles to the intersection with Mountain Base Road.

Alternately, you may go north on CO-119 for 5.3 miles from Blackhawk and then east on CO-46 for another 4.0 miles to reach Mountain Base Road. Proceed north on Mountain Base Road to the Coyote Trailhead at Bootleg Bottom. Park there on the right (east) side of the road.

The Hike

Begin by going east, and up, on the Coyote Trail for about one quarter mile to a sharp turn of the trail to the southeast, at about 9400 feet. Leave the trail at this point and head northeast, up to the western (left) side of Tremont Mountain. The slope is quite steep near the top, before you gain a ridge which leads southeast to the rocky summit. There is some easy hand work on this short, summit ridge. A hole drilled into the rock and an upright piece of wood are the only markers. The best route down is as you came up.

FYI

Tremont Mountain is the highest point in Golden Gate Canyon State Park. From the summit, you have a spectacular view west of an over 100-mile stretch of the Continental Divide.

This park is well maintained and contains nearly 60 miles of clearly marked hiking trails. After your hike, stop again at the visitor center, located just inside the southeast corner of the park, off Golden Gate Canyon Road. Here you will find displays and the *Wilbur and Nellie Larkin Memorial Nature Trail.* This trail is designed to be accessible to persons with disabilities and winds around the park's rainbow trout show pond.

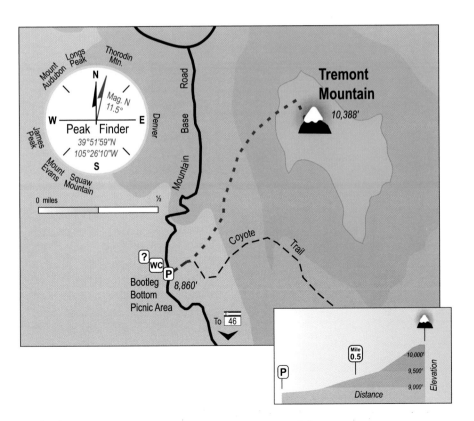

Looking west from the summit of Tremont Mountain at the Indian Peaks section along the Continental Divide. (Terry Root)

35 MOUNT SHERIDAN 13,748 Feet

Rich mining history is featured along the way to this high alpine summit.

Distance: 1.25 miles each way
Hiking Time: Up in 90 minutes, down in 60 minutes
Starting Elevation: 12,200 feet
Elevation Gain: 1,548 feet
Trail: Part of the way, plus off-trail tundra walking
Season: Early June to early October
Jurisdiction: Pike National Forest
Maps: *USGS 7 ½'* — Mount Sherman and Fairplay West;
County — Park #1 and Lake; *USFS* — Pike National Forest; *Trails Illustrated* — #110

Directions to the Trailhead

From the junction of CO-9 and US-285 in Fairplay, drive south on US-285 for 1.25 miles. Then turn west (right) and follow Park County 18 (also known as the Fourmile Creek Road) for 12.3 miles to two metal posts on each side of the road. (Keep right at the fork near the Leavick town site.) In most years, regular cars can drive to this point or close to it. Park here.

The Hike

Proceed west, up the road to the old Dauntless Mine. Then leave the road and hike up, and southwest, to the saddle between Peerless Mountain to the south and Mount Sheridan to the north. A faint trail goes up the ridge to a small cairn and a makeshift register atop Mount Sheridan. Descend as you came up, by way of the abandoned Dauntless Mine.

For extra credit, you may wish to hike up Peerless Mountain to the south, adding 0.4 miles each way and 208 feet of elevation gain. Mount Sherman, a popular fourteener, is accessible via the ridge to the north.

FYI

This area is rich in mining history. The Last Chance Mine was located on the side of Mount Sheridan. Another large producer was the Hilltop Mine, located at the saddle between Mount Sheridan and Mount Snerman. Many of the miners lived in the nearby towns of Leavick and Horseshoe, which you pass in your car en route to the trailhead. The Denver and South Park Railroad once reached Leavick, whose population approximated 200 before the turn of the century.

While you may have the summit of Mount Sheridan to yourself, you will likely spot several hikers trudging up nearby Mount Sherman's south ridge. Many consider Sherman to be one of the easiest fourteeners because of its high start. Both Sheridan and Sherman were named for Civil War-era generals on the Union side.

Trudging up to the Peerless-Sheridan saddle in early summer. (Linda Grey)

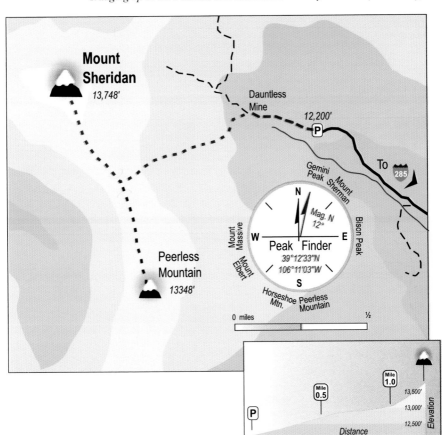

Mount Sheridan
13,748'

Dauntless Mine

12,200'
P

Gemini Peak

Mount Sherman

To 285

Mount Massive

N
Mag. N 12°

W Peak Finder E
39°12'33"N
106°11'03"W

Bison Peak

Mount Elbert

S

Peerless Mountain
13348'

Horseshoe Mtn.   Peerless Mountain

0 miles   ½

Mile 0.5
Mile 1.0
13,500'
13,000'
12,500'
P
Distance
Elevation

36 REVENUE MOUNTAIN 12,889 Feet

*E*asy ridge walking from this peak leads to other close-by summits for extra credit.

Distance: 1.9 miles each way
Hiking Time: Up in 85 minutes, down in 70 minutes
Starting Elevation: 10,850 feet
Elevation Gain: 2,039 feet
Trail: Initial 1.0 mile, tundra and talus beyond
Season: Early June to early October
Jurisdiction: Arapaho National Forest
Maps: *USGS 7 ½'* — Montezuma; *County* — Summit #2; *USFS* — Arapaho National Forest, *Trails Illustrated* — #104

Directions to the Trailhead

Drive via I-70 and US-6 to the Keystone Ski Resort, which lies east of Lake Dillon. Turn south off US-6 onto the Montezuma Road. In fifty yards, jog left, and then right once past the ski area parking lot. Drive east up this road for 4.8 miles from US-6 to the Peru Creek Road, which begins on the left at a curve in the road. Drive northeast up Peru Creek for 3.8 miles and turn right off the main road onto an unmarked road. This is the road up Cinnamon Gulch. Park here, before Peru Creek is crossed. (With four-wheel drive, you can travel 0.85 miles up into the basin for a higher starting point. The hike information given is based on a start from Peru Creek.)

The Hike

Peru Creek Road is the CDT

Go south, cross Peru Creek and stay on the mining road, which rises into Cinnamon Gulch. Several side roads lead to old mining operations. At the first three forks go left, right and right as you head toward the basin. In a little less than a mile, you arrive at a large, open area and a road fork. Take the right fork and continue south as you ascend further into the basin. Revenue Mountain will be visible to the southeast. Just below timberline, leave the road and go directly south, over easy tundra, to the saddle between Silver Mountain on the right and Revenue Mountain on the left. An old mining cabin lies below the

A skiff of early snow dusts the slopes of Revenue Peak in this late season view.

(*Eric Wiseman*)

> ### FYI
>
> Revenue Mountain lies on the boundary between Summit and Clear Creek Counties. Peru Gulch was the site of extensive mining in the late eighteen hundreds. This hike should be attempted late in the season when Peru Creek will be lower and more easily crossed.

Revenue Mountain summit. Follow the ridge, then go eastward to the top, where there is a cairn and a small register jar. Decatur Mountain to the northeast, Silver Mountain to the west and Brittle Silver Mountain to the northwest are all accessible by easy ridge walks from Revenue Mountain. Descend as you came up, unless you wish to walk the ridge to some of these other nearby peaks.

Looking out the door of the old miner's cabin reveals the summit of Revenue Mountain, just a short walk away. (Eric Wiseman)

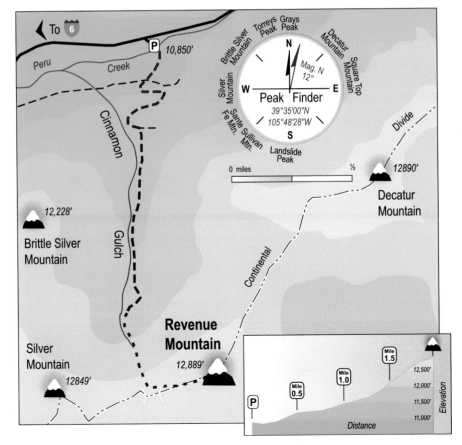

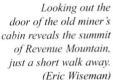

To 6

P 10,850'

Peru   Creek

Cinnamon   Gulch

12,228'

Brittle Silver Mountain

Brittle Silver Mountain Torreys Peak Grays Peak

Decatur Mountain

Square Top Mountain

Peak Finder

Silver Mountain

N

Mag. N 12°

W   E

39°35'00"N
105°48'28"W

Santa Sullivan Fe Mtn. Mtn.

S

Landslide Peak

0 miles   ½

Divide

12890'

Decatur Mountain

Continental

Revenue Mountain

12,889'

Silver Mountain

12849'

P

Mile 1.5

Mile 1.0

Mile 0.5

12,500'
12,000'
11,500'
11,000'

Elevation

Distance

37 WOODS MOUNTAIN 12,940 Feet

Descend by your ascent route or create an interesting loop trip with more summits to explore.

Distance: 2.55 miles each way
Hiking Time: Up in 88 minutes, down in 70 minutes
Starting Elevation: 10,800 feet
Elevation Gain: 2,190 feet (includes 25 feet extra each way)
Trail: Initial 1.5 miles, tundra walking beyond
Season: Early June to early October
Jurisdiction: Arapaho National Forest
Maps: *USGS 7 ½'* — Berthoud Pass and Grays Peak;
County — Clear Creek; *USFS* — Arapaho National Forest; *Trails Illustrated* — #104

Directions to the Trailhead

Drive west from US-40 on the Henderson Mine cutoff road, 5.9 miles south of Berthoud Pass or 7.4 miles west of Empire. In 0.4 miles, turn left toward Urad Lake. You will drive a total of 3.65 miles southwest from US-40 to a creek crossing at the inlet to Urad Lake. Park here. En route to this point, go straight at 1.7 miles, keep right at 2.7 miles, keep left at 2.8 miles and continue straight at 3.1 miles, staying above Urad Lake.

The Hike

Proceed on the road, as it curves north and then returns to a southwesterly direction into the gulch along Woods Creek. After 0.5 miles, take the right fork and keep the creek on your left. In 0.6 miles further, follow the road as it crosses the creek and soon ends just below timberline. Continue south-southwest toward the head of the valley. Turn south and gain the ridge over tundra, wherever the route appears easiest. At the ridge, follow a faint trail which goes east over a false summit to the nondescript, flat, unmarked top of Woods Mountain. To return, retrace your ascent route, or descend to the north-northwest over steep tundra to Woods Creek and the road back to your vehicle.

An alternate, loop trip is possible by descending the northeast ridge to an old mine at the 12,000-foot level. A jeep trail switchbacks down from here into the Ruby Creek drainage, leading back north to the access road.

 FYI

From Woods Mountain, one can ascend the ridge to the east-southeast and easily reach Mount Parnassus and Bard Peak. If you do so, then the easiest descent is to return to the saddle between Woods Mountain and Mount Parnassus. Descend northeast from here to Ruby Creek. Pick up the jeep trail where it crosses Ruby Creek, at just below timberline. Follow this jeep trail north, along the east bank of the creek, down to the intersection with the access road. Turn left here and walk west back up the road to your car in a little more than 1.0 mile.

Woods Mountain, as viewed from the access road to the north. The described route goes up the right hand ridge. Mount Parnassus is on the left. (Eric Wiseman)

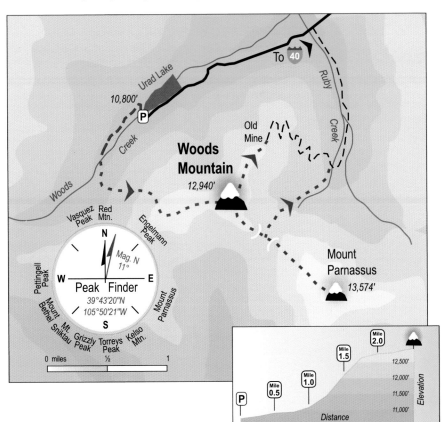

38 LITTLE BALDY MOUNTAIN 12,142 Feet

Easily spotted from South Park, Little Baldy Mountain is a favorite with the locals.

Distance: 2.0 miles each way
Hiking Time: Up in 88 minutes, down in 76 minutes
Starting Elevation: 10,240 feet
Elevation Gain: 2,002 feet (includes 50 feet extra each way)
Trail: Initial 0.5 miles, bushwacking beyond
Season: Early June to early October
Jurisdiction: Pike National Forest
Maps: *USGS 7 ½'* — Como; *County* — Park #1;
USFS — Pike National Forest; *Trails Illustrated* — #109

Directions to the Trailhead

From 10.0 miles north of Fairplay on US-285, drive north on the Boreas Pass Road (Park County Road 33) through the town of Como for 3.4 miles and arrive at a fork. The right fork goes to Boreas Pass. Take the left fork, west and then northwest, for 0.8 miles, avoiding another right fork. Take a faint road going off to the left (southwest) for 0.06 miles and park at a barrier blocking further vehicular traffic.

The Hike

Along Boreas Pass Road

Continue on the road, pass under the chain preventing vehicular access and cross Tarryall Creek on an earthen bridge. Follow the road as it curves to the left (southeast). In about eight minutes from the trailhead, take a right fork and continue southeast. The road soon ends at two private cabins. Avoiding any private property, hike due south and lose 50 feet of elevation as you descend toward South Tarryall Creek. Keep to the right of the creek and three abandoned cabins. Little Baldy Mountain may now be visible directly south. Enter the woods, following an abandoned road which heads west. When the road becomes obscure, continue to bushwhack up and south through the relatively sparse forest. You eventually reach a talus slope, followed by some more trees and then more talus. Above timberline, a cairn on top of a false summit marks the route. The high point lies at the south end of a mesa and is marked by a rock cairn with an embedded pole. An animal skull was on the pole on the day I was there. Retrace your ascent route for the return.

FYI

This is the prominent peak at the southwest end of the Boreas Pass Road, easily seen from South Park. It is a favorite with the locals in Como, the little town that sits at the foot of the mountain. Como was orignally the Stubbs Ranch and was named after Lake Como by the many Italian workers who lived there.

Some private homes exist in the area but no prohibitive signs are to be seen throughout this route.

Little Baldy Mountain forms the backdrop for the South Park town of Como. (Eric Wiseman)

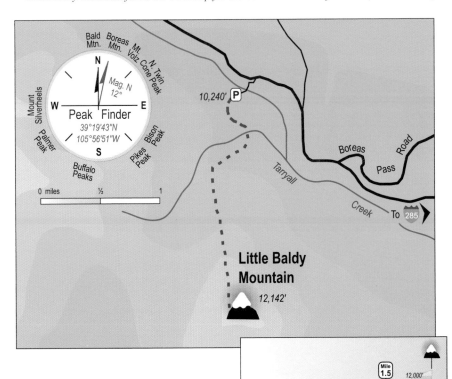

39 KELSO MOUNTAIN 13,164 Feet

A stunning view of the Fourteeners, Grays and Torreys, can be enjoyed from the summit of Kelso Mountain.

Distance: 2.75 miles on ascent, 1.5 miles on descent
Hiking Time: Up in 93 minutes, down in 54 minutes
Starting Elevation: 11,230 feet
Elevation Gain: 1,934 feet
Trail: Initial 1.9 miles on ascent, final 1.0 mile on descent
Season: Early June to early October
Jurisdiction: Arapaho National Forest
Maps: USGS 7 ½' — Grays Peak; County — Clear Creek; USFS — Arapaho National Forest; Trails Illustrated — #104

Directions to the Trailhead

Drive south from the Bakerville Exit (Exit # 221) of I-70 for 3.4 miles to the trailhead. The road is blocked just before the defunct Stevens Mine, further south. En route to the parking area near the trailhead, take left forks at mile 1.35 and mile 2.3. A regular car can make it up this steep, rough road to the trailhead area. Restrooms and an information board are next to the large, gravel parking area. On summer weekends, the parking lot fills up very early with hikers intent on climbing the twin fourteeners. Late arrivals may be forced to park alongside the access road.

The Hike

Cross the pedestrian bridge over the creek and quickly access the old mining road going southwest up Stevens Gulch. This road is closed to vehicles. In almost two miles, the road becomes a trail and crosses the creek amid two cairns. Leave the trail (which continues southwest up to Grays Peak) at this point and ascend north-northwest over steep tundra to gain Kelso's south ridge. Alternately, you may continue southwest on the Grays Peak Trail (a section of the Continental Divide Trail) for another

Grays Peak Trail is the CDT

0.25 mile before heading directly for the Torreys/Kelso saddle. An old miner's cabin still stands here, just below the saddle.

Once on the ridge, continue north to the summit cairn. The best descent route is over the steep tundra to the east, to regain the trail which leads back to the trailhead. In early June, when snow still blankets this slope, bring your ice axe for an enjoyable glissade down to the trail.

FYI

This mountain is named after William Fletcher Kelso, a local prospector in the mining era. The mountain was to be pierced by a railroad tunnel that would pass beneath the Continental Divide to reach the rich mining regions on the Western Slope. But only a small portion of the tunnel was completed and the scheme ran out of funds when the rails reached Bakerville in the 1880s.

North ridge of Kelso Mountain from the Grays Peak Trail

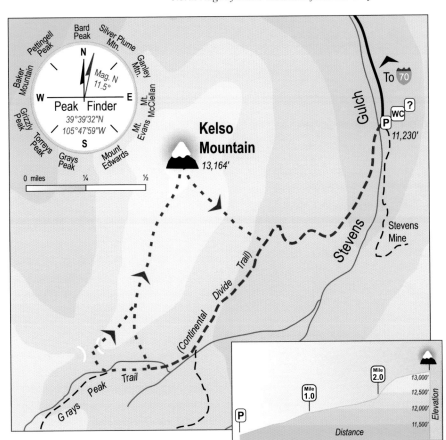

40 BOTTLE PEAK 11,584 Feet

In winter this valley is "the icebox of the nation," but in season, this little peak is a summer delight.

Distance: 1.75 miles each way
Hiking Time: Up in 57 minutes, down in 35 minutes
Starting Elevation: 10,440 feet
Elevation Gain: 1,194 feet (includes 25 feet extra each way)
Trail: All the way
Season: Late May to mid October
Jurisdiction: Arapaho NF, Byers Peak Wilderness Area
Maps: *USGS 7 ½'* — Bottle Pass; *County* — Grand #4; *USFS* — Arapaho National Forest; *Trails Illustrated* — #103

Directions to the Trailhead

From US-40 at the town of Fraser (northwest of Winter Park and southeast of Granby), drive west on Eisenhower Drive at a sign directing you to Town Park. Drive past the library on your left, cross the railroad tracks and make an immediate left turn onto Leonard Lane. This road runs parallel to the train tracks and curves right to become Mills Avenue and Forest Road 160. Continue on this good dirt road as it leads southwest up the valley. From US-40, you will take the following forks: right at mile 2.8, left at mile 4.7, straight at a four-way intersection at mile 4.8, right at mile 6.5, right at mile 7.2 (at the Byers Creek Campground sign), right at mile 7.5 (follow the sign to the Bottle Pass Trail), right at mile 9.5, left at mile 9.6, right at mile 9.9, right at mile 10.5, left at mile 10.7 and reach the trail to Bottle Pass, on the right, at mile 12.0. Park off the road here. Regular cars can reach this point and the road-end, 0.4 miles further.

The Hike

Begin west up the trail. After some switchbacks, you will reach a ridge and tundra just below timberline after 0.8 miles. Then turn right and follow a series of cairns north-northwest up to the top of Bottle Peak. A pole in a rock pile marks this point. (Bottle Pass is a few hundred yards to the west, with Ptarmigan Peak not far beyond.) Return as you ascended.

FYI

Grand County is named after its Grand Lake and the Grand River, the original name of the Colorado River. The town of Fraser, and the Fraser River running through it, were named for Reuben Frazier, an early settler of the area. The re-spelling occured after a post office was begun in the town. Fraser calls itself "the icebox of the nation" due to the frequently recorded low temperatures there.

On the drive in, you will pass the headquarters for the Fraser Experimental Forest. They have been studying the effect of management practices here on water yield and quality since 1937.

Ptarmigan Peak (left) and Bottle Peak (right) straddle Bottle Pass in this view from the south.

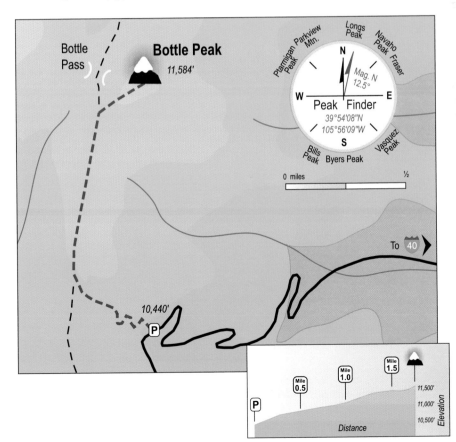

41 GRIFFITH MOUNTAIN 11,558 Feet

Hike through an historic mining district where the hills once echoed with the sound of pick and shovel.

Distance: 2.5 miles each way
Hiking Time: Up in 100 minutes, down in 60 minutes
Starting Elevation: 9,100 feet
Elevation Gain: 2,568 feet (includes 50 feet extra each way)
Trail: Initial 1.25 miles, bushwack beyond
Season: Late May to late October
Jurisdiction: Arapaho National Forest
Maps: *USGS 7 ½'* — Georgetown; *County* — Clear Creek; *USFS* — Arapaho National Forest; *Trails Illustrated* — #104

Directions to the Trailhead

From Exit #240 of I-70 at the town of Idaho Springs, drive southwest on CO-103 for 6.7 miles. At a sharp bend in the road, a dirt road leads southwest up West Chicago Creek. Drive up this road for 1.1 miles to an area on the right (north), just before a group of houses and a creek flowing under the road to the southeast. Being careful to avoid private property, park off the road in this general area.

The Hike

Continue on foot up the public road, about 200 yards southwest of the creek crossing. Just past some houses on your right, leave the road and ascend steeply northwest. Within one hundred feet, gain an abandoned mining road passing to the west. Take this road, continuing your ascent to the west. Stay on the road, which crosses a ridge and descends a bit, before resuming its upward, west-northwest direction. Eventually an old cabin is reached in a clearing, to the left of the road. Leave the road at this point and enter a relatively sparse area of forest on your right, ascending northwest over many decaying tree fragments, all the way to the top. The summit lies on a small natural rock formation and has no identifying markers. Return by the same route, bushwhacking southeast about a mile until you reach the trail.

FYI

This mountain is named after two early Clear Creek miners, the Griffith brothers, David and George. Georgetown was named after the later. There are several mines on the mountain, mostly on the Georgetown side. As opposed to gold mining in nearby Idaho Springs and Central City, the mines around Georgetown were among the first in the state to be developed on silver ore.

This hike passes by a large aspen forest carpeting the south slope of the peak and involves one mile of bushwhacking to and from the top. The views from the summit are best to the south, southeast and southwest, with many trees obscuring vistas in the other directions.

A backpacker descends through aspen on an abandoned road on Griffith Mountain's south slope. (Eric Wiseman)

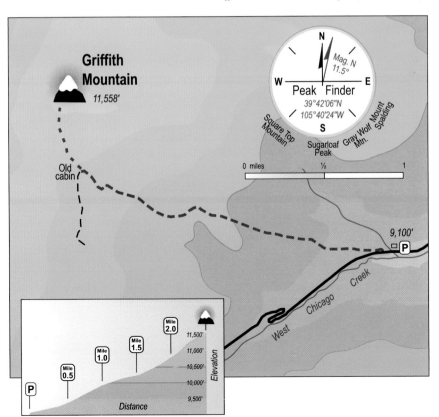

42 HORSETOOTH PEAK 10,344 Feet

Explore a remote corner of spectacular Rocky Mountain National Park on the way to this rocky summit.

Distance: 2.2 miles each way
Hiking Time: Up in 110 minutes, down in 68 minutes
Starting Elevation: 8,740 feet
Elevation Gain: 1,604 feet
Trail: Most of the way, with some bushwacking near the top
Season: Early May to early November
Jurisdiction: Roosevelt NF and Rocky Mountain NP
Maps: *USGS 7 ½'* — Allens Park; *County* — Boulder; *USFS* — Roosevelt National Forest; *Trails Illustrated* — #200

Directions to the Trailhead

Either drive south on CO-7 for 12.0 miles from US-36 in Estes Park or go 22.3 miles north on CO-7, from the junction with US-36 in Lyons, to Meeker Park. Opposite the Meeker Park Lodge is Colorado Road 113, going west past some cabins. This dirt road has a "Dead End" sign at its beginning. Follow this road west, a total of 0.7 miles, to where it ends near a cabin. En route, avoid side roads to cabins and stay on the well-maintained main road. Park off the road.

The Hike

Unmarked trails pass east and west from where you have parked at road end. Take the trail west, and in a minute you will enter Rocky Mountain National Park at a sign. Continue on the trail for about eight minutes, with Horse Creek on your left, until the trail clearly crosses the creek, rises and curves southwest, and then south, to reach a saddle between Horsetooth Peak on your left (northeast) and Lookout Mountain to your right (southwest). Bushwhack northeast up from the saddle to a prominent, unmarked rocky summit. Ascending the summit boulder is somewhat demanding and requires the use of hands. Descend by way of your ascent route.

FYI

Horsetooth Peak is named for the configuration of its summit. The distinctive summit boulder may prove unnegotiable for the solo hiker. A second person can provide the necessary support. No entrance fee is required to access Rocky Mountain National Park by this route. This is in a remote part of the park, most often used by mountaineers intent on climbing Mount Meeker's east ridge.

Pope John Paul II stayed at nearby Camp St. Malo on his visit to Colorado in 1993 and hiked on a portion of this trail. After your hike, you might want to drive north for 1.0 mile on CO-7 for a look at the dramatic statue of Christ erected on the site after founder Msgr. Joseph J. Bosetti saw a fiery meteor fall from the sky in 1916.

Aspen leaves along Horse Creek.
(Steve Waterman)

The distinctive outcropping
on its summit, as viewed
here from the saddle, gives
Horsetooth Peak its name.

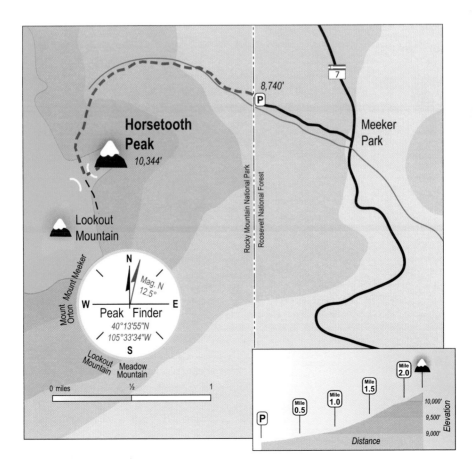

43 RED MOUNTAIN 12,315 Feet

This prominent peak west of Empire has collapsed on its northwest flank from intense mining.

Distance: 1.2 miles each way
Hiking Time: Up in 90 minutes, down in 75 minutes
Starting Elevation: 10,115 feet
Elevation Gain: 2,200 feet
Trail: Bushwack all the way, with some easy scrambling up top
Season: Early June to early October
Jurisdiction: Arapaho National Forest
Maps: *USGS 7 ½'* — Berthoud Pass; *County* — Clear Creek; *USFS* — Arapaho National Forest; *Trails Illustrated* — #103

Directions to the Trailhead

Drive west on US-40 (Main Street) in the town of Empire, toward Berthoud Pass, for 7.4 miles or drive 5.9 miles on US-40 south from Berthoud Pass. Then turn west off the main road at the Big Bend Picnic Area sign and drive 0.4 miles west to a fork. Take the left fork toward the Urad Mine, drive southwest for 1.05 miles, and park off the road in a large, open, flat area. Red Mountain is directly to the west.

The Hike

Cross the flat area to the west and ascend quite steeply into an avalanche couloir. As you gain altitude, cross an old mining road and continue west and up, until you reach the northeast ridge of Red Mountain. Continue up along the ridge, to the southwest, and reach timberline. Continue past some old mine ruins and ascend a talus slope to a false summit. Go over an easy rocky traverse, staying mostly to the southwest, to the summit cairn, a red and white metal pole and a register cylinder. Hands may occasionally be necessary in negotiating the rocky traverse before the summit, but there is no special risk or danger.

The best descent is your ascent route. However, if a loop trip is desired, you may descend steeply from the saddle, between the true and

The old Urad Mine.

(Terry Root)

FYI

Red Mountain, one of several so-named in Colorado, is a prominent, pyramidal-shaped peak, southwest of Berthoud Pass. This hike requires bushwhacking all the way to timberline but the summit ridge is visible for virtually the entire route.

The Urad Mine, at the peak's southern base, processed mostly molybdenum ore, closing in 1974. From the summit area, you'll be able to peer down into the peak's collapsed northwest flank — a dramatic legacy of mining.

false summits, east into another couloir, southwest of the one in which you ascended. This connects eventually with an old mining road, bringing you down and southwest of the abandoned Urad Mine buildings and your car.

Red Mountain, as viewed from the east. The ascent route climbs up to the right hand ridge.
(Terry Root)

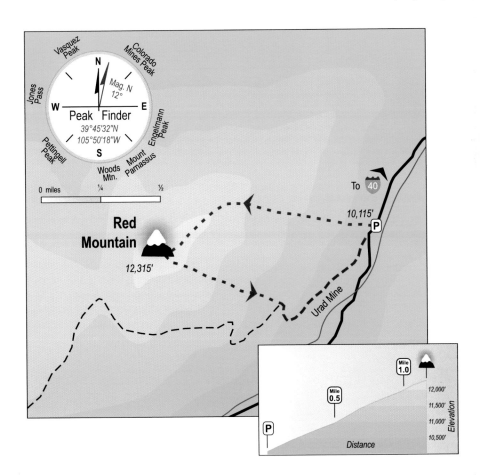

44 ESTES CONE 11,006 Feet

This perfectly formed cone offers 360 degree, panoramic views of Rocky Mountain National Park.

Distance: 3.0 miles each way
Hiking Time: Up in 87 minutes, down in 80 minutes
Starting Elevation: 9,400 feet
Elevation Gain: 2,206 feet (includes 300 feet extra each way)
Trail: All the way, with easy scrambling up top
Season: Early May to early November
Jurisdiction: Rocky Mountain National Park
Maps: *USGS 7 ½'* — Longs Peak; *County* — Larimer #3;
Trails Illustrated — #200; Rocky Mountain National Park Map

Directions to the Trailhead

Drive north from Lyons on CO-7 from its junction with US-36 for 25.1 miles or go south from Estes Park on CO-7 from its junction with US-36 for 9.2 miles. Turn west at the sign to Longs Peak Campground and drive for 1.1 miles to the parking area at road end, at the Longs Peak Ranger Station and trailhead. This parking lot fills to overflowing on summer weekends by mid-morning with climbers intent on scaling Longs Peak. Either do this hike mid-week or plan on an early start.

The Hike

Classics

Begin south on the excellent trail from the Longs Peak Ranger Station. Pass a trail register and follow the trail northwest, through the trees, to a fork, a half-mile from the trailhead. Go to the right and pass the ruins of the Eugenia Mine in 0.9 more miles. Continue north on the trail and descend into Moore Park. A corral and fork are reached 0.6 miles from the Eugenia Mine. Ascend the left fork to the north-northwest and, after a somewhat steeper six-tenths of a mile, reach a rock pile at a final fork. Take the right fork to the north, following a fainter trail and a series of cairns as the going becomes steeper. At the rocky summit block, follow the trail and cairns through a notch. Then descend briefly, before the final ascent to a large rock pile on top of Estes Cone. Some easy hand work may be needed. Enjoy the fantastic, 360 degree panorama, especially west to Mount Meeker and Longs Peak. Be careful to retrace your ascent route, following the cairns back down to the rock pile and taking the left fork.

FYI

This peak is prominent from CO-7 in the Longs Peak area. It is named after Joel Estes, who is said to have been the first settler in what is now called Estes Park. No admission fee is required for entering Rocky Mountain National Park at this trailhead.

The abandoned Eugenia Mine, with its spoil heap and rusty boiler, was not a success. Lack of valuable mineralization throughout most of the Park prevented widescale mining.

Estes Cone, shown here from Lily Lake, has excellent views of Longs Peak and Mount Meeker behind it. (Brent J. Murphy)

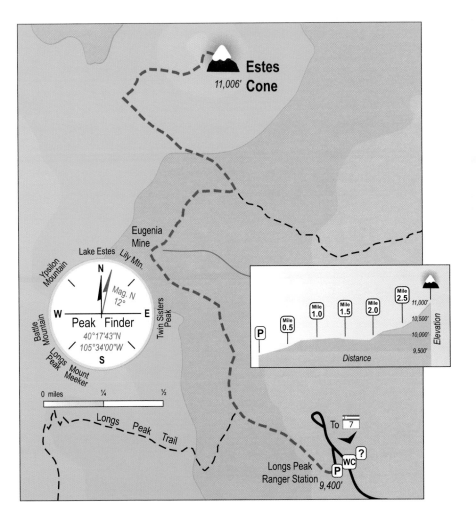

Estes Cone

11,006'

Eugenia Mine

Ypsilon Mountain

Lake Estes

Lily Mtn.

N

Mag. N 12°

W Peak Finder **E**

40°17'43"N
105°34'00"W

S

Battle Mountain

Longs Peak

Mount Meeker

Twin Sisters Peak

0 miles ¼ ½

Longs Peak Trail

To 7

Longs Peak Ranger Station *9,400'*

P WC ?

Mile 2.5

Mile 2.0

Mile 1.5

Mile 1.0

Mile 0.5

P

Elevation

11,000'
10,500'
10,000'
9,500'

Distance

45 VASQUEZ PEAK **12,947 Feet**

*V*asquez is a popular early season hike for good reason; snow melts quickly from its south-facing slopes.

Distance: 2.0 miles each way
Hiking Time: Up in 107 minutes, down in 55 minutes
Starting Elevation: 10,800 feet
Elevation Gain: 2,147 feet
Trail: Initial 0.33 miles, tundra and talus beyond
Season: Late May to early October
Jurisdiction: Arapaho NF, Vasquez Peak Wilderness
Maps: *USGS 7 ½'* — Berthoud Pass; *County* — Clear Creek; *USFS* — Arapaho National Forest; *Trails Illustrated* — #103

Directions to the Trailhead

Drive west on US-40 from its junction with I-70 for 9.6 miles, passing through the town of Empire. Turn left (west) at the big bend in the road, 5.9 miles south of Berthoud Pass. Continue west on this paved road, bypassing a left fork at 0.4 miles, for a total of 1.75 miles to the Henderson Mine entrance, where a dirt road goes off to the right, ascending to Jones Pass. Drive northwest up this road for 1.45 miles to some old ruins on the right, just before the road crosses the creek. Park off the road to the right. Many regular cars can drive this far. (Note that sometimes this road is closed to vehicles at a point 0.5 miles from the mine turnoff, lengthening your hike).

The Hike

Future crossing of CDT near treeline

Classics

Follow the old mining road to the north-northeast for one-third of a mile, until it ends. Then turn right (northeast) and ascend steeply through a bare area with a few dead trees. About 33 minutes from the trailhead, you will reach timberline. Turn left (north) and cross boulders, scree and tundra along the base of a false summit to your right (east). When you reach the drainage, turn right (northeast) and ascend to the saddle. Turn left (northwest) at the saddle and ascend the ridge, gaining the summit in eleven minutes or so. A large cairn and a register-jar mark the top.

To descend, return to the saddle and descend the drainage to the southwest, until around timberline. At timberline, go directly south (left), angling through the trees and back to the trailhead to complete the loop. If you prefer less tree cover and a less gradual loss of elevation, follow your ascent route.

FYI

This mountain is named after Louis Vasquez, one of the earliest settlers of Colorado. Vasquez was a hunter, explorer and fur trader. It is believed that he built the first cabin in Clear Creek County.

Vasquez Peak lies astride the Continental Divide. With its open, south facing slopes, Vasquez Peak is known as a fine, early season hike. An as-yet unbuilt portion of the Continental Divide Trail will traverse this slope in the future, crossing the route of this hike at treeline.

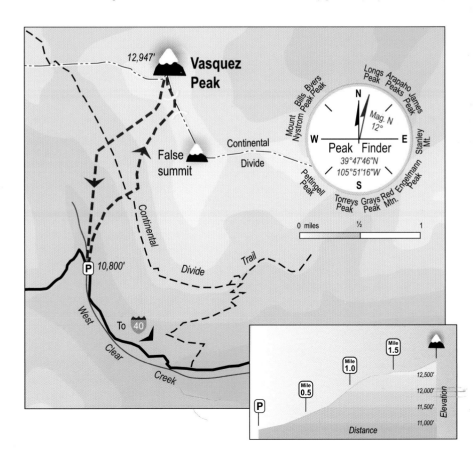

Hikers rest on Vasquez Peak in June, as snow still blankets nearby peaks. (Lloyd McClendon)

12,947'

Vasquez Peak

False summit

Continental Divide

Continental

Divide

Trail

P 10,800'

West Clear Creek

To 40

Peak Finder
39°47'46"N
105°51'16"W

N

W — E

S

Mag. N 12°

Mount Nystrom
Bills Peak
Byers Peak
Longs Peak
Arapaho Peaks
James Peak
Stanley Mt.
Engelmann Peak
Red Mtn.
Grays Peak
Torreys Peak
Pettingell Peak

0 miles   ½   1

P

Mile 0.5

Mile 1.0

Mile 1.5

12,500'
12,000'
11,500'
11,000'

Elevation

Distance

46 CARIBOU PEAK 12,310 Feet

The view from this gentle summit takes in the southernmost, glacier-fed lakes in the Rockies.

Distance: 3.9 miles each way
Hiking Time: Up in 115 minutes, down in 85 minutes
Starting Elevation: 9,960 feet
Elevation Gain: 2,640 feet (includes 145 feet extra each way)
Trail: To within 100 feet of the top
Season: Early June to early October
Jurisdiction: Roosevelt NF, Indian Peaks Wilderness Area
Maps: USGS 7 ½' — Ward; *County* — Boulder;
USFS — Roosevelt National Forest; *Trails Illustrated* — #102

Directions to the Trailhead

From the traffic circle in Nederland at the junction with CO-119, drive north on CO-72 for 7.0 miles and turn left onto Road 116 to the Rainbow Lakes Campground. Follow this dirt road for eight-tenths of a mile and take the left fork for the next 3.4 miles. Go right at another fork for the final eight-tenths of a mile to a parking area, located on the right at the Arapaho Glacier Trailhead. Regular cars can readily reach this trailhead.

The Hike

The trail begins at the left side of the parking area at a sign stating, "Glacier Rim Trail, Arapaho Glacier Overlook 6 (miles), Arapaho Pass Trail 8 (miles)." Follow this clear trail, generally north and then west, as it rises above timberline along the boundary of the Boulder watershed area, and then up the northern flank of Caribou Peak. About 100 feet below the top, leave the trail and ascend south to a huge cairn with an embedded metal pole. The only other marker on the summit is a small adjacent cairn.

Descend by your ascent route. Or if you would like to make a loop out of it, then descend southeast, along faint jeep trails across the tundra, to near treeline. Pick up a trail here, descending northeast to Rainbow Lakes. Follow the trail around the north side of the lakes, as it tracks east, back to your trailhead.

FYI

Look north from the summit to see the shimmering, green lakes that catch the silt out of the Arapaho Glacier. This peak is officially unnamed; "Caribou" is actually the annotation of the USGS benchmark on top.

That name comes from the nearby, former Caribou Mine and the ghost town of Caribou. Silver was mined in this area. For President Grant's visit to Central City in 1882, silver bricks were sent from Caribou to line the walkway to the Teller House. The town of Caribou had as many as 3,000 residents in the mid-1870s. But fires devastated the town on several occasions, and after the last in 1889, most residents moved on. The townsite slowly drifted back to a natural state, with only a few foundations visible today.

The massive cairn on Caribou Peak is probably due to its significance as a USGS Benchmark location.

Caribou Peak from Rainbow Lakes.

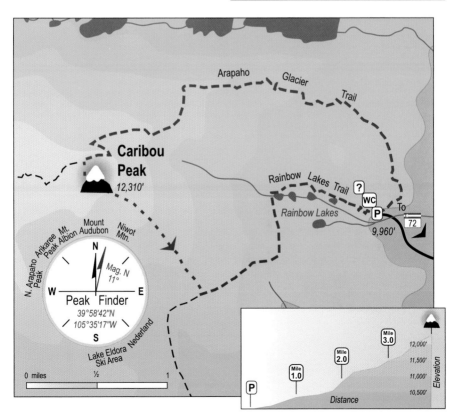

Arapaho Glacier Trail

Caribou Peak 12,310'

Rainbow Lakes Trail

? WC P

To 72

Rainbow Lakes

9,960'

N. Arapaho Peak Arikaree Mt. Peak Mount Albion Audubon Niwot Mtn.

N

Mag. N 11°

W E

Peak Finder

39°58'42"N 105°35'17"W

S

Lake Eldora Nederland Ski Area

0 miles ½ 1

P

Mile 1.0

Mile 2.0

Mile 3.0

12,000'

11,500'

11,000'

10,500'

Distance

Elevation

47 MOUNT TRELEASE 12,477 Feet

Hike up this summit, and while you are at it, grab another peak for extra credit.

Distance: 3.2 miles each way
Hiking Time: Up in 125 minutes, down in 95 minutes
Starting Elevation: 10,720 feet
Elevation Gain: 2,021 feet (includes 132 feet extra each way)
Trail: Initial 1.3 miles, bushwack beyond
Season: Early June to early October
Jurisdiction: Arapaho National Forest
Maps: *USGS 7 ½'* — Loveland Pass; *County* — Clear Creek; *USFS* — Arapaho National Forest; *Trails Illustrated* — #104

Directions to the Trailhead

From I-70, between Bakerville and the Eisenhower-Johnson Tunnel, take Exit 216. The exit road passes south under I-70 on its way to Loveland Pass. Instead, turn right (north and then northeast) and park alongside a neglected access road, blocked to vehicles in about a half mile.

The Hike

Proceed around the barrier and follow the access road northeast. You will pass two other barriers as the road rises, curves north and then northwest and enters Dry Gulch. After the road ends, hike about 0.4 miles further northwest, keeping to the right of the creek. There is only a faint trail from here onward. At about the 11,000-foot level, turn southwest, cross the creek and ascend Mount Trelease directly for about one mile, gaining about 1500 feet. The summit is visible to the right of a smaller subpeak. The top has no special marking. Take the same route back to the trailhead.

FYI

The Eisenhower-Johnson Tunnel was cut through the southwestern flank of Mount Trelease. It is the highest automobile tunnel in the world. The summit of Mount Trelease overlooks the Loveland Basin Ski Area to the south and Loveland Valley Ski Area to the southeast.

This hike is to a sub-peak identified on most maps as Mount Trelease. But the actual highpoint on the mountain is one-half mile west and some 500 feet higher. For extra credit, you may drop west off the summit and into a small saddle, before trudging up to the actual highpoint on the Continental Divide in about 40 minutes. You can return by the same route or drop north from the saddle into Dry Gulch. Follow the gulch down to the east, avoiding most of the willows by crossing to the north side of the creek.

Mount Trelease (foreground) and the actual highpoint on the Divide (left), as viewed from the south. (Eric Wiseman)

Hikers on the summit after a fall snow storm.

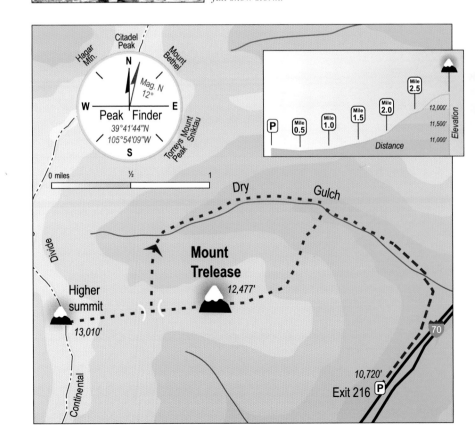

48 GRIZZLY PEAK 13,427 Feet

This is a wonderful hike for those that enjoy ridge walking above timberline — the views are endless.

Distance: 2.6 miles each way
Hiking Time: Up in 122 minutes, down in 95 minutes
Starting Elevation: 11,990 feet (Loveland Pass)
Elevation Gain: 2,387 feet (includes 475 feet extra each way)
Trail: All the way, with occasional gaps
Season: Early June to early October
Jurisdiction: Arapaho National Forest
Maps: *USGS 7 ½'* — Grays Peak; *County* — Clear Creek; *USFS* — Arapaho National Forest; *Trails Illustrated* — #104

Directions to the Trailhead

Drive to Loveland Pass on US-6, either south from I-70 via Exit 216 or west from Dillon and the Keystone resort area. Park at the summit of the pass, on the east side of the highway.

The Hike

Classics

Proceed up the ridge to the northeast on a clear trail. In about 25 minutes, leave this trail and turn right (southeast) before you reach the ridge. A trail passes in this direction, but is not essential to the hike. Contour until you eventually reach the ridge and continue southeast. You will lose elevation as you pass over or near several unnamed highpoints. The final saddle on the ridge lies 660 feet below the Grizzly Peak summit. A trail, present for most of the ridge, is very distinct on the scree for the final ascent. At the top is a semi-open rock shelter. The summit ridge extends toward Torreys Peak to the east. (The routes up that fourteener from this point, and from Chihuahua Gulch to the southeast, appear relatively easy.) Descend by your ascent route back to Loveland Pass, which can be seen throughout most of the hike.

FYI

Grizzly Peak, and much of this hike, are on the Continental Divide and the boundary between Clear Creek County and Summit County. This is a wonderful hike for those who enjoy ridge walking above timberline. The views are seemingly endless in all directions.

Get an early start, as the Colorado Rockies are infamous for brewing some fast-moving, afternoon thunderstorms. There have been several incidents on the ridges above Loveland Pass involving lightning. In each case, the hikers put themselves in jeopardy by staying high. If caught in the open on this ridge during an approaching storm, drop at least a few hundred feet off the ridge to wait things out.

A view down Chihuahua Gulch from the summit of Grizzly Peak.

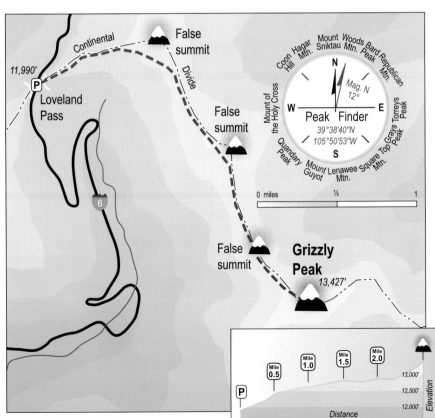

49 MOUNT BETHEL 12,705 Feet

*I*t is a short but steep climb to this prominent I-70 landmark — and well worth it.

Distance: 2.75 miles on ascent, 1.5 miles on descent
Hiking Time: Up in 93 minutes, down in 54 minutes
Starting Elevation: 11,230 feet
Elevation Gain: 1,934 feet
Trail: Initial 1.9 miles on ascent, final 1.0 mile on descent
Season: Early June to early October
Jurisdiction: Arapaho National Forest
Maps: *USGS 7 ½'* — Grays Peak, *County* — Clear Creek, *USFS* — Arapaho National Forest, *Trails Illustrated* — #104

Directions to the Trailhead

From I-70, between Bakerville and the Eisenhower-Johnson Tunnel, take Exit 216. The exit road passes south under I-70 on its way to Loveland Pass. Instead, turn right (north and then northeast) and park alongside a neglected access road, blocked to vehicles in about a half mile.

The Hike

Walk northeast on the frontage road, as it ascends and curves north, and then northwest, into Dry Gulch. The road is blocked to vehicles, but accessible on foot.

As you enter the basin, Mount Bethel will be visible on your right and is distinguishable by two rows of snow barricades on its southwest flank. At road end, keep a few hundred yards to the right of Dry Creek and soon begin to hike up and north, toward the saddle west of Mount Bethel. Before you reach the saddle, angle steeply northeast, gain the ridge and proceed to the cairn at the summit. Some easy hand work may be necessary, just before the ridge, but there is no special risk.

The descent can be made more directly due south, to the place where the road ended on your ascent. Aim downhill, passing between the snowfences. Once you reach the trees, it is steep but easy going through the scattered forest, down to the road.

FYI

The triangular top of this mountain dominates the western horizon, as one drives from Bakerville on I-70 toward Loveland Basin. The snowfences protect I-70 from snow accumulating in the obvious avalanche chute that faces the highway. Mount Bethel lies between Dry Gulch to the southeast and Herman Gulch to the northeast.

Formerly called Little Professor Peak, Mount Bethel was renamed to honor Ellsworth Bethel, a pathologist with the U.S. Department of Agriculture, who while a leader in the Colorado Mountain Club named several Front Range summits, including the Indian Peaks.

Mount Bethel from along the frontage road.

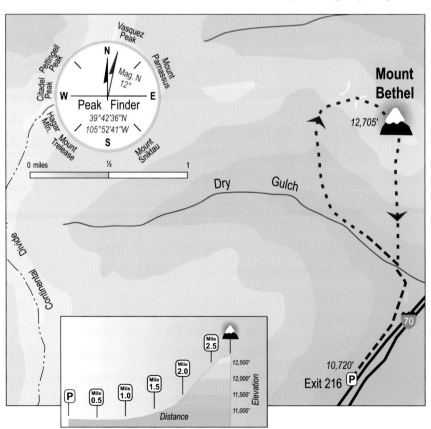

50 BERGEN PEAK 9,708 Feet

After a beautiful forest walk, you are rewarded with a fine view of the Mount Evans massif.

Distance: 4.6 miles each way
Hiking Time: Up in 120 minutes, down in 80 minutes
Starting Elevation: 7,760 feet
Elevation Gain: 2,708 feet (includes 380 feet extra each way)
Trail: All the way
Season: Mid April to late November
Jurisdiction: Jefferson County Open Space
Maps: *USGS 7 ½'* — Squaw Pass and Evergreen;
County — Jefferson #1; *Trails Illustrated* — #100; Elk Meadow Park Map

Directions to the Trailhead

Either drive south for 5.3 miles from the first traffic light, after crossing over I-70, at Exit #252 or drive north from Evergreen on CO-74 from the junction with Jefferson County Road 73 for 2.1 miles. Then turn west onto Stage Coach Boulevard, and in 1.1 miles, park on the right (north) in the trailhead parking area.

The Hike

Classics

Proceed to the northeast on a trail, past the picnic tables and toilets, to a junction in 0.3 miles. Take the left fork and continue along the Meadow View Trail for 0.6 miles. Then at another fork, go left again and head west, and then northwest, on the Bergen Peak Trail for 2.7 miles. Yet another left fork leads you in a counterclockwise route of one more mile to the Bergen Peak summit. The trail passes a scenic overlook and gets a bit faint later near the summit. You pass a wooden shack and a radio tower just before reaching the top, marked by a wooden elevation sign.

Take the same route back. If you want more exercise or variety, head back to the first trail intersection, one mile down from the summit, and take the left fork onto the Too Long Trail. This trail eventually curves around to connect with the beginning segments of your ascent route.

FYI

Bergen Peak is named after Thomas C. Bergen who came from Illinois seeking gold and settled west of Denver in 1859. His combined hotel and post office was a busy spot along the toll road west from Mount Vernon. He was one of the first three Jefferson County Commissioners.

Near the summit there are fine views of the Mount Evans massif, as it shimmers above the foreground foothill peaks. There are several other enjoyable trails in this Jefferson County Open Space Park, free and open to the public. If you bring your dog, enjoy the designated off-leash area, in a pretty meadow south of the parking lot, complete with water for cooling off.

There is information about Elk Meadow Open Space Park's extensive trail system at the trailhead for Bergen Peak. (Linda Grey)

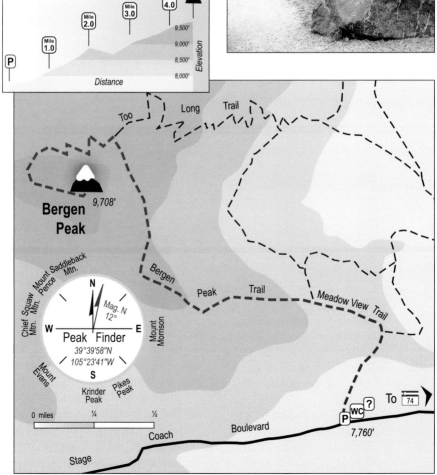

Mile 1.0
Mile 2.0
Mile 3.0
Mile 4.0
9,500'
9,000'
8,500'
8,000'
Elevation
P
Distance

Too   Long   Trail

Bergen Peak   9,708'

Chief Squaw Mtn.
Mount Pence
Saddleback Mtn.

Bergen   Peak   Trail

Meadow View Trail

N
Mag. N 12°
W   E
Peak Finder
39°39'58"N / 105°23'41"W
S

Mount Morrison

Mount Evans

Krinder Peak
Pikes Peak

0 miles   ¼   ½

P WC ?
7,760'
To 74

Coach   Boulevard

Stage

51 RALEIGH PEAK 8,183 Feet

*E*njoy a segment of the famous Colorado Trail on your hike to this interesting rocky summit.

Distance: 3.4 miles each way
Hiking Time: Up in 113 minutes, down in 85 minutes
Starting Elevation: 6,120 feet
Elevation Gain: 2,203 feet (includes 70 feet extra each way)
Trail: Initial 2.8 miles, faint trail beyond
Season: Mid April to mid November
Jurisdiction: Pike National Forest
Maps: *USGS 7 ½'* — Platte Canyon; *County* — Jefferson #2; *USFS* — Pike National Forest; *Trails Illustrated* — #135

Directions to the Trailhead

Drive southwest on US-285 through Aspen Park and Conifer. Just beyond Conifer, turn south onto Jefferson County Road 97, which passes through Reynolds Park. After 8.3 miles from US-285, turn left onto Jefferson County Road 96, which parallels the North Fork of the Platte River for 10.6 miles to the boarded-up South Platte Hotel at the South Platte townsite. Continue over the bridge where the road becomes Douglas Co Rd-97 and go 0.7 mile further to a widened spot in the road. A long footbridge and a Colorado Trail sign identify this spot.

The Hike

To within 0.5 miles of the summit

From the parking area, cross the South Platte River on the long, sturdy footbridge. On the opposite bank, descend to the level of the river and wrap back under the bridge. The trail follows the river upstream (southeast) for a few hundred feet, then ascends on the mountainside. Go through nine switchbacks, then pick up the route of an old quarry road. After about 1.5 miles, Raleigh Peak will come into view. After another 1.3 miles, keep right at two successive forks and reach a semi-open area with trails to the left and right. The main road continues ahead around a solitary tree. Leave the road here and bushwhack 150 degrees southeast, directly toward Raleigh Peak. As you ascend, you may find a faint trail. Proceed toward the right side of the rocky summit and pick your way to the top. Some easy hand work will be needed. The summit contains some old wood and wire with a USGS marker nearby. Use your compass to retrace your route back to the trailhead.

FYI

This is a good early or late season hike with an interesting, rocky summit. The route, after leaving the trail, is faint and may require some bushwhacking and compass work. There is quite a lot of burned-over area, a legacy of the 1996 Buffalo Creek fire.

The fine footbridge over the Platte at the start of this hike is named for Gudy Gaskill, the "mother" of the Colorado Trail. This spot is the start of Segment 2 of the 468-mile, Denver to Durango trail.

Despite its appearance, Raleigh Peak requires only easy scrambling around the summit block.
(Maureen McCarty)

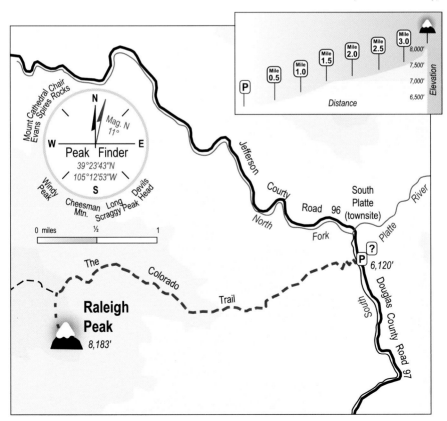

52 RESOLUTION MOUNTAIN 11,905 Feet

Camp Hale, training ground for the famed 10th Mountain Division, forms the backdrop for this hike.

Distance: 3.0 miles each way
Hiking Time: Up in 120 minutes, down in 70 minutes
Starting Elevation: 11,905 feet
Elevation Gain: 2,227 feet
Trail: Initial 2.0 miles, bushwack beyond
Season: Late May to mid October
Jurisdiction: White River National Forest
Maps: USGS 7 ½' — Pando; County — Eagle #4;
USFS — White River National Forest; Trails Illustrated — #109

Directions to the Trailhead

Drive north of Leadville on US-24 from the intersection with CO-91 for 14.8 miles. Or if you come from the north, drive 15.2 miles south on US-24 from Minturn. Either of these routes brings you to a turnoff that goes east through two stone pillars into the former site of Camp Hale. After proceeding off US-24 through the pillars for 0.2 miles, turn left at a "T" and drive for 0.9 miles, to a turnoff to the right and a creek crossing. You are now on Resolution Road #702. Keep on this road as it ascends northeast, alongside Resolution Creek, for 1.9 miles to a fork. You will want the left fork, often blocked to vehicles at this point. Park here.

The Hike

Continue northeast on foot up the left-hand road along Resolution Creek for about two miles, where the road turns sharply to the right (east). Leave the road at this sharp bend and ascend up the gulch going northwest, keeping to the left of the creek. Stay left at the confluence of two creeks, continue northwest and gain the ridge at a low point. Then turn left (south) to the summit, which lies a total of one mile from where you left the Resolution Road. At the top there is a metal pole marker, and nearby, a cement slab with two embedded metal rods. To descend, you may retrace your route or make a loop by descending south, to the unnamed creek which passes east through the aspens by way of an abandoned mine, to the Resolution Road.

(If the Resolution Road is open to vehicles, a regular car can ascend to the sharp bend in the road at 10,382 feet. The hike can begin there and continue northwest, up the gulch away from the road. This would save 2 miles and 704 feet in elevation gain on the ascent.)

FYI

To reach the trailhead, one must pass through the ruins of Camp Hale which was established to train ski troops of the U.S. Army 10th Mountain Division for World War II and also as a camp for German prisoners of war. The Forest Service discourages on-foot exploration of the site because of possible unexploded ordinance.

Approaching Resolution Mountain.

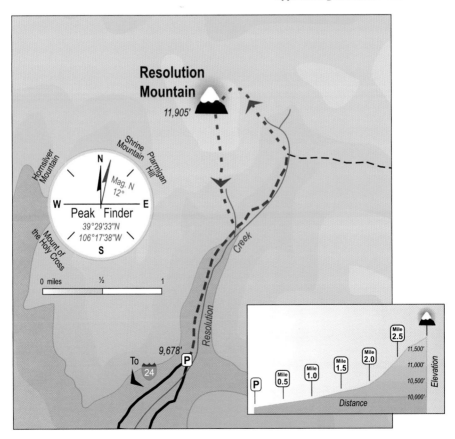

53 BALD MOUNTAIN 13,684 Feet

*H*old on to your hat — the God of the North Wind may visit you on this beautiful ridge walk.

Distance: 2.0 miles each way
Hiking Time: Up in 130 minutes, down in 90 minutes
Starting Elevation: 11,390 feet
Elevation Gain: 2,602 feet (includes 154 feet lost between summits)
Trail: None, all off-trail on tundra and talus
Season: Early June to early October
Jurisdiction: Arapaho National Forest
Maps: *USGS 7 ½'* — Boreas; *County* — Summit #2;
USFS — Arapaho National Forest; *Trails Illustrated* — #109

Directions to the Trailhead

Drive to the south end of the town of Breckenridge on US-9 and turn east onto Summit County Road 10, the Boreas Pass Road. The pavement ends in 3.5 miles. Continue driving on the road for a total of 9.65 miles toward Boreas Pass. Park at the bend in the road, 0.6 miles short of the pass. From the southeast, this trailhead can be reached by turning west off US- 285, 10.0 miles north of Fairplay, onto the Boreas Pass Road (Park County Road 33). Drive through the town of Como for a total of 11.3 miles to the pass. The trailhead is 0.6 miles further north beyond the pass. Regular cars can easily traverse Boreas Pass when there is no blockage by snow. Park off the road.

The Hike

Along Boreas Pass Road

Classics

Head northeast and up, staying to the left of the creek, and quickly pass timberline. Proceed to the ridge at the left of the saddle, between Bald Mountain on your left and Boreas Mountain on your right. Ascend this ridge and traverse several false summits, heading north. The true summit is marked by a large cairn and a circular rock shelter. Two other large cairns lie further to the northwest, down from the summit. To descend, stay on the summit ridge and keep to the west (right) of the last two false summits, returning as you came up.

Old Section House/Boreas Pass

(*Terry Root*)

FYI

This is a good hike for those who enjoy ridge walking and being above timberline. Now named for the God of the North Wind, Boreas Pass had been called Hamilton, Tarryall and then Breckenridge Pass. In 1882, track was laid over the pass and it was a Denver, South Park and Pacific Railroad Company route until 1937. A town called Boreas was located at the pass for the railroad workers and travelers. This was the highest post office in the country in 1898.

A restored, 1882 Section House stands on top of the pass. It hosts visitors as part of the Summit Huts Association.

Bald Mountain is in view from just below treeline. (Terry Root)

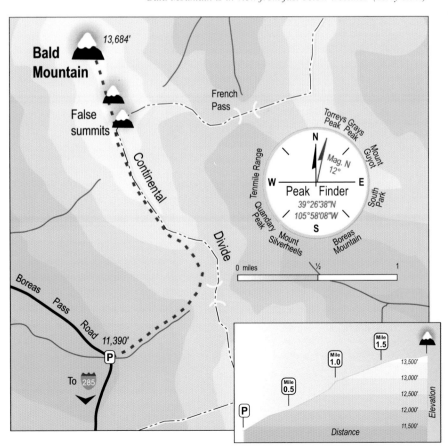

54 HORNSILVER MOUNTAIN 11,572 Feet

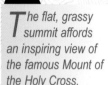

The flat, grassy summit affords an inspiring view of the famous Mount of the Holy Cross.

Distance: 4.0 miles each way
Hiking Time: Up in 120 minutes, down in 100 minutes
Starting Elevation: 9,020 feet
Elevation Gain: 2,552 feet
Trail: All the way
Season: Late May to mid October
Jurisdiction: White River National Forest
Maps: *USGS 7 ½'* — Red Cliff and Pando; *County* — Eagle #4; *USFS* — White River NF; *Trails Illustrated* — #108 & 109

Directions to the Trailhead

4WD option for Road 747

From US-24, about 9.5 miles south of the intersection with I-70, turn east on the Shrine Pass Road. From the town of Red Cliff, drive for 2.45 miles. Alternately, drive west over Shrine Pass toward Redcliff from the Shrine Pass cutoff of I-70 (Exit #190) for a total of 8.5 miles. Park here off the road, as the side road to Hornsilver Mountain requires four-wheel drive.

The Hike

Leave the Shrine Pass Road and hike south on Road 747. Follow this rough road for 0.65 miles, crossing Wearyman Creek at several points and taking the right fork onto Road 708. Follow this road up, and generally south, in a counterclockwise direction to the flat, grassy summit at timberline. A few rocks, old boards and wire mark the high point, just west of the road. Return by the same route.

There are wonderful views of Mount of the Holy Cross from Hornsilver Mountain.

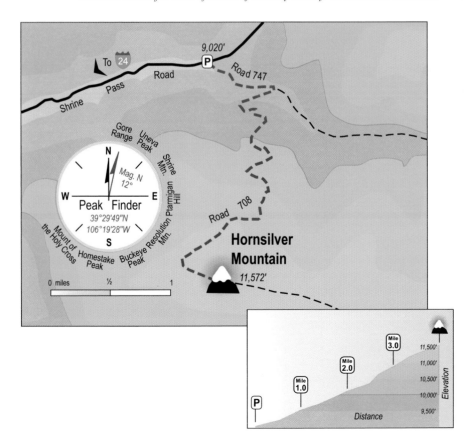

55 TWIN CONES 12,060 & 12,058 Feet

There are stunning views on this hike that follows a portion of the Continental Divide National Scenic Trail.

Distance: 4.0 miles each way
Hiking Time: Up in 120 minutes to southern Cone, 20 minutes to northern Cone, and back in 115 minutes
Starting Elevation: 11,315 feet
Elevation Gain: 1,645 feet (includes 340 feet extra on ascent and 560 feet extra on return)
Trail: Initial 1.5 miles, off-trail on tundra beyond
Season: Early June to early October
Jurisdiction: Arapaho NF, Vasquez Peak Wilderness
Maps: USGS 7 ½' — Berthoud Pass; *County* — Grand #4; *USFS* — Arapaho National Forest; *Trails Illustrated* — #103

Directions to the Trailhead

Drive to Berthoud Pass on US-40, between Empire to the south and Winter Park to the north. Park off the road. There is abundant parking area on the east side of the road.

The Hike

Cross the highway and ascend the rough road to the west-southwest, about 100 feet south of Berthoud Pass. A barrier prevents vehicular access to this service road for the one-time ski area. After 0.7 miles on this road, you will reach a ridge at the end of the ski lift at timberline. (Note that as of 2003, the lifts for this area were being removed.) Follow the faint trail up to the west and onto a mesa. Numerous large cairns mark the trail. Turn right (north) at the mesa and follow a faint trail (the Mt. Nystrom Trail) north to two conical projections. These cones are 0.5 miles apart. Each highpoint is marked only by a few loose rocks.

The return is a little more demanding, due to elevation gain, and does not offer as clearly visible a destination. Keep south-southwest until you reach the ridge, going east back to the trailhead.

Alpine sunflowers dot the ridge in June. (Terry Root)

FYI

There are several named "Twins" in the Colorado Rockies — cones, lakes, peaks and mountains. This leisurely ridge walk, partly along the Continental Divide, is mostly above treeline; so there are stunning views in all directions. Your route for the first mile or so follows the *Continental Divide National Scenic Trail,* which passes through five states as it winds its way along the backbone of the continent. The Colorado segment is over 90% complete, at some 759 miles. Only about a dozen people undertake the complete journey from Canada to Mexico each year.

Twin Cones, as viewed from the south.

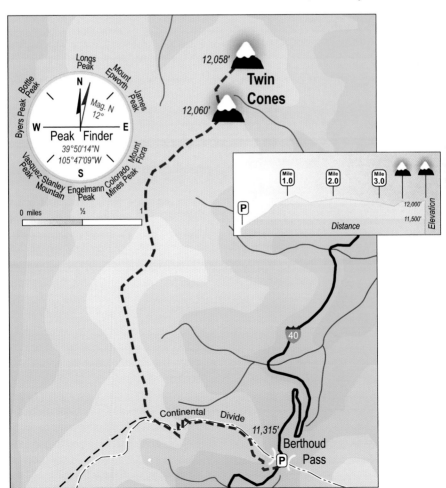

56 JAQUE PEAK 13,205 Feet

Enjoy gorgeous summer wildflowers in the lush meadows on the approach to Searle Pass.

Distance: 4.1 miles on ascent, 1.4 miles on descent
Hiking Time: Up in 145 minutes, down in 55 minutes
Starting Elevation: 10,980 feet
Elevation Gain: 2,225 feet
Trail: Initial 2.6 miles, tundra and talus beyond
Season: Mid June to early October
Jurisdiction: Arapaho National Forest
Maps: USGS 7 ½' — Copper Mountain; County — Summit #2; USFS — Arapaho National Forest; Trails Illustrated — #109

Directions to the Trailhead

Drive south from I-70 at Copper Mountain (Exit #195) toward Leadville on CO-91 for 4.0 miles. Or drive north from Fremont Pass on CO-91 for 7.45 miles. Turn off CO-91 onto a paved road going northwest for 0.9 miles. Then take the dirt road going to your right and ascend northwest for 3.4 miles. Park at an open area on your left at a sign saying, "Searle Pass Parking Area." The road is passable for regular cars.

The Hike

Cross the road and head northwest up an old mining road into Searle Gulch. Continue on this road until it disappears in scrub oak. Then follow the pink ribbons on the trees, directing you toward Searle Pass which is the lowest point on your right, to the northwest. As you approach the pass, you will likely encounter the Colorado Trail as it drops south off the pass. From Searle Pass, follow a trail going east over grassy slopes, to the right of a subpeak, and on to the impressive, true highpoint, marked by a cairn and a simple jar register. It will take about 90 minutes from Searle Pass to the Jaque Peak summit. Descend directly downward, steeply to the southwest, over tundra and then through the trees to your vehicle, visible from the top of the peak.

--- **FYI** ---

This peak is named after Captain J.C. Jaque, a well-known character who lived in Leadville and died there in 1890.

From Searle Pass onward, you will have fine vistas of the Gore and Tenmile Ranges, marred only by the massive tailings ponds around Climax. The pass itself has a reputation for being a windy place. Be sure that you do not accidently follow the Colorado Trail north from the pass, but instead follow the fainter trail east up the ridge.

This hike is best done in early to mid summer, when wildflowers are abundant in Searle Gulch. Or you may be lucky enough to spot elk, trekking through the pass on the way to the lush meadows on the north side of Jaque Peak.

Jaque Peak, as viewed along the access raod.

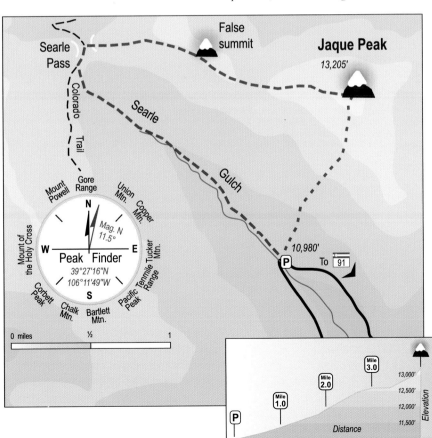

57 QUAIL MOUNTAIN 13,461 Feet

This gentle, Sawatch Range peak has impressive views of some of Colorado's highest.

Distance: 3.1 miles each way
Hiking Time: Up in 140 minutes, down in 90 minutes
Starting Elevation: 9,870 feet
Elevation Gain: 3,651 feet (includes 30 feet extra each way)
Trail: Initial 2.4 miles, off-trail tundra beyond
Season: Late June to early October
Jurisdiction: San Isabel National Forest
Maps: USGS 7 ½' — Mount Elbert and Winfield;
County — Chaffee #1; USFS — San Isabel NF; Trails Illustrated — #127 & 129

Directions to the Trailhead

Drive west on Chaffee County Road 390 from US-24 between Leadville and Buena Vista. This road is 4.3 miles south of CO-82 and 15.3 miles north of the stop light in Buena Vista (at CO-306). On this good dirt road, keep left at mile 3.5 and at mile 6.0. Pass the ghost town of Vicksburg at mile 8.0. Just past a pond and a camp site on the left at mile 9.4, the trailhead sign stating "Colorado Trail" will lie off the right side of the road. Park around here.

The Hike

Begin north on the trail, which leads steeply up into Sheep Gulch. On the way, you will soon pass an abandoned mine shaft on the left, and higher in the gulch, an old cabin lies off the trail on your right. Around timberline, the trail is marked by a series of cairns, as it rises with switchbacks to the saddle between Mount Hope on your left (west) and Quail Mountain on your right (east). From this saddle at 12,530 feet, leave the trail and ascend 0.7 miles east over tundra to the top of Quail Mountain. Descend as you ascended.

FYI

Quail Mountain is the location of a proposed ski area in the Twin Lakes area. This peak has a gentle, rounded summit which provides extensive views of many high mountains, including several fourteeners and Colorado's highest peak, Mount Elbert, to the northwest.

From the saddle to the west, Mount Hope, one of the 100 highest peaks in Colorado, is a 65 minute ridge hike with no real difficulties along the way.

The trail over this saddle is no longer the official route of the Colorado Trail. The actual route has been relocated on the east side of Quail Mountain. However. the Colorado Trail Foundation still lists this route as a strenuous, optional route for backpackers interested in geting a taste of Colorado's alpine.

The gentle slopes of Quail Mountain as viewed from Mount Hope.

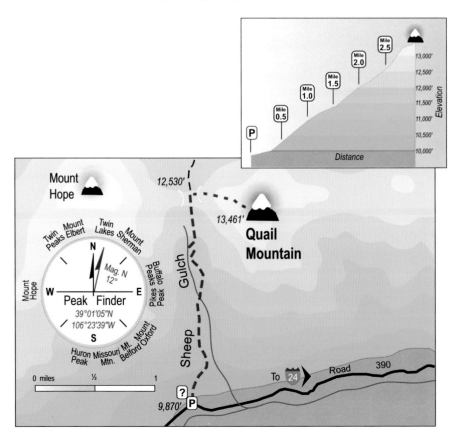

Mount Hope

12,530'

13,461'
Quail Mountain

Mile 0.5
Mile 1.0
Mile 1.5
Mile 2.0
Mile 2.5

13,000'
12,500'
12,000'
11,500'
11,000'
10,500'
10,000'

Elevation

P

Distance

Twin Peaks
Mount Elbert
Twin Lakes
Mount Sherman

N
Mag. N 12°

Buffalo Peaks
Pikes Peak

Mount Hope

W — Peak Finder — E
39°01'05"N
106°23'39"W

S

Huron Peak
Missouri Mtn.
Mt. Belford
Mount Oxford

0 miles   ½   1

Gulch

Sheep

To 24
Road 390

?
P
9,870'

58 MOUNT WILCOX 13,408 Ft. & OTTER MOUNTAIN 12,766 Ft.

A ghost town, once with the highest post office in the country, is the starting point for this high-altitude loop.

Distance: 1.95 miles to Mount Wilcox, 1.85 miles from Mount Wilcox to Otter Mountain, 2.0 miles from Otter Mountain to trailhead
Hiking Time: 116 minutes to Mt. Wilcox, 46 minutes from Mt. Wilcox to Otter Mountain, 68 minutes from Otter Mountain to trailhead
Starting Elevation: 11,594 feet
Elevation Gain: 2,394 feet
Trail: Initial 0.5 mile, off-trail tundra and talus beyond
Season: Mid June to early October
Jurisdiction: Arapaho National Forest
Maps: *USGS 7 ½'* — Montezuma, Grays Peak, and Georgetown; *County* — Clear Creek; *USFS* — Arapaho National Forest; *Trails Illustrated* — #104

Directions to the Trailhead

From the intersection of Sixth and Rose Streets in Georgetown, drive south and up toward Guanella Pass for 2.8 miles, to a dirt road on your right. Turn off onto this road, take the right fork at 0.25 miles, another right fork at 0.5 miles and also at 1.0 miles from the paved road. In 0.2 miles further, take the sharp left fork and continue up the basin for a total of 6.25 miles from the Guanella Pass Road, to the substantial ruins of the Waldorf Mine, just above timberline. Park here. Although this road can be quite rough in spots, passenger cars with good clearance can usually negotiate the road to this point. Mount Wilcox is the prominent peak to the southwest.

The Hike

Go east over Leavenworth Creek to two abandoned cabins on the east side of the creek, near some power lines. Follow an old mining road across the creek and through the marshes toward these cabins, thereby avoiding most of the scrub oak on the basin floor. At the cabins, the trail ends. Continue steeply up to the east and gain the ridge. This part will require about 84 minutes. Turn south on the ridge, and soon, the Mount Wilcox summit will come into view. Cross the tundra and ascend easily to a large cairn at the top. This will require about 32 minutes from the ridge.

Continue this loop hike by descending from Mount Wilcox

> ## FYI
>
> Mount Wilcox was named on August 1, 1948 after Edward John Wilcox, who owned the nearby Waldorf Mines. In fact, the ghost town of Waldorf was once called Wilcox. A railroad, which ran up Mount McClellan, opened on August 12, 1906 and passed through Waldorf, which then was called the site of the highest post office in the United States. The train line could only operate three months out of each year and was eventually torn up in 1919.

and heading northeast to Otter Mountain. Keep to the south of an unnamed peak with a rocky wind shelter on top. This peak lies about halfway between Mount Wilcox and Otter Mountain. Continue northeast over the gently rising tundra to another large cairn at the Otter Mountain summit.

The summit cairn on Mount Wilcox, with Argentine Peak beyond.

Descend directly west to the ridge, then to the two cabins and pick up the old road back across Leavenworth Creek to your car.

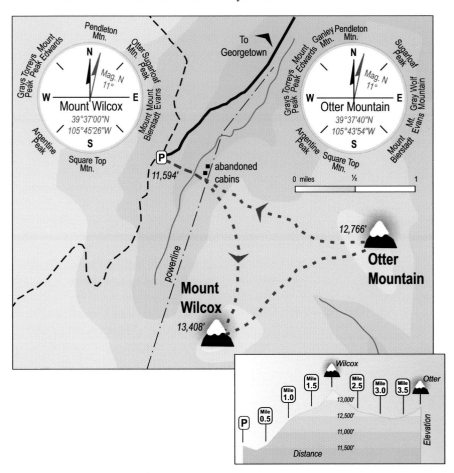

59 HORSESHOE MOUNTAIN 13,898 Feet

Ancient glaciers carved one of the highest peaks in the state into its distinct shape.

Distance: 3.1 miles each way
Hiking Time: Up in 145 minutes, down in 95 minutes
Starting Elevation: 11,480 feet
Elevation Gain: 2,418 feet
Trail: All the way
Season: Mid June to early October
Jurisdiction: Pike National Forest
Maps: *USGS 7 ½'* — Mount Sherman and Fairplay West; *County* — Park #1 and Lake; *USFS* — Pike National Forest; *Trails Illustrated* — #110

Directions to the Trailhead

Drive south on US-285 from Fairplay from the junction with CO-9 for 1.25 miles. Then turn right (west) on Park County Road 18 (also called the Fourmile Creek Road) and continue up the valley on the main road for 11.3 miles to a four-way intersection at the ghost town of Leavick. Take the left (west) turn, staying to the left at the first fork, and drive about 0.6 miles to around timberline. Park off the road. Regular cars should be able to make it this far.

The Hike

Classics

Continue on the road as it curls up west into Horseshoe Gulch. Horseshoe Mountain, with its impressive cirque, lies before you. Follow the road as it eventually angles northwest up to a ridge, just south of Peerless Mountain. Evidence of abandoned mining efforts can be seen below and on this ridge. Then continue south on a gently ascending, faint trail to a summit cairn and register cylinder. Return by the same route.

(If you wish to hike up Peerless Mountain on your descent, it will add about 14 minutes and 168 feet of elevation gain to your outing.)

FYI

As you drive west on the Fourmile Creek Road, you pass the site of the former town of Horseshoe, which once had a population of as much as 800 and was called East Leadville.

This hike lies totally above timberline and takes you through many abandoned mines to an extensive view from the summit, which divides Park from Lake County. Horseshoe Mountain is named after its configuration, with a nearly perfect, glacier-carved cirque on its east face. The peak has added significance because it is one of the 100 highest peaks in Colorado, and a coveted mountain for peakbaggers.

Horseshoe Mountain is named for the distinctive cirque on its east face. (Terry Root)

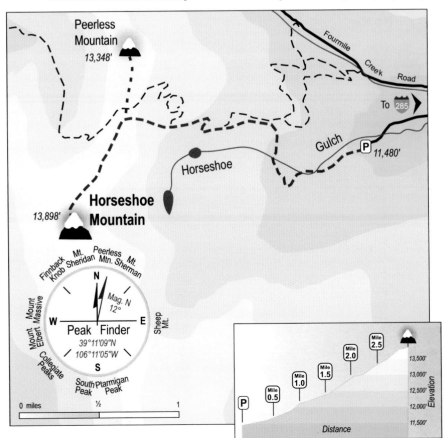

60 SUGARLOAF PEAK 12,513 Feet

The Mount Evans Wilderness offers fourteeners, rare pockets of acrtic tundra and mountain goats.

Distance: 4.4 miles each way
Hiking Time: Up in 142 minutes, down in 96 minutes
Starting Elevation: 9,640 feet
Elevation Gain: 3,073 feet (includes 100 feet extra each way)
Trail: Initial 2.8 miles, bushwacking and tundra walking beyond
Season: Early June to early October
Jurisdiction: Arapaho NF, Mount Evans Wilderness Area
Maps: *USGS 7 ½'* — Georgetown; *County* — Clear Creek; *USFS* — Arapaho National Forest; *Trails Illustrated* — #104

Directions to the Trailhead

From Exit 240 off I-70 at Idaho Springs and drive southwest on CO-103 for 6.7 miles. At a sharp bend in the highway, Road 114, also called the West Chicago Creek Road, leads southwest. Follow this excellent dirt road until it ends after 3.0 miles in a parking area, just past the West Chicago Creek Campground. Park here.

The Hike

The trail begins at a sign at the south end of the parking area. Follow this clear trail as it ascends to the south. After about 75 minutes, leave the trail and bushwhack west-southwest to the saddle at the left (south) of Sugarloaf Peak. Ascend through sparse forest, willows and scrub to the ridge. Then travel north-northwest over tundra to the summit which is marked by a red and white pole, embedded in a rockpile and with a nearby USGS marker in the midst of a smaller pile of rocks. Descend by your ascent route.

FYI

Several Colorado Mountains are named Sugarloaf Peak, due to a conical configuration. This peak can be seen from the northern segments of the Guanella Pass Road and from numerous Clear Creek County high points. Lake Edith to the northeast lies within private property. A loop return from the summit to the northeast, via an old mining road and Lake Edith, is therefore not recommended.

Your route lies within the magnificent Mount Evans Wilderness Area, offering several unique features worthy of a visit. Rare south of the Arctic Circle, the wilderness contains small pockets of arctic tundra. Unlike typical Colorado alpine tundra, which is dry and brittle once the snow recedes, arctic tundra holds numerous small pools of water. Mountain goats, introduced in the 1940s, gambol on Gray Wolf Mountain, across the basin from Sugarloaf to the southeast. The area also holds two popular fourteeners, Mount Evans and Mount Bierstadt.

Sugarloaf Mountain, as viewed at treeline from a north approach.

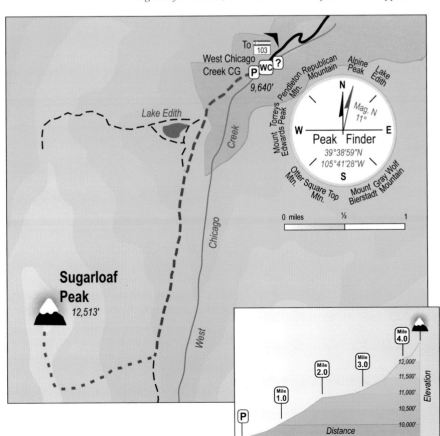

To 103

West Chicago
Creek CG

P **WC** **?**

9,640'

Lake Edith

Creek

Chicago

West

**Sugarloaf
Peak**

12,513'

Mount Torreys
Edwards Peak
Pendleton
Mtn.
Republican
Mountain
Alpine
Peak
Lake
Edith

W **Peak   Finder** **E**
39°38'59"N
105°41'28"W

N
Mag. N
11°

S

Otter
Mtn.
Square Top
Mtn.
Mount
Bierstadt
Gray Wolf
Mountain

0 miles   ½   1

**Mile
4.0**

**Mile
3.0**

**Mile
2.0**

**Mile
1.0**

12,000'

11,500'

11,000'

10,500'

10,000'

Elevation

P

Distance

61 WHALE PEAK 13,078 Feet

In the fall, aspen of the Hall Valley are at a golden peak and the tundra on Whale Peak turns to a deep crimson.

Distance: 4.0 miles each way
Hiking Time: Up in 148 minutes, down in 95 minutes
Starting Elevation: 10,316 feet
Elevation Gain: 2,832 feet (includes 35 feet extra each way)
Trail: Most of the way, faint in places
Season: Early June to early October
Jurisdiction: Pike National Forest
Maps: *USGS 7 ½'* — Jefferson; *County* — Park #1;
USFS — Pike National Forest; *Trails Illustrated* — #104

Directions to the Trailhead

From US-285 at the ghost town of Webster, (4.4 miles east of Kenosha Pass or 3.25 miles west of Grant), turn west on Road 120 and drive up Hall Valley for 5.3 miles, past the Handcart Campground, to the Hall Valley Campground. En route, take the right fork at 3.3. miles and the left fork at 5.2 miles from US-285. Continue on the rough road up the valley for 1.25 more miles past the Hall Valley Campground, to a parking area on the left. Park here. Regular cars can usually make it this far.

The Hike

Follow the trail which begins west of the parking area, at a sign. Descend slightly to the south, cross the creek on a small wooden bridge and proceed southwest, and then west, up the valley on the clear trail, keeping to the right of the Lake Fork of the South Platte River until you cross it near timberline. In about 40 minutes from the trailhead, take the left fork, staying lower in the valley and closer to the creek. Avoid the right fork which ascends steeply into the northern edge of the basin. In about forty more minutes past the fork, you will arrive at Gibson Lake. If you lose the trail, just continue close to the creek and toward the southwest corner of the basin and Gibson Lake. Pass to the left of the lake and ascend talus and tundra on the south to gain a trail leading to a saddle on the southwest ridge of Whale Peak. Then continue northwest up this ridge to the summit cairn. Descend as you came up.

FYI

Whale Peak lies on the Continental Divide, on the boundary between Park and Summit Counties and also between Pike and Arapaho National Forests. The Hall Valley is named after Colonel William Jairus Hall, a local mine owner.

Whale Peak is an excellent hike in late September, when the aspen stands of the Hall Valley are at their golden peak and the tundra above Gibson Lake turns to a deep, autumn crimson.

On the summit of Whale Peak, looking north. (Terry Root)

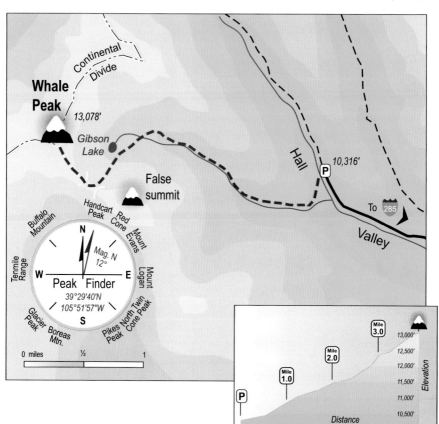

62 MOUNT MANITOU 9,460 Ft. & ROCKY MOUNTAIN 9,250 Ft.

Follow the historic Barr Trail to reach these two rocky summits in the shadow of Pikes Peak.

Distance: 3.4 miles to Mt. Manitou, 0.5 miles Mt. Manitou to Rocky Mountain, 3.3 miles from Rocky Mountain to trailhead
Hiking Time: Up to Mt. Manitou in 120 minutes, Mt. Manitou to Rocky Mtn. in 33 minutes, down from Rocky Mtn. in 83 minutes
Starting Elevation: 6,680 feet
Elevation Gain: 3,060 feet
Trail: Most of the way, off-trail close to top of Mt. Manitou and between summits, plus some easy scrambling
Season: Late April to late November
Jurisdiction: Pike National Forest
Maps: *USGS 7 ½'* — Manitou Springs; *County* — El Paso #1; *USFS* — Pike National Forest; *Trails Illustrated* — #137

Directions to the Trailhead

From Manitou Avenue in the town of Manitou Springs (west of Colorado Springs) drive southwest up Ruxton Avenue for 0.8 miles to the end of the public road. Turn right (northwest) and go 0.1 miles to a parking area, rest rooms and a bulletin board adjacent to the trail head. Park here.

The Hike

Classics

Follow the Barr Trail steeply up and to the west, in a series of switchbacks. The trail is very well maintained and has wooden fencing along it for most of the first two miles. After about 80 minutes, you will reach a fork. Continue to the left (west) on the Barr Trail. In about five more minutes, another fork at a metal sign is reached. Take the right fork toward the former Fremont Experimental Forest and leave the Barr Trail. After passing some old cement foundations on your right, in 17 minutes from the Barr Trail, you arrive at a saddle and a "T". Take the right fork, going northeast, and ascend another seven minutes, before leaving the old road and proceeding due north to Mount Manitou. Near the top, some easy scrambling is necessary. At the tree-covered summit, there is a large rock with a register jar on its top.

To reach Rocky Mountain, descend toward the southeast and stay close to the ill-defined ridge. Cross the old road, left earlier, and continue generally east and upward, past a false summit, to reach the treeless, rocky top of Rocky Mountain. There are four embedded metal poles and a fixed

FYI

The first part of this loop hike involves the historic Barr Trail, which is the major hiking route to the top of Pikes Peak. This trail, completed by Fred Barr in 1921, is extensively maintained and includes the Barr Camp, an overnight accommodation at about the halfway point.

Manitou is an Algonquin Indian word meaning "great spirit."

wooden plank to assist you in ascending the summit boulder.

Descend Rocky Mountain to the east and pick up a faint trail that winds past some rocky projections, reaching the upper terminus of the Mount Manitou Incline Railway in about 15 minutes. (If you find no trail, just continue east.) From there, take the trail west and upward 150 feet, leading to the Barr Trail. After nine minutes, take the left fork, descend and reach the fork that meets the Barr Trail in four more minutes. Turn left (east) and descend on the trail on which you ascended, reaching the trailhead in 55 minutes.

The route travels over the Barr Trail, very popular with climbers, hikers and runners. (Terry Root)

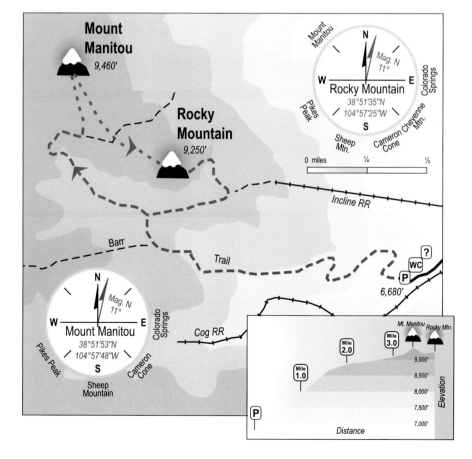

63 BUFFALO MOUNTAIN 13,164 Feet

The trail is a bit steep, but your well-earned reward is fantastic views and mountain goats.

Distance: 1.8 miles each way
Hiking Time: Up in 150 minutes, down in 90 minutes
Starting Elevation: 9,560 feet
Elevation Gain: 3,217 feet
Trail: Most of the way, talus and tundra beyond
Season: Mid June to early October
Jurisdiction: Arapaho National Forest
Maps: *USGS 7 ½'* — Frisco & Vail Pass; *County* — Summit #2; *USFS* — Arapaho National Forest (Dillon Ranger District); *Trails Illustrated* — #108

Directions to the Trailhead

From I-70, take Exit #205 (the Dillon-Silverthorne exit) and drive northwest about one block. Turn left (south) onto the Wildernest Road. Follow this road which becomes Ryan Gulch Road, passing through an area of condominiums, for 3.5 miles to the trailhead on the right (north), at a sign stating "Buffalo Cabin Trail." Park off the left (south) side of the road at a National Forest bulletin board.

The Hike

Cross Ryan Gulch Road and proceed northwest on the Buffalo Cabin Trail. In 15 minutes, take a left fork, and a minute later, you arrive at a four-way intersection. A severe right turn takes you to Mesa Cortina. A milder right turn leads to Willow Creek. Take the left turn which goes past a ruined cabin on the right in twelve minutes, and five minutes later, to the ruined, so-called, Buffalo Cabin. You now have a choice of two routes to the top of Buffalo Mountain. A trail to the left of Buffalo Cabin passes steeply up through the trees to the west, over considerable scree and loose rocks. This trail ends above timberline, as the summit comes into view on your left (south). The other choice is a trail which begins to the right of Buffalo Cabin and continues northwest behind the cabin. Faint at times, it passes under two large logs and eventually arrives at a lengthy, steep slope of talus and boulders on your left (west). Some easy hand work is needed to ascend this slope. After the rocks,

- - - **FYI** - - - - - - -

There are a number of Buffalo Mountains in Colorado. This one is the dome which dominates the western view from the Eisenhower-Johnson Tunnel. The view of Lake Dillon and rough Gore Range from the top is truly exceptional.

Mountain goats patrol the rugged north slopes of Buffalo Mountain. Even if you are not lucky enough to spot one, you may find a tuft of coarse,white fur, left from shedding their winter coats, stuck in the summit rocks.

proceed up and southwest, through more trees and over a talus slope. The trail reaches timberline, at the same point as the first trail. Be sure to keep left of the rocky crag.

By either route, it is about an hour hike from the Buffalo Cabin to this spot and another thirty minutes over tundra and talus to the top. The summit is on the right

Mountain goats perched on an overlook near the summit of Buffalo Mountain. (Eric Wiseman)

(north) side of a ridge and it has a small cairn. (Some hand work will be necessary if you wish to traverse to a subpeak at the south end of the ridge, for views of the valley.) Descend via first route mentioned, picking up a clear trail from where the bushes begin below the talus and tundra.

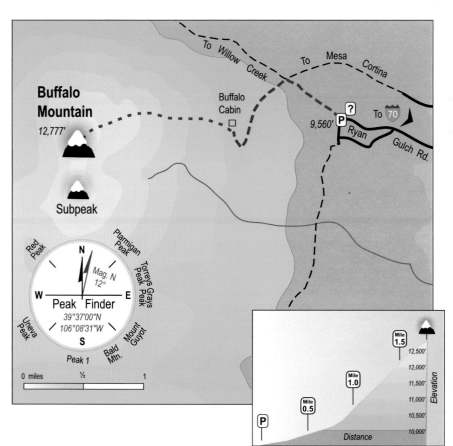

64 PEAK 8 12,987 Feet

S*ummer wildflowers are everywhere on this high alpine hike into the heart of the Tenmile Range.*

Distance: 4.4 miles each way
Hiking Time: Up in 160 minutes, down in 115 minutes
Starting Elevation: 11,000 feet
Elevation Gain: 2,187 feet (includes 100 feet extra each way)
Trail: Initial 3.6 miles, off-trail tundra and talus beyond
Season: Mid June to early October
Jurisdiction: Arapaho National Forest
Maps: *USGS 7 ½'* — Breckenridge; *County* — Summit #2; *USFS* — Arapaho National Forest; *Trails Illustrated* — #109

Directions to the Trailhead

From Ski Hill Road in Breckenridge, drive south on CO-9 for 2.2 miles and turn right onto Crown Road. Follow Crown Road for a half mile and take a right fork, joining the Spruce Creek Road. Keep straight on the Spruce Creek Road, past several side roads, for 1.4 miles from the Crown Road fork, keeping left at a fork and sign. (The right fork leads to Lower Crystal Lake.) Continue up the left fork for another half mile to a junction with the Wheeler Trail, at a sign. Turn right (north) and ascend the road for fifty yards and park near a road barrier. Regular cars with good clearance can reach this point.

The Hike

Head up the road for 35 yards, then northwest on the Wheeler Trail, up and over logs at Crystal Creek. Ascend a ridge, continuing northwest (straight at a four-way junction,) and traverse the eastern flanks of Peaks 10 and 9, en route to a saddle between Peaks 8 and 9. The trail continues west and north from this saddle down to Copper Mountain. However, leave the trail at the saddle and proceed north, up a ridge for 0.8 miles to a cairn at the summit. Descend via the same route.

(From the Peak 8 summit, it is only 0.45 miles north and mostly downhill to the lower, Peak 7 with no special danger or difficulty, if you wish to

Alpine forget-me-nots along the Wheeler Trail.

(Eric Wiseman)

FYI

The eastern slopes of Peak 8 and 9 constitute the Breckenridge Ski Area. Breckenridge was named after President Buchanan's Vice President, John Cabell Breckinridge of Kentucky. When he became a Confederate general, Union supporters in the area agitated to change the first I to an E.

This hike is mostly above timberline with wonderful views all around. From the top, Copper Mountain, Breckenridge and Lake Dillon can all be seen. The best time to visit is June, when fragrant alpine forget-me-nots dot the landscape.

extend your outing. However, you will have to regain nearly 400 feet on your return, back over Peak 8.)

Gentle tundra slopes lead up Peak 8 from the saddle where the Wheeler Trail crosses the range.

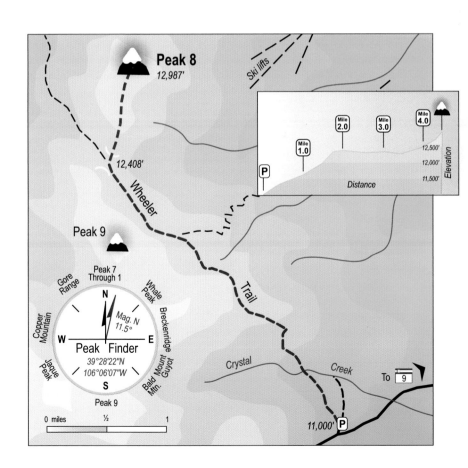

65 MATTERHORN PEAK 13,590 Feet

*D*ramatic peaks of volcanic origin tower above the trail in this breath-taking corner of the San Juan Mountains.

Distance: 4.5 miles each way
Hiking Time: Up in 143 minutes, down in 103 minutes
Starting Elevation: 10,390 feet
Elevation Gain: 3,200 feet
Trail: Initial 3.6 miles, mostly trailless tundra and talus beyond
Season: Mid June to early October
Jurisdiction: Uncompahgre NF, Big Blue Wilderness Area
Maps: *USGS 7 ½'* — Uncompahgre Peak; *County* — Hinsdale #1; *USFS* — Uncompahgre National Forest; *Trails Illustrated* — #141

Directions to the Trailhead

From CO-149 in Lake City, drive west on Second Avenue, just north of the Henson Creek Bridge. This road quickly turns left (south) and then follows Henson Creek to the west. It eventually leads over Engineer Pass to Ouray and Silverton, but you will not go that far. Instead, drive 9.3 miles from CO-149 to a fork at the old site of Capitol City. Turn right (northwest) up the North Fork of Henson Creek for 2.0 miles. Park around Matterhorn Creek and a road leading north and up the creek. Regular cars can come this far, but four-wheel drive is required for the 0.7 miles north up Matterhorn Creek, where the road is blocked.

The Hike

Classics

Hike up this rough road to the north, marked by a sign, "Ridge Stock Driveway Trail." This road keeps to the right of Matterhorn Creek and is quite steep to above timberline. In half an hour, you will reach the vehicle barricade, and in another 30 minutes, you pass a wilderness sign (The Big Blue Wilderness.) Follow the road as it passes timberline, curves northeast away from the creek, and then north again. Matterhorn Peak lies directly ahead. Do not confuse it with the taller Wetterhorn Peak, to the left (west). When you can see a direct route up Matterhorn's southeast ridge, without losing any elevation, leave the road and proceed northwest, up over steep tundra. When the tundra ends and the rocks begin, a trail emerges and continues up an easily negotiated couloir to the unmarked summit rock pile. Descend by your ascent route.

FYI

This hike requires less elevation gain, route finding, rock work and risk than nearby Wetterhorn Peak. In naming these two peaks after their Swiss counterparts, the names seemingly should have been reversed, since in Switzerland, the Matterhorn is the higher, more dramatic summit.

The immense hulk of Uncompahgre Peak, 6th highest peak in Colorado, sits to the east. These peaks are remnants of volcanic activity in the San Juans, with Wetterhorn Peak believed to be an ancient plug.

Matterhorn Peak, as viewed at treeline from the south.

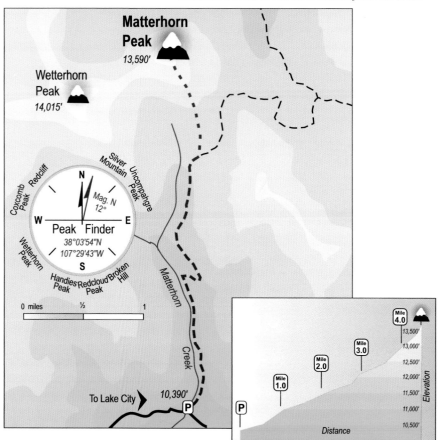

66 BILLS PEAK 12,703 Feet

A hike to remote Bills Peak features an exceptionally well-marked trail and an option to visit a pretty alpine lake.

Distance: 4.8 miles each way
Hiking Time: Up in 151 minutes, down in 110 minutes
Starting Elevation: 9,708 feet
Elevation Gain: 3,195 feet (includes 100 feet extra each way)
Trail: Most of the way, with off-trail tundra near the top
Season: Mid June to early October
Jurisdiction: Arapaho NF, Byers Peak Wilderness Area
Maps: *USGS 7 ½* — Byers Peak and Ute Peak; *County* — Grand #4; *USFS* — Arapaho NF; *Trails Illustrated* — #103

Directions to the Trailhead

From the Dillon and Silverthorne area at the intersection of I-70 and CO-9, drive north on CO-9 for 12.8 miles. Turn right (east) on Summit County Road 15, also known as the Ute Pass Road. After 5.4 miles on this paved road, cross Ute Pass. In 2.2 more miles, take the left fork and bypass the Henderson Mine. Keep left after 0.7 miles, and in 0.9 more miles, turn right at a sign onto Grand County Road 30. Follow this good road for 2.6 miles, turning left (east) onto Grand County Road 302 and at a sign directing you east to the Kinney Creek Trail. After 3.6 miles on this road, at a bend in the road just past Kinney Creek, is the well-marked trailhead. Park here off the road.

The Hike

Proceed east at the trail sign and register. Kinney Creek remains on your right as you ascend the valley. In 50 minutes, you reach a fork and a sign. The right fork leads to Horseshoe Lake in 2.5 miles. Take the left fork which leads to Evelyn Lake and the St. Louis Divide Trail. In another 44 minutes, you will arrive at a saddle and a sign, having passed several poles in cairns. The sign points left to the Keyser Ridge Road (2 miles) and right to the Keyser Creek Road (2 miles) and to St. Louis Lake (4 miles). Turn right (east) and follow the trail past timberline. At a ridge, turn right (south) and pick up the trail which continues along the west side of the ridge. In about 54 minutes from the saddle, leave the trail at a cairn and ascend steeply east to the summit, which has an erroneous elevation sign in a cairn. Return by your ascent route, unless you wish to loop back by way of Horseshoe Lake.

FYI

The trail for this hike is clear and exceptionally well-marked. Horseshoe Lake to the southwest of Bills Peak is very pretty with few visitors, can readily be reached, and while worth the effort, makes for a long day. You will have to bushwack down the steep, west side of Bills Peak to meet the trail along the south fork of Kinney Creek. From there, go left (south) for one mile and another 400 feet in gain to the lake. Return by following the Horseshoe Lake Trail northwest and back to the Kinney Creek Trail in 2.5 miles. Turn left (west) there to return to your car.

Bills Peak.

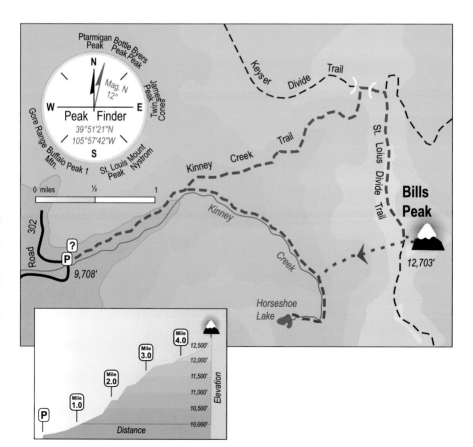

67 BIRTHDAY PEAK 12,730 Feet

*B*ask on this summit, surrounded by giants — the skyscraping Collegiate Peaks.

Distance: 4.6 miles each way
Hiking Time: Up in 153 minutes, down in 107 minutes
Starting Elevation: 9,840 feet
Elevation Gain: 2,890 feet
Trail: Initial 1.8 miles, intermittent trail beyond
Season: Mid June to early October
Jurisdiction: San Isabel NF, Collegiate Peaks Wilderness Area
Maps: *USGS 7 ½'* — Mount Harvard and Mount Yale;
County — Chaffee #2; USFS — San Isabel National Forest; *Trails Illustrated* — #129

Directions to the Trailhead

Drive north on US-24 from the only stoplight in Buena Vista for 0.4 miles, or drive south on US-24 from the intersection with CO-82 for 19.3 miles. Turn west onto Crossman Avenue, which is also Chaffee County Road 350. Drive 2.1 miles to a "T" and turn right on Chaffee County Road 361. After 0.9 miles, turn sharply left onto Chaffee County Road 365 at a sign, "North Cottonwood Creek 4 miles." Stay on this road for 5.3 miles, as it goes west and up into the valley, to a road end and a parking area. A sign alongside the trail reads: "North Cottonwood Creek Trail, Bear Lake 5 miles, Kroenke Lake 4 miles, Browns Pass 6 miles."

The Hike

Classics

Proceed west up into the basin on the clear trail and cross two wooden bridges. About 1.8 miles from the trailhead, there is a fork. Keep left and continue toward Kroenke Lake. (The right turn goes to spectacular Horn Fork Basin at the foot of Mount Harvard and Mount Columbia.) After about 1.6 miles from the fork, you will reach a creek flowing toward the southeast. Just before this creek, leave the main trail and hike northwest, up along the creek. A faint trail is present at first, and then intermittently as you ascend. It is 0.9 miles from the main trail to the saddle, left of Birthday Peak, and 0.3 miles more over tundra and talus to the top, which holds a small cairn and some scattered wooden poles and wire. Be sure to identify Birthday Peak to the northwest as you follow the creek to timberline. A slightly higher, unnamed peak lies directly to the north as you arrive at timberline.

FYI

This mountain forms part of the Continental Divide and lies on the boundary between Chaffee and Gunnison Counties. The trail, which is used for the initial part of this hike, continues to Kroenke Lake, Browns Pass and over to the Cottonwood Pass Road. Birthday Peak is in a section of the Sawatch Range known as the Collegiate Peaks for its impressive collection of skyscraping fourteeners, with names like Harvard, Columbia, Yale and Princeton.

Birthday Peak.

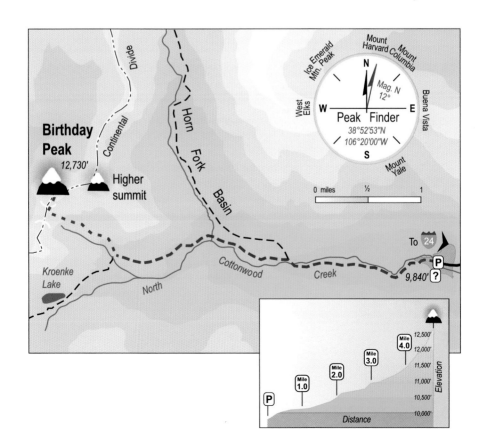

68 NORTH TWIN CONE PEAK 12,319 Ft. & MT. BLAINE 12,303 Ft.

This hike is not to be missed in the fall — the aspen are ablaze with fire red and golden yellow.

Distance: 4.5 miles each way
Hiking Time: Up to N. Twin Cone in 149 minutes, from N. Twin Cone to Mount Blaine in 32 minutes, down in 128 minutes
Starting Elevation: 10,050 feet
Elevation Gain: 2,489 feet (includes 110 feet extra each way)
Trail: Initial 2.6 miles, with some off-trail walking on tundra
Season: Early June to early October
Jurisdiction: Pike National Forest
Maps: *USGS 7 ½'* — Jefferson and Mount Logan;
County — Park #2; *USFS* — Pike National Forest; *Trails Illustrated* — #105

Directions to the Trailhead

From Kenosha Pass on US-285, between Jefferson to the south and Bailey to the north, dirve east on a wide, dirt road. After 0.2 mile, go right at a four-way intersection (toilets on the left.) Then follow a bumpy, main road for 0.8 mile to a locked gate. Park nearby and don't block the road.

The Hike

Classics

Start hiking to the east around the locked gate. Follow the rough road in open terrain, past several beaver dams and a private cabin on the left. After 1.25 miles, hike around a second locked gate and continue up the main road as it rises more steeply, with several switchbacks through thick aspen groves. At mile 2.5 of the hike, keep right at a road fork and continue upward another 0.5 mile to a key point for this hike. A blue diamond marker will be on a tree to the left, and a pole with an arrow on the right side of the road. The main road circuitously leads to the summit, but the shorter, more direct route will be described here.

Enter the trees to the left (southwest) on a faint trail and follow it generally north-northeast through a large clearing. Briefly rejoin the road, and then either follow it or proceed directly to the top of North Twin Cone Peak,

Aspen at Kenosha Pass.
(Eric Wiseman)

> ## FYI
>
> Kenosha Pass and Creek were named after Kenosha, Wisconsin, the home town of a local stage coach driver.
> In July, the understory of the aspen forest here is filled with colorful columbine, golden banner, and larkspur. But this hike is not to be missed in September! The slopes on the east side of Kenosha Pass are ablaze with colors ranging from fire red to golden yellow, with one of the most magnificent displays of aspen in the Front Range.

which will be visible over the last third of your ascent. An antenna, a benchmark and some metal remants mark the summit.

To reach Mount Blaine, proceed east using the four-wheel drive road briefly, before heading directly to the

North Twin Cone Peak, as viewed fron near treeline.

collection of large boulders at the Mount Blaine summit. To descend, head southwest and regain the four-wheel drive road, following it to just below timberline, where you may pick up your ascent route.

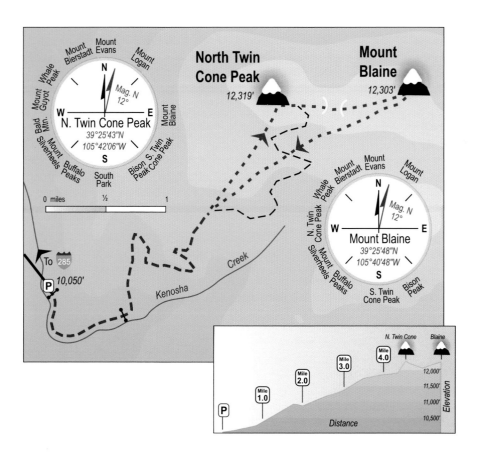

69 REPUBLICAN MOUNTAIN 12,386 Feet

As you approach this rocky summit, keep a sharp eye out for bighorn sheep.

Distance: 5.6 miles each way
Hiking Time: Up in 157 minutes, down in 106 minutes
Starting Elevation: 9,000 feet
Elevation Gain: 3,506 feet
Trail: Most of the way to treeline, easy tundra walking beyond
Season: Mid June to early October
Jurisdiction: Arapaho National Forest
Maps: *USGS 7 ½'* — Georgetown and Empire;
County — Clear Creek; *USFS* — Arapaho National Forest; *Trails Illustrated* — #104

Directions to the Trailhead

Drive south from Empire on the Bard Creek Road, as it cuts off US-40 from the center of town. Continue on this road for 2.0 miles, as it curves west past Empire Pass, overlooking I-70, until reaching a rough road on your left. Park here. A regular car can come this far. Difficult four-wheel driving would be required beyond this point toward Republican Mountain.

The Hike

To within 0.5 mile of top

Start your hike, going south up the rough side road. After a few hundred yards, take a left fork and stay on the main ascending road. After several curves in the road and after passing several mining ruins, you will arrive at the high point of the road, 4.5 miles from the trailhead. The top of Republican Mountain will now be visible ahead. The road continues down and east, through Silver Gulch, toward Georgetown. But leave the road and its highpoint, angling up and west about a hundred yards through the sparse trees to the ridge. Then ascend west-southwest along the ridge, over the tundra, to the rocky

Bighorn sheep runs across tundra on Republican Mountain.

(Sandra Miller)

FYI

The route up Republican Mountain should be free of snow between June and October. Four nearby fourteeners can be seen from the top — Grays Peak, Torreys Peak, Mount Evans and Mount Bierstadt. Approaching the summit, be on the lookout for bighorn sheep, often spotted along the top of this ridge in the summer. They are part of the large Georgetown herd, who winter on the lower, south-facing slopes between Idaho Springs and Georgetown and are often seen by I-70 motorists. This successful herd is often trapped for restocking operations around the state.

The names of Republican Mountain and others along this ridge are of Ciivl War vintage and reflect the political loyalties of the day.

summit. Keep to the right of any residual snow. A benchmark and a pole mark the mountain top. Enjoy the sights before retracing the lengthy ascent route.

Republican Mountain, as viewed from near treeline.

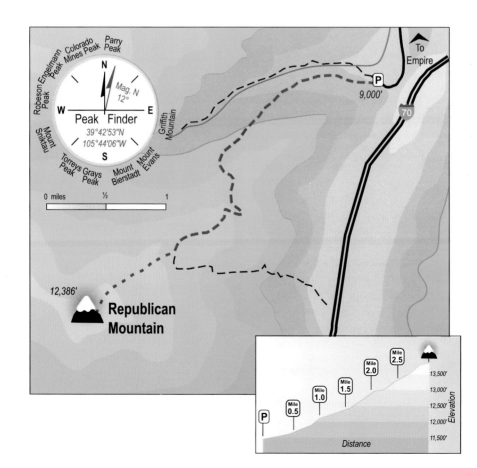

70 PAIUTE PEAK 13,088 Feet

*P*aiute Peak has a wilder, less-crowded feel than other summits in the popular Indian Peaks Wilderness.

Distance: 4.0 miles each way
Hiking Time: Up in 165 minutes, down in 125 minutes
Starting Elevation: 10,470 feet
Elevation Gain: 2,718 feet (includes 50 feet extra each way)
Trail: Initial 3.0 miles, tundra and talus beyond
Season: Mid June to early October
Jurisdiction: Roosevelt NF, Indian Peaks Wilderness
Maps: *USGS 7 ½'* — Monarch Lake and Ward; *County* — Boulder; *USFS* — Roosevelt National Forest; *Trails Illustrated* — #102

Directions to the Trailhead

From the town of Nederland, drive west and then north on CO-72 for about 11.7 miles. Turn left (west) onto the road to Brainard Lake. Soon you will come to a entrance station, where you must pay a day use fee. After 4.9 miles on this road, keep left and cross two bridges at the edge of Brainard Lake. Take right forks at 5.35 miles, at 5.5 miles and at 5.7 miles. Park in the lot for access to Mitchell Lake and Blue Lake, a total of 5.85 miles from CO-72. Get an early start, as lots fill up quickly on weekends.

The Hike

Classics

Take the trail leading west. It begins to the left of a wooden sign and map. Soon a bridge crosses a creek. Later you will cross another creek over logs, with Mitchell Lake reached in about 18 minutes. Follow the clear trail for another 42 minutes to Blue Lake, with Mount Toll looming impressively to the west. Continue on the trail as it curves to the right, around the lake, and continues upward to the west, ending near a smaller lake. Leave this lake and ascend to your right (northwest) over boulders. Then continue up a moderately steep gulch to the northwest. The footing is loose at times, as you ascend to a saddle and then north to a flat summit. A boulder with a pile of rocks and a makeshift register mark the highpoint. Avoid the temptation to descend to the east toward Mount Audubon (unless you wish to hike to that summit,) and instead, return more securely by your ascent route.

FYI

The Indian Peaks Wilderness, with its pristine lakes, remnant glaciers and rugged peaks, long has been a favorite with Front Range residents. The danger of this place being loved to death prompted the Forest Service to institute a use fee and overnight permit system.

Many of the summits, including Paiute Peak, have wonderful, evocative names that honor American Indian tribes that lived in the shadow of the Rockies, a suggestion pushed by Ellsworth Bethel in the 1920s. Paiute Peak, tucked away behind the bulk of Mount Audubon, has a wilder, less-crowded feel than the other summits in this popular playground.

A hiker ascends the final few feet to the summit of Paiute Peak. (Nelson Chenkin)

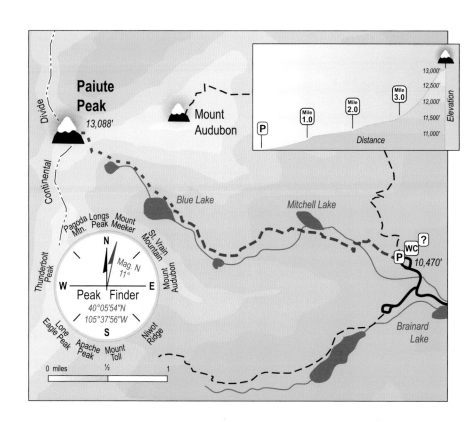

71 GANLEY MTN. 12,902 Feet & PENDLETON MTN. 12,275 Feet

This hike through the high alpine has rewarding views of two famous fourteeners.

Distance: 4.3 miles to Ganley Mountain, 1.7 miles from Ganley Mountain to Pendleton Mtn., 5.5 miles on return

Hiking Time: Up Ganley Mtn. in 145 minutes, Ganley Mountain to Pendleton Mtn. in 40 minutes, down in 140 minutes

Starting Elevation: 11,594 feet

Elevation Gain: 1,808 feet (includes 500 feet extra on return)

Trail: Most of the way, with some off-trail tundra walking

Season: Mid June to early October

Jurisdiction: Arapaho National Forest

Maps: *USGS 7 ½'* — Grays Peak; *County* — Clear Creek; *USFS* — Arapaho National Forest; *Trails Illustrated* — #104

Directions to the Trailhead

From the intersection of Sixth and Rose Streets in Georgetown, drive south and up toward Guanella Pass for 2.8 miles, to a dirt road on your right. Turn off onto this road, take the right fork at 0.25 miles, another right fork at 0.5 miles and also at 1.0 miles from the paved road. In 0.2 miles further, take the sharp left fork and continue up the basin for a total of 6.25 miles from the Guanella Pass Road, to the substantial ruins of the Waldorf Mine, just above timberline. Park here. Although this road can be quite rough in spots, passenger cars with good clearance can usually make it to this point.

The Hike

Begin hiking north up the road. After 0.65 miles, take the right fork. Just beyond, at a four-way intersection, continue straight (north). In 0.3 miles, take the right fork and a sharp left fork in 0.3 more miles. The road continues in switchbacks. In 0.6 miles, take the right fork and again 0.1 miles later. In another 1.4 miles, take another right fork and soon thereafter, leave the road and ascend to the left (northwest) over tundra to the summit of Ganley Mountain. A small cairn lies at the top. The view southwest to Stevens Gulch and two fourteeners, Grays and Torreys Peaks, is especially rewarding.

Descend northeast, losing about 600 feet over the 1.7 miles of tundra to the top of Pendleton Mountain. Note that this peak is lower than the intervening high points. The summit is marked by a small cairn.

Return to your car at the Waldorf site as you ascended, bypassing slightly below the summit of Ganley Mountain. Be sure on the drive back down Leavenworth Gulch to take the sharp right fork, after 5.0 miles from Waldorf.

FYI

This hike is completely above timberline. Ganley Mountain is named for John W. Ganley, the first postmaster of Silver Plume. Pendleton Mountain is named after George H. Pendleton, the vice presidential running mate of General George McClellan on the unsuccessful Democratic ticket of 1864.

Hikers heading toward Pendleton Mountain. (Eric Wiseman)

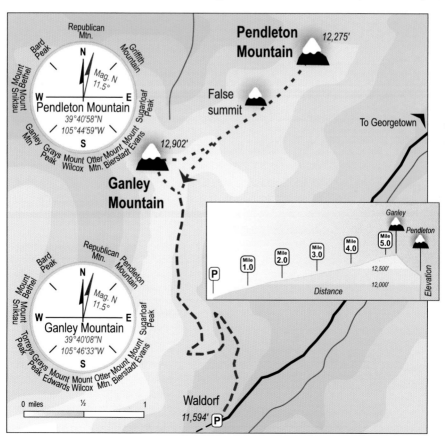

72 GRAYS PEAK 14,270 Feet & TORREYS PEAK 14,267 Feet

These two popular fourteeners are fun to bag, with easy access and an established trail.

Distance: 4.3 miles to Grays Peak, 0.7 miles from Grays Peak to Torreys Peak, 4.5 miles on return
Hiking Time: Up Grays Peak in 135 minutes, Grays Peak to Torreys Peak in 35 minutes, down in 90 minutes
Starting Elevation: 11,230 feet
Elevation Gain: 3,944 feet (includes 894 ft. extra between summits)
Trail: All the way
Season: Late June to early October
Jurisdiction: Arapaho National Forest
Maps: USGS 7 ½' — Grays Peak; *County* — Clear Creek; *USFS* — Arapaho National Forest; *Trails Illustrated* — #104

Directions to the Trailhead

Drive south from the Bakerville exit (Exit # 221) of I-70 for 3.4 miles to the trailhead. The road is blocked just before the defunct Stevens Mine, further south. En route to the parking area near the trailhead, take left forks at mile 1.35 and mile 2.3. A regular car can make it up this steep, rough road to the trailhead area. Restrooms and an information board are next to the large, gravel parking area. On summer weekends, the parking lot fills up very early with hikers intent on climbing the twin fourteeners. Late arrivals may be forced to park alongside the access road.

The Hike

Classics

Hike southwest over the bridge. Follow the wide trail up past timberline, with Kelso Mountain on the right. After 1.25 miles from the trailhead, cross the creek. The top of Grays Peak and the trail are plainly visible to the south from here. Near the summit, there are several connecting trails which all lead to the top. The final thousand feet of elevation is over a talus trail, reaching a rock shelter at the highpoint.

To continue over to Torreys Peak, descend northwest on a faint trail to the saddle. Then ascend the ridge, over talus, to a rock pile atop Torreys Peak. Enjoy the views.

Descend to the saddle and continue 50 feet up toward Grays Peak, before turning left on a trail and cutting back across the face to the Grays Peak Trail. This segment is snow-covered most of the hiking season. Early in the season, many people choose to glissade back down into the basin.

FYI

These peaks were named after the famous botanists, Asa Gray and John Torrey by colleague Charles C. Parry. They are considered two of the easier fourteeners to climb. Oddly enough, they are the only fourteeners that lie on the Continental Divide.

These are very popular hikes due to their proximity to Denver. A herd of mountain goats are often present near the trail, seemingly oblivious to a steady stream of climbers.

Grays Peak (left) and Torreys Peak (right), as viewed from the Grays Peak Trail.

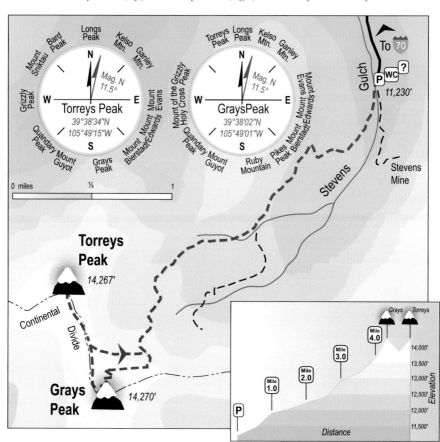

73 ROSEDALE PEAK 11,825 Feet

Explore some odd geology on the edge of the Mount Evans Wilderness.

Distance: 5.1 miles each way
Hiking Time: Up in 186 minutes, down in 134 minutes
Starting Elevation: 8,960 feet
Elevation Gain: 2,865 feet
Trail: Initial 4.0 miles, bushwack beyond
Season: Late May to late October
Jurisdiction: Pike NF, Mount Evans Wilderness Area
Maps: *USGS 7 ½'* — Harris Park; *County* — Park #2;
USFS — Pike National Forest; *Trails Illustrated* — #104

Directions to the Trailhead

From US-285, 2.7 miles east of Bailey or 4.5 miles west of Pine Junction, turn north on Park County Road 43 and continue for 6.9 miles to a fork. Take the right turn, which is Park County Road 47. After 1.5 miles further, a dirt road leads off left (north), with a sign indicating 1.0 mile to the trailhead for the Meridian Trail. Follow this narrow road, passing Camp Rosalie after 0.3 mile. Continue on to the trailhead parking area.

The Hike

From the signed trailhead, hike north along the Meridian Trail. After about five minutes from the trailhead, a fork is reached. The left route is Church Fork Road. Take the right fork, which is the Meridian Trail. Continue north on the trail, soon reaching a clearing and a horse corral on your left. A sign indicates that the road will dead end. The trail cuts off to the right, crosses Elk Creek by way of a small wooden bridge and then cuts left (north), gradually ascending to an unnamed, unmarked pass at 10,700 feet. Continue north on the trail about 200 yards past the pass and then bushwhack left (west), steeply up for 0.9 miles to a summit ridge and then to a summit boulder. Keep north on the ridge. The highpoint is on the west end of the ridge. There are no markers at the top. Descend by the ascent route.

FYI

Rosedale Peak lies at the eastern edge of the so-called Pegmatite Points. Pegmatites are very coarse-grained, granitic rocks that typically form in dikes and isolated stocks. They have an unusual chemistry that often includes rare-elements and sometimes, gems such as aquamarine, garnet and topaz. This ridge is studded with several of these odd outcrops.

The summit ridge forms part of the boundary between the Pike and the Arapaho National Forests. The trail over the unnamed pass continues north, penetrating into the eastern half of the wonderful Mount Evans Wilderness.

Rosedale Peak rises above Harris Park near the trailhead for the Meridian Trail. (Eric Wiseman)

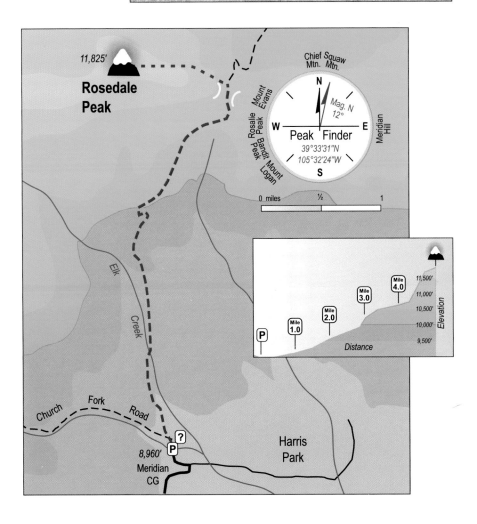

11,825'

Rosedale Peak

Chief Mtn.   Squaw Mtn.

Mount Evans
Rosalie Peak
Bandit Peak
Mount Logan
Meridian Hill

N
Mag. N 12°
W   **Peak Finder**   E
39°33'31"N
105°32'24"W
S

0 miles   ½   1

Mile 1.0   Mile 2.0   Mile 3.0   Mile 4.0

11,500'
11,000'
10,500'
10,000'
9,500'

Elevation

P

Distance

Elk

Creek

Church   Fork   Road

8,960'
Meridian CG

P   ?

Harris Park

74 BRECKINRIDGE PEAK 12,889 Feet

A hike up this ridge in June is a delightful experience with miniature alpine plants to charm the senses.

Distance: 5.1 miles each way
Hiking Time: Up in 165 minutes, down in 110 minutes
Starting Elevation: 9,800 feet
Elevation Gain: 3,419 feet (includes 165 feet extra each way)
Trail: Initial 4.0 miles, bushwack beyond
Season: Mid June to early October
Jurisdiction: Arapaho NF, James Peak Wilderness Area
Maps: *USGS 7 ½'* — Empire; *County* — Clear Creek;
USFS — Arapaho National Forest; *Trails Illustrated* — #103

Directions to the Trailhead

From the center of Empire on US-40, drive north on Main Street. Take right forks at 0.7, 1.1, 1.6, 1.8 and 1.9 miles. Stay on the main road, which is rough and a bit steep in spots towards the end. Park at mile 2.3 from US-40 at the former Conqueror Mine.

The Hike

Begin southwest on the road, which soon becomes rougher. Stay on the main road and avoid side roads to the left at mile 0.1, 0.2 and 0.3. The road then curves left. Keep straight at a four-way intersection at mile 0.6. 100 yards farther, go right. Take another right fork in 0.2 more miles and within 100 yards farther, take the first of five consecutive left forks over the next mile. The last of these leads steeply north-northwest to a "T". Go left, make a

Alpine flowers near the summit.

(Terry Root)

FYI

The Conqueror group of mines numbered over ten and were begun in 1881 to mine gold and silver. After closing down, they reopened again in 1901. The striking, abandoned mine building north of the trailhead was part of this complex.

The peak maintains the original spelling of President Buchanan's Vice President, John Cabell Breckinridge. Named by E.H.N. Patterson on October 4, 1860, this is actually a subpeak of Mount Flora to the west. Mount Flora, in turn, was named by Dr. Charles Parry, who explored this group of peaks on the east side of Berthoud Pass in 1861, and as a botanist, was charmed by the great profusion of miniature alpine plants. A hike along this ridge in June is still a delightful experience with *alpine forget-me-nots, mountain avens* and *old-man-of-the-mountain* to charm the senses.

quick right fork and ascend to a ridge. Keep west on the ridge and take two more left forks before arriving at the foot of Breckinridge Peak. Leave the road and ascend west-northwest up the ridge for another 1.5 mile to a cairn at the summit. You may intersect a segment of the Continental Divide Trail, which

Breckinridge Peak from near Empire. The route hikes up the right hand ridge. (Terry Root)

as envisioned will traverse this ridge, passing close by the summit. Return by retracing your ascent route. Be careful to take the correct trail forks.

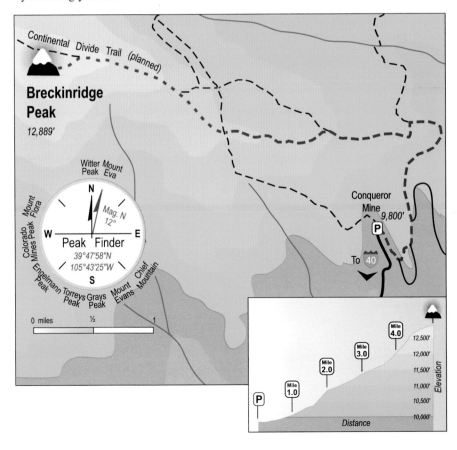

75 ENGELMANN PEAK 13,362 Ft. & ROBESON PEAK 13,140 Ft.

The hike is a very steep pull but you are likely to have these two fine summits all to yourself.

Distance: 1.65 miles to Engelmann Pk., 0.9 miles from Engelmann Peak to Robeson Peak, 2.7 miles on return
Hiking Time: Up in 180 minutes, down in 95 minutes
Starting Elevation: 10,200 feet
Elevation Gain: 3,502 feet (includes 340 ft. extra between summits)
Trail: Mostly bushwacking, with 1.75 miles of trail on descent
Season: Mid June to early October
Jurisdiction: Arapaho National Forest
Maps: *USGS 7 ½'* — Berthoud Pass and Grays Peak; County — Clear Creek; *USFS* — Arapaho NF; *Trails Illustrated* — #103 & 104

Directions to the Trailhead

On US-40, drive 7.4 miles west from Main Street in Empire toward Berthoud Pass or drive 5.9 miles south of Berthoud Pass. Turn left at the bend in the road, following the road toward the Henderson Mine. Pass the Big Bend Picnic Ground. After 0.4 miles from US-40, take the left fork toward the old Urad Mine. This road becomes unpaved. After 0.9 miles from the fork, park off the road at a spacious flat area.

The Hike

Proceed due east, over grass and rock above a tailings pond. Enter the trees, ascending steeply to the east, until you gain a ridge below timberline. Turn right (south) on this ridge and continue to ascend past timberline to another ridge. From here, the Engelmann summit becomes visible. This is all steep going, but the footing is firm. Continue south over tundra to a talus slope, where there is a faint trail to the top of Engelmann Peak. A small cairn is the only marking.

Continue south for a mile to Robeson Peak, mostly over tundra. Lose about 560 feet to the saddle and then ascend 340 feet to the flat, unmarked top of Robeson Peak.

FYI

The higher peak is named after George Engelmann, a botanist and physician from St. Louis. The Engelmann Spruce is also named in his honor. The lower peak is named after the well-known mining family of Georgetown. Solomon Robeson discovered many mines in Clear Creek County and his son, Jacob H. Robeson, was superintendent of the Dives Pelican Mine and mayor of Georgetown in 1898.

The impressive bulk of Engelmann Peak is a familiar sight along US-40, with a reputation for spewing deadly avalanches unto the highway in winter. Perhaps that is why few venture up its steep slopes. You are likely to have these summits to yourself. The hike is best done in September, when the creek along the descent will be at its lowest level.

To descend, return to the Robeson-Engelmann saddle and then pass downward and west into a chute of scree and talus. A creek begins in this chute. Follow the creek to an abandoned mine below timberline. A trail begins here and continues west and north, until it

A view of Engelmann Peak from the north. The route climbs the steep slopes on the right hand side. (Eric Wiseman)

meets an old mining road running parallel to Ruby Creek. Turn right (north) onto this mining road, until it ends at a locked fence. Pass around the fence and reach the Urad Mine Road. Walk about 0.5 mile north on this road to your car.

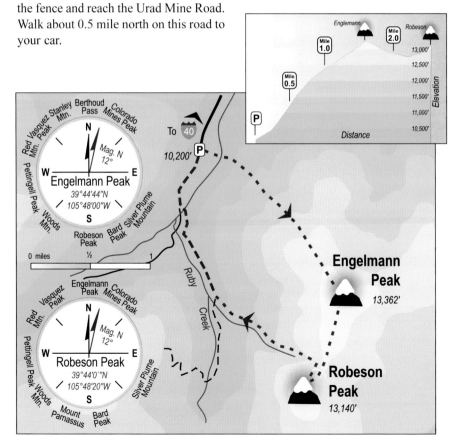

76 BISON PEAK 12,431 Feet

*E*xplore the Lost Creek *Wilderness with its striking rock formations and herd of bighorn sheep.*

Distance: 6.7 miles on ascent, 4.1 miles on descent
Hiking Time: Up in 180 minutes, down in 105 minutes
Starting Elevation: 9,910 feet
Elevation Gain: 2,521 feet
Trail: Most of the way, with some bushwacking
Season: Early June to early October
Jurisdiction: Pike NF, Lost Creek Wilderness Area
Maps: *USGS 7 ½'* — Farnum Peak, McCurdy Mountain, and Topaz Mountain; *County* — Park #2; *USFS* — Pike NF; *Trails Illustrated* — #105

Directions to the Trailhead

Drive on US-285 for 3.2 miles south Kenosha Pass and turn east onto a good dirt road marked by a sign, "Lost Creek Road." (This road lies just north of the town of Jefferson.) Stay on this main dirt road going east-southeast for 19.7 miles and park. This trailhead is just west of the Lost Park Campground. Regular passenger cars should have no trouble.

The Hike

Classics

Cross to the south side of the creek, where there are some signs and a trail passing east-west. Take a trail going south, passing up into the trees at a clearing, called the Indian Creek Trail # 607. Follow this trail south into Willow Gulch, eventually reaching a large open valley. After about 4.7 miles, the Indian Creek Trail reaches Bison Pass at 11,100 feet. Here lies a three-way trail intersection. Signs direct you to Tarryall Creek: 4 miles to the south, to Lost Creek: 5.25 miles north (the route you have just taken) and McCurdy Park: 5.75 miles to the east. Follow the McCurdy Park Trail up and to the east, to above timberline, where numerous and impressive, red granite formations are encountered. As the trail turns south, leave it and head northeast to Bison Peak, and its clearly visible, rocky summit. Avoid the labyrinth of boulders lying to the south of the peak and reach the unambiguous summit, where the ruins of an old platform, a stone

FYI

Bison Peak is the highest in the Tarryall Range. The name Tarryall is said to have originated when miners found such abundant gold in this area that they believed there was enough for all (Tarry-all). McCurdy Mountain is an easy tundra walk of 2.0 miles along the McCurdy Park Trail to the southeast, if you have the time and the energy.

This hike enters the Lost Creek Wilderness, with its fascinating domes and knobs of pink, Pikes Peak granite. Lost Creek gets its name from it habit of disappearing into piles of rock, only to reappear further downstream. Be on a sharp lookout for bighorn sheep, very common around Bison Peak.

stove and a register jar can be found.

For the descent, hike northwest on the ridge tundra and pick your way down. Bushwhack mostly to the northwest to regain the Indian Creek Trail in the large open valley visible below. Then continue north, retracing your ascent route back to your car.

Hikers explore the top of Bison Peak.
(Terry Root)

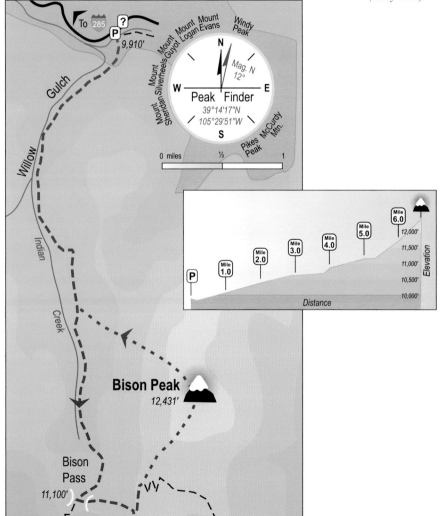

77 CORBETT PEAK 12,583 Feet

The sound of falling water is always near and alpine wildflowers grow in great profusion along Cataract Creek.

Distance: 4.8 miles on ascent, 3.4 miles on descent
Hiking Time: Up in 190 minutes, down in 100 minutes
Starting Elevation: 9,560 feet
Elevation Gain: 3,023 feet
Trail: Trail to timberline, intermittent beyond
Season: Early June to early October
Jurisdiction: Arapaho NF and White River NF
Maps: *USGS 7 ½'* — Pando and Copper Mountain; *County* — Summit #2 and Eagle #4; *USFS* — Arapaho NF and White River NF; *Trails Illustrated* — #109

Directions to the Trailhead

Either drive on US-24 north from Leadville for 11.3 miles or south from Minturn for 18.8 miles. Turn northeast onto a dirt road (Road 726). After 2.9 miles the road arrives at a "T". Turn right for 0.7 more miles and park off the road. This point can be easily reached by regular passenger cars.

The Hike

The trail begins on the north side of the road at a "No Motor Vehicles" sign. Continue north for about 180 yards to a fork, where the Colorado Trail is intercepted. Turn right (east) onto the trail, an old logging road which climbs rather steeply to an abandoned cabin and sawmill, crosses Cataract Creek and generally proceeds to the east. After some switchbacks just before timberline, the creek is crossed again and the trail passes through lovely alpine meadows, before a final short, steep ravine to Kokomo Pass at 12,022 feet, low point on the ridge to the east. From the unmarked pass, leave the

Cairn just below Kokomo Pass.
(Julie Mesdag)

r- **FYI** ----

Kokomo Pass lies west of Kokomo Gulch and the now-abandoned town of Kokomo. These places were named after Kokomo, Indiana, the home town of some of the area residents. Corbett Peak lies on Elk Ridge which divides Eagle and Summit Counties, and offers excellent views of Mount of the Holy Cross to the west.

Cataract Creek leaves rolling apine meadows, filled with flowers, and tumbles down a steepening gorge. The sound of falling water is always near. Since 2002, the Forest Service requires hikers to stay on the Colorado Trail along the Cataract Creek corridor because of old munitions found in the Camp Hale area. Camping or wandering off the trail are not permitted. Any munitions discovered should be reported.

Colorado Trail, following the ridge trail north, and then northwest, to gain the rocky outcroppings at the unmarked top of Corbett Peak.

Descend over the tundra to the southwest, rejoin the trail of your ascent route just below timberline, and follow it west and southwest back to the trailhead.

A hiker descends the Colorado Trail, at a point just above the Cataract Creek bridge crossing. (Julie Mesdag)

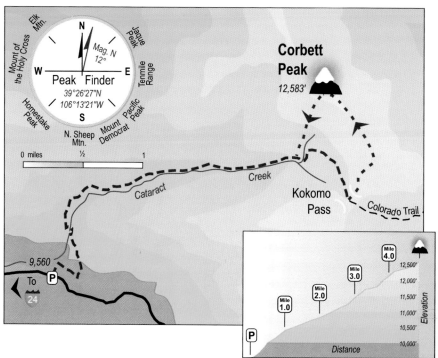

78 LONG SCRAGGY PEAK 8,812 Feet

Looming up like a splendid battleship, Long Scraggy Peak rises out of the ashes.

Distance: 6.3 miles each way
Hiking Time: Up in 240 minutes, down in 200 minutes
Starting Elevation: 7,442 feet
Elevation Gain: 2,770 feet (includes 700 extra feet each way)
Trail: Initial 2.3 miles, intermittent beyond, plus some scrambling
Season: Early May to late November
Jurisdiction: Pike National Forest
Maps: USGS 7 ½'— Deckers and Platte Canyon;
County — Jefferson #2; USFS — Pike National Forest; Trails Illustrated — #135

Directions to the Trailhead

Drive south from US-285 at Pine Junction onto Jefferson County Road 126 for 11.8 miles. A dirt road on the left (east), the former Top-of-the-World Campground Road, is now closed to vehicles because of damage from the Buffalo Creek fire. Park off the highway.

The Hike

Walk the dirt access road east, southeast and then north. After 1.7 miles, there is a fork. The right turn goes to the now-removed campground. Take the left fork for 0.6 more miles to a parking area on the right. Follow the trail, heading southeast from the parking area. After 0.2 mile, leave the trail and proceed to your right, directly toward Long Scraggy Peak, visible in the distance. Another 0.2 mile brings you to the valley floor. Pick up an old road and follow it east along the creek. There are several paths in the area. Continue east and east-northeast, taking a right fork at two consecutive intersections. You are now 1.4 miles from the point where you left the access road. Continue south along Spring Creek. At 0.5 mile from the last fork, go right at another junction and head southeast. At 0.75 mile past the last fork, leave the trail and bushwack to the left (southeast). You are heading toward the northern ridge of Long Scraggy Peak. As you continue southeast, you may encounter an intermittent trail, occasional ribbons and cairns. There are some steep segments along the western side of the ridge and two rocky, false summits before reaching the flat, treeless summit with two benchmarks. Some easy hand work will be needed over the final boulders.

FYI

Long Scraggy Peak looms like a splendid battleship, southeast of the town of Buffalo Creek. To reach the summit requires good bushwhacking and compass skills. The area of this hike is traversed by many bicycle trails which are heavily used on non-winter weekends.

The disastrous 1996 Buffalo Creek fire consumed some 12,000 acres. Much of this hike is through this charred forest, which is slowly beginning to come back as plants and animals re-colonize.

Enjoy the fine views from the summit, especially of Pikes Peak to the south-southeast, before retracing your ascent route. Avoid the steep dropoffs on the east and west sides of the summit ridge on your way back.

Long Scraggy Peak rises above the burnt-over forest.
(Terry Root)

The Buffalo Creek fire and private property in the area may necessitate altering your route. If so, generally head directly toward Long Scraggy Peak, bushwacking up to its north ridge, then follow the west side of the ridge to the summit.

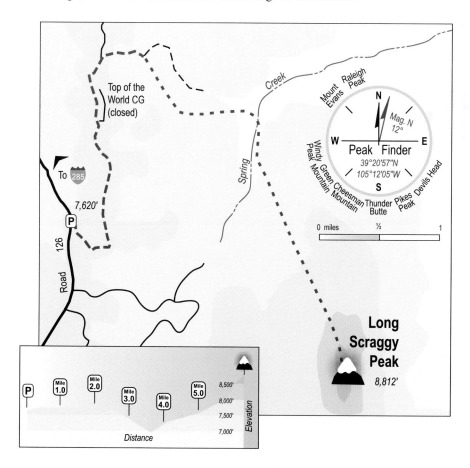

79 MOUNT GUYOT 13,370 Feet

This impressive peak is a climbers' favorite, with a handsome cirque visible for miles around.

Distance: 5.25 miles on ascent, 2.4 miles on descent
Hiking Time: Up in 212 minutes, down in 122 minutes
Starting Elevation: 10,390 feet
Elevation Gain: 3,164 feet (includes 75 feet extra each way)
Trail: All the way on ascent, final 0.8 mile on descent
Season: Mid June to early October
Jurisdiction: Arapaho National Forest
Maps: USGS 7 ½' — Boreas Pass; *County* — Summit #2; *USFS* — Arapaho National Forest; *Trails Illustrated* — #109

Directions to the Trailhead

Drive 0.8 miles north from the stop light in Breckenridge (Lincoln Street) on CO-9. Turn right (east) onto Summit County Road 450, and drive generally south up French Gulch for 4.65 miles and park off the road at a locked gate. The left fork leads up Little French Gulch and ends in 1.5 miles. En route to this parking spot from CO-9, keep right at mile 0.4, left at mile 1.1, straight at mile 3.9, left at mile 4.0, and left at mile 4.55. Regular passenger cars can reach this point.

The Hike

Proceed south around the gate and avoid two roads on the left after 0.5 mile. Pass through an open meadow and enter the forst as the road steepens. At mile 2.3, reach a meaningless fork, as both roads quickly converge at another locked gate. Pass around the gate and soon cross a creek. It is 1.2 miles further, mostly over tundra, to a cairn at French Pass. Bald Mountain is on your right (west) and Boreas Mountain lies straight ahead (south). From the pass, ascend a faint trail to the left (east-northeast), following it along the western

slopes of the ridge (the Continental Divide.) This trail eventually turns to the northeast to gain the cairn-marked summit. A register cylinder and some rock shelters are also at the top.

Classics

Descend over talus to the northwest, to a ridge separating French Gulch from Little French Gulch. Around timberline, veer to your left (northwest) and bushwhack down to the road leading back to your vehicle.

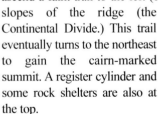

 FYI

Mount Guyot is named after the Swiss surveyor, Professor Arnold Henry Guyot. Climbers, when perched on other summits, love to pick out this big, impressive peak. The huge, handsome cirque on the east face can be seen for miles around.

Mount Guyot and French Pass also form part of the Continental Divide, the boundary between Summit and Park Counties and also between the Arapaho and Pike National Forests. Mount Guyot can also be climbed easily from Georgia Pass on the east.

Mount Guyot from the south, showing its prominent and steep, east-facing cirque.

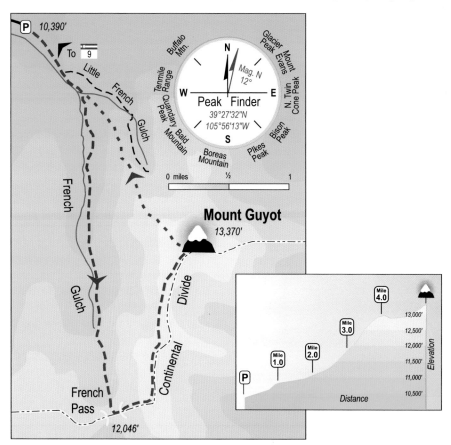

80 SATANTA PEAK 11,979 Feet and MOUNT NEVA 12,814 Feet

A colorful riot of alpine wildflowers in this magnificent wilderness area leads you up to a pair of peaks on the Continental Divide.

Distance: 2.8 miles to Arapaho Pass, 1.3miles from Arapaho Pass to Satanta Peak, 1.25 miles from Arapaho Pass to Mt. Neva.

Hiking Time: Up to Arapaho Pass 93 minutes, Arapaho Pass to Satanta Peak in 26 minutes, back to Arapaho Pass in 26 minutes, Arapaho Pass to Mount Neva in 88 minutes, down from Mount Neva in 130 minutes.

Starting Elevation: 10,180 feet

Elevation Gain: 3,157 feet for both peaks (includes 225 feet extra)

Trail: Most of the way, with some scrambling on final ridges

Season: Early June to early October

Jurisdiction: Arapaho NF & Roosevelt NF, Indian Peaks WA

Maps: USGS 7 ½' — East Portal and Monarch Lake; County — Boulder & Grand #4; USFS — Arapaho NF & Roosevelt NF; Trails Illustrated — #102

Directions to the Trailhead

From the junction of CO-72 and CO-119 in Nederland, drive south on CO-119 for 0.65 miles and turn right (west). Drive a total of 9.1 miles from CO-119 on this road, through the town of Eldora, to a parking area at the trailhead at the Fourth of July Campground. En route keep right at 1.5 miles and at 4.9 miles. Keep left at 7.7 miles and then right to the parking area at 9.0 miles. This road, rough in a few spots after a rain, is normally suitable for a regular car.

The Hike

Classics

Proceed north and then west from the clearly marked trailhead. Take a right fork after 27 minutes (the left fork goes to Diamond Lake) and a left fork after 24 more minutes (the right fork goes to the Arapaho Glacier and the Arapaho Peaks). Continue west above timberline on the excellent trail, which now consists of mostly flat talus, to Arapaho Pass, just northeast of Lake Dorothy. For Satanta Peak, continue southwest to the vicinity of Lake Dorothy and then descend west, contouring around the north ridge of Mount Neva. The trail becomes a bit narrow at times, but is adequate. In 13 minutes, the trail brings you to a sign marking Caribou Pass. A trail leads northwest from the pass and the Caribou Pass Trail. Follow this trail for only a few hundred feet and then leave the trail, ascending

FYI

Arapaho Pass and Mount Neva are on the Continental Divide and on the boundary between Grand and Boulder Counties and the Roosevelt and Arapaho National Forests. This hike lies in the very popular Indian Peaks Wilderness Area.

Ths sunny, south-facing slopes leading up to Arapaho Pass are a riot of colors in July, with one of the finest displays of alpine wildflowers in the Front Range.

north over tundra to a large cairn atop Satanta Peak. Return to Arapaho Pass by the same route.

For Mount Neva, continue west up the north ridge on a faint trail from the area of Lake Dorothy. Follow the ridge as it turns south. At a few points along this ridge, some moderate hand work is necessary. Continue south and eventually reach a grassy area, leading to a cairn at the summit. Return to Arapaho Pass and the trailhead by your ascent route. (For an alternate descent route from Mount Neva, go south along the Divide to a saddle and then descend east into the basin toward Diamond Lake, where you may gain a trail leading east back to the Arapaho Pass Trail.)

Mount Neva, from the flower-strewn meadows along the Arapaho Pass Trail.

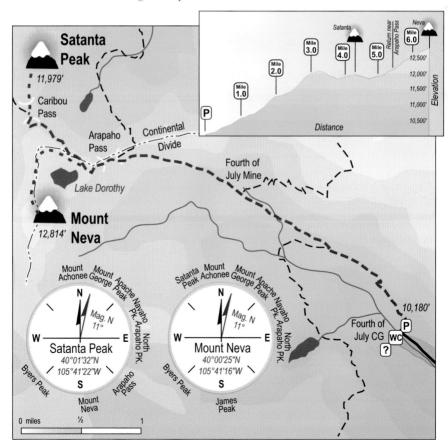

81 MOUNT BUCKSKIN 13,370 Feet

Flower-strewn meadows and spectacular vistas await you on this hike into the scenic Elk Range.

Distance: 4.5 miles each way
Hiking Time: Up in 190 minutes, down in 135 minutes
Starting Elevation: 9,600 feet
Elevation Gain: 4,170 feet (includes 200 feet extra each way)
Trail: Initial 3.7 miles, tundra walking beyond
Season: Early June to early October
Jurisdiction: White River NF, Maroon Bells/Snowmass Wilderness
Maps: *USGS 7 ½'* — Maroon Bells; *County* — Pitkin #1;
USFS — White River National Forest; *Trails Illustrated* — #128

Directions to the Trailhead

The Maroon Lake area is one of the most heavily used in Colorado. The Maroon Creek Road is closed to private motor vehicles from 9:00 A.M. until 5:00 P.M. daily, during the hiking season. Shuttle buses transport visitors from a parking area at the mouth of the valley, for the nine miles to Maroon Lake. Drive west on CO-82 from Aspen. Cross the Castle Creek bridge and take the first left turn, after the stop light. This turn directs you to Aspen Highlands. After 0.1 miles on this road, take the right fork to Maroon Creek. Soon, you will notice the parking area for the shuttle buses. The paved road continues up the valley for a total of 9.9 miles from CO-82, until the road ends at a parking area at Maroon Lake, above the Maroon Lake Campground.

The Hike

Classics

Take the trail, starting at the west end of the parking area at a sign, "Maroon Snowmass Trail #1975". This leads south, then turns southwest, before the lake. Take two right forks, en route to a sign and trail fork near Crater Lake. This fork will be reached in about 45 minutes. Take the right fork and ascend southwest into Minnehaha Gulch. In about thirty minutes from the fork at Crater Lake, take the right fork, reaching timberline in forty minutes more. About ten minutes above timberline, take the left fork at a sign. (The right fork goes to Willow Pass.) In another thirty

FYI

This hike brings you to one of the most scenic passes in Colorado, with fantastic flower-strewn meadows to please the senses along the way. The view of the Maroon Bells, from your starting point at Maroon Lake, has to be one of the most photographed scenes in Colorado. Despite the very rugged nature of the peaks in the Elk Range, Mount Buckskin poses no special risks and offers spectacular vistas.

As of 2003, hikers are required to obtain a free permit to enter the Maroon Bells/Snowmass Wilderness, available at self-serve stations at the trailhead. There are no restrictions on the number of permits granted each day (although that could be the future for this popular area.)

minutes, you will arrive after a series of switchbacks to unmarked, scenic Buckskin Pass. From the pass, proceed north over tundra. The Mount Buckskin summit is visible, 0.8 miles from the pass. En route, you will lose about one hundred feet of elevation, as you pass through a saddle. Continue north, over some rocky false summits, to the top which has a cairn, USGS marker and a small register jar. Retrace the ascent route back to the trailhead.

Buckskin Pass is to the left of Mount Buckskin (center) in this view from the east. (Eric Wiseman)

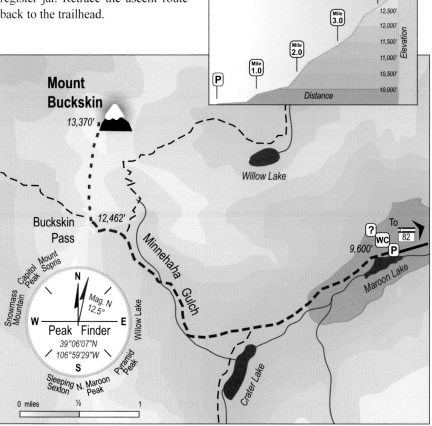

82 UNEVA PEAK 12,522 Feet

With scant mining history, the Gore Range still retains much of its rugged, wilderness character.

Distance: 6.5 miles on ascent, 5.5 miles on descent
Hiking Time: Up in 210 minutes, down in 160 minutes
Starting Elevation: 9,711 feet
Elevation Gain: 2,811 feet
Trail: Initial 4.3 miles on ascent, tundra walking beyond
Season: Early June to early October
Jurisdiction: Arapaho National Forest, Eagles Nest Wilderness
Maps: *USGS 7 ½'* — Vail Pass; *County* — Summit #2; *USFS* — Arapaho National Forest; *Trails Illustrated* — #108

Directions to the Trailhead

At the Copper Mountain/Leadville/CO-91 exit of I-70 (Exit # 195), cross south on the overpass and turn left onto a side road opposite the ski area. Park at the trailhead parking lot on the right, past the gas station. Do not park on the off ramp!

The Hike

Walk north across the overpass to pick up the trail, which begins just north of the bridge. The trail quickly ascends to the northwest, across from the Copper Mountain Resort. Keep left at a fork in the trail, as the right fork leads to Wheeler Lakes. The clear trail progresses west, and then curves north, to reach Uneva Pass at 11,900 feet. Uneva Peak will now be visible to the northwest, at the end of a cirque. Proceed west to gain the ridge and then turn north to the summit, marked by an USGS marker and two nearby cairns. The best descent route passes directly to the south-southeast over a grassy ridge. At the final subpeak of this ridge, pass to the left, and soon thereafter, regain the trail.

FYI

This hike travels into the beautiful Eagles Nest Wilderness, which is dominated by the rocky backbone of the Gore Range. Uneva Peak lies at the southern tip of the the range, on the boundary between Eagle and Summit Counties, and has more in common with the gentler Tenmile Range, south of the highway, than the sharp peaks that make up the rest of the Gores. There was almost no mining in the range, so that the area still retains much of its rugged, wilderness character. The wildlife have fully recovered from the exploits of Sir St George Gore, an Irish baronet, who devastated the local fauna in the 1850s.

Uneva Lake is located east of the peak and doesn't intersect this hiking route. It was an early recreational area for the residents of Frisco. The Wheeler Lakes are named after Judge John S. Wheeler, a South Park rancher who grazed his cattle in this area.

Uneva Peak, as viewed from Uneva Pass.

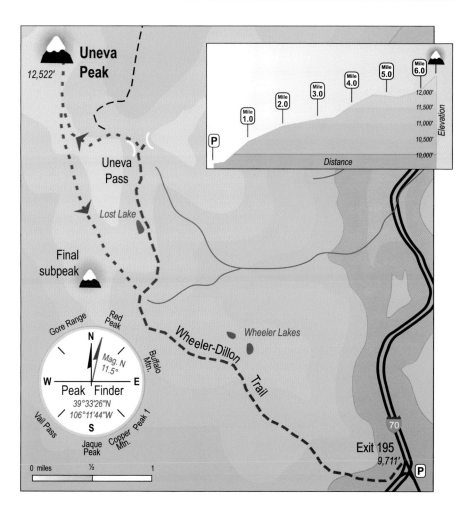

83 BANDIT PEAK 12,444 Feet

*B*ighorn sheep make this peak their home and can often be spotted on the open slopes in early summer.

Distance: 5.0 miles on ascent, 3.2 miles on descent
Hiking Time: Up in 214 minutes, down in 122 minutes
Starting Elevation: 9,248 feet
Elevation Gain: 3,246 feet
Trail: Initial 2.25 miles on ascent, final 2.0 miles on descent
Season: Late May to mid October
Jurisdiction: Plke National Forest, Mount Evans Wilderness
Maps: *USGS 7 ½'* — Harris Park; *County* — Park #2;
USFS — Pike National Forest; *Trails Illustrated* — #104

Directions to the Trailhead

From US-285, 2.7 miles northeast of Bailey or 4.5 miles southwest of Pine Junction, drive north, then northwest, on Park County Road 43 for 8.3 miles to Deer Creek Campground. Then go 0.8 miles further to a parking area and a trail sign. Park here. (En route to this trailhead, take the left fork after 7.0 miles, then the right fork 1.3 miles further at the campground.)

The Hike

Take the trail to the right, labeled "Tanglewood Trail." (The trail to the left is the Rosalie Trail # 603, which ultimately reaches Guanella Pass.) Lose a little altitude and continue northwest along Tanglewood Creek, keeping right at a fork one mile from the trailhead. After 2.25 miles, the trail reaches a pass at just above treeline, with Mount Rosalie on your left and several rocky knobs, the Pegmatite Points, to your right. (The trail continues north, down to Roosevelt Lakes and Beartrack Lakes.) Leave the pass and the trail by contouring to the west (left), then southwest around a cirque beneath Mount Rosalie for about 1.5 miles, to the north ridge of Bandit Peak. Ascend to the south easily from there, to the cairn on top.

Classics

Descend by continuing south over tundra. At a point just above treeline, follow a prominent gully south, down through the trees to meet the Rosalie Trail, paralleling Deer Creek. This will require about 60 minutes. Then turn left (east) onto this trail. It is about two miles, and another hour, to complete the loop back to the trailhead.

Bandit Peak is a subpeak of Rosalie Peak, on the southeastern arm of the Mount Evans massif. The southern flanks of Bandit Peak are important winter range for bighorn sheep, as those slopes are often snow free for a good part of the winter. Sheep can usually be spotted in the large open meadows on the south side in spring. By June, they move up the mountain to drop their lambs, then continue to drift higher on the massif. By November, they are back and the echo of crashing horns can sometimes be heard on Bandit Peak.

Looking north from the summit of Bandit Peak at Mount Rosalie.

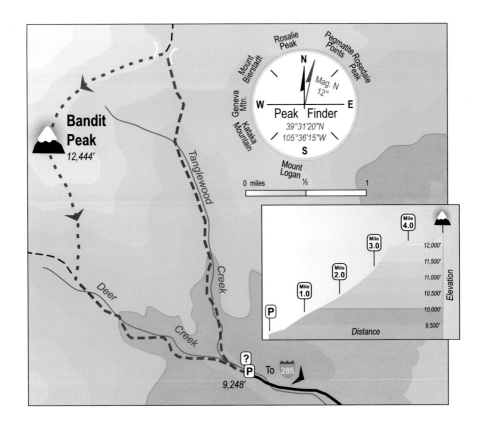

84 KATAKA MOUNTAIN 12,441 Feet

Views of the popular fourteeners, Mount Bierstadt and Mount Evans, fill up the horizon on this hike.

Distance: 5.7 miles on ascent, 3.6 miles on descent
Hiking Time: Up in 250 minutes, down in 122 minutes
Starting Elevation: 9,610 feet
Elevation Gain: 2,831 feet
Trail: Initial 4.5 miles on ascent, final 2.1 mile on descent
Season: Mid June to early October
Jurisdiction: Pike NF, Mount Evans Wilderness Area
Maps: USGS 7 ½' — Mount Evans; *County* — Park #2;
USFS — Pike National Forest; *Trails Illustrated* — #104

Directions to the Trailhead

Either drive north from US-285 at the town of Grant on Park County Road 62 (Guanella Pass Road) for 5.3 miles or drive south from Guanella Pass on Park County Road 62 for 8.1 miles to a parking area on the east side of the road. (Geneva Park is the name given to the meadow on the west side of the road.) Park here.

The Hike

The trailhead is well-marked, past an open wooden fence, by a sign indicating that the intersection for the Rosalie Trail is 4.0 miles and that Abyss Lake is 8.0 miles away. Since this is part of the Mount Evans Wilderness Area, the trail is closed to motorized vehicles (but open to horseback travel.) Hike northeast on this trail, paralleling Scott Gomer Creek. After 2.1 miles from the trailhead, the trail crosses the creek at a wooden bridge. In another 20 minutes, the trail crosses the creek again, back to the west side.

After about two hours from the trailhead, you reach an open basin and a confluence of Scott Gomer Creek, coming from the northwest, with the Lake Fork, coming from the northeast. Cross Scott Gomer Creek, near the confluence; and very quickly, the trail reaches a fork. The left fork continues northeast to Abyss Lake. Take the right fork, the Rosalie Trail (which eventually leads to Deer Creek.) Continue east on this trail, which rises to timberline after crossing the Lake Fork. When at about 11,400 feet (just below timberline), where a subpeak of Mount Bierstadt lies directly

FYI

This gentle, rounded summit in Park County isn't visited frequently, yet it affords wonderful views of Kenosha Pass, South Park and the surrounding high peaks. The popular fourteeners, Mount Bierstadt and Mount Evans, fill up the horizon to the north. Make this a fall hike, with grand aspen displays along the Guanella Pass Road.

Park County, named after South Park, was one of the original territorial counties of Colorado.

north, leave the trail and proceed up and south over tundra, past sparse trees. A ridge, below the Kataka summit, lies to your south. It is about 1.2 miles from the trail, over this ridge, to a small pile of rocks on the flat summit.

Mount Bierstadt (left) and Mount Evans (right) from Kataka Mountain.

For the return, make a loop by proceeding due west, bushwacking down to regain the trail near the southernmost bridge which crosses Scott Gomer Creek. The trail then returns you southwest to the trailhead.

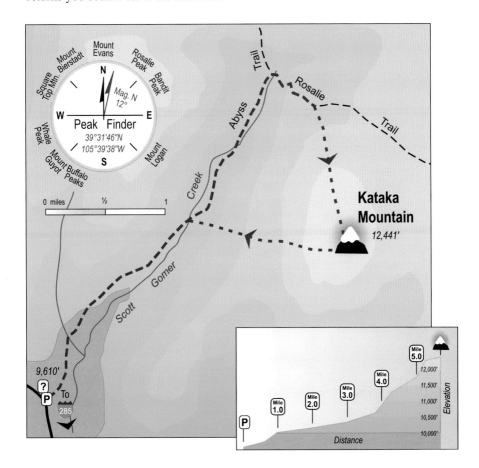

85 COMANCHE PEAK 13,277 Feet

*I*t is striking how abruptly these classic fault-block mountains soar above the valleys on either side.

Distance: 5.4 miles each way
Hiking Time: Up in 214 minutes, down in 142 minutes
Starting Elevation: 8,940 feet
Elevation Gain: 4,337 feet
Trail: All the way
Season: Mid June to early October
Jurisdiction: Rio Grande NF & San Isabel NF, Sangre de Cristo WA
Maps: USGS 7 ½' — Horn Peak; County — Custer #1 and
Saguache #5; USFS — Rio Grande NF & San Isabel NF; Trails Illustrated — #138

Directions to the Trailhead

Drive south on CO-69 from Westcliffe at the junction with CO-96 for 3.4 miles. Turn right on Schoolfield Road (Custer County Road 140) and drive for 4.5 miles to a "T". Turn left onto Custer County Road 141. After 1.9 miles, reach an intersection and take the right fork 0.3 mile to the Comanche-Venable Trailhead. Regular cars can easily reach this point, 6.75 miles from CO-69.

The Hike

Classics

A signed trail at the southwest corner of the parking area rises almost 0.5 mile to reach an intersection with the Rainbow Trail. Proceed to the right on the Rainbow Trail and quickly reach the Comanche Lake Trail on your left. Continue on this trail, up the valley to the west. Eventually, Horn Peak comes into view on your left, across the valley. In 3.4 miles from the Rainbow Trail, you will arrive at a point overlooking Comanche Lake, with Comanche Peak looming impressively at the end of the basin. Continue on the trail, rising to the right of the lake in a series of switchbacks, to an unnamed pass at 12,750 feet. Descend about forty feet from the pass to a saddle on your left. From here, take the faint ridge trail south, over tundra, to the summit and a small cairn. Descend as you ascended.

You may combine this hike with Hike #86, descending on the Venable

FYI

The very authentic, western town of Westcliffe lies in the idyllic Wet Mountain valley, bounded on the west by the Sangre de Cristo Mountains. Formerly called Clifton, the town was renamed by Dr. W. A. Bell after his home town of Westcliff-on-the-Sea, England.

It is striking how abruptly the Sangre de Cristo Range soars 7,000 above the valleys on either side. The Sangres are classic fault-block mountains, situated along massive fault lines. As the range began to thrust upward some 25 million years ago, almost as a single block, the valleys slid down. The actual basement rock is now hidden under thousands of feet of sediment. Evidence of large earthquakes in the San Luis Valley in recent geologic time indicates continued movement.

Trail, for a wonderful loop trip through the Sangre de Cristo Wilderness. Retrace your steps to the unnamed pass, then continue on the trail north for 1.0 mile, along the west flank of Spring Mountain, to another unnamed pass. Pick up the Venable Trail here, following the directions for Hike #86 in reverse to the Rainbow Trail. Turn right (south) at the Rainbow Trail, passing the Comanche Lake Trail in about 0.5 mile. Soon afterwards, turn left (east) to return to your car.

Comanche Peak and Comanche Lake.

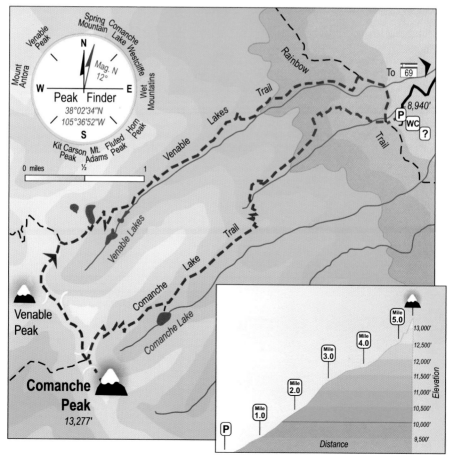

86 VENABLE PEAK 13,334 Feet

Link this route with Hike #85 for an outstanding loop trip through the Sangre de Cristo Wilderness.

Distance: 6.8 miles each way
Hiking Time: Up in 205 minutes, down in 140 minutes
Starting Elevation: 8,930 feet
Elevation Gain: 4,404 feet
Trail: Initial 6.5 miles, off-trail tundra and talus beyond
Season: Mid June to early October
Jurisdiction: Rio Grande NF & San Isabel NF, Sangre de Cristo WA
Maps: *USGS 7 ½'* — Horn Peak and Rito Alto Peak; *County* — Saguache #5 and Custer #1; *USFS* — Rio Grande NF & San Isabel NF; *Trails Illustrated* — #138

Directions to the Trailhead

Drive south on CO-69 from Westcliffe at the junction with CO-96 for 3.4 miles. Turn right on Schoolfield Road (Custer County Road 140) and drive for 4.5 miles to a "T". Turn left onto Custer County Road 141. After 1.9 miles, reach an intersection and take the right fork 0.3 mile to the Comanche-Venable Trailhead. Regular cars can easily reach this point, 6.75 miles from CO-69.

The Hike

Classics

A signed trail at the southwest corner of the parking area rises almost 0.5 mile to reach an intersection with the Rainbow Trail. Proceed to the right on the Rainbow Trail, and in less than 0.5 mile, take the left fork at a sign, "Venable Lakes 5 miles." Continue southwest up the valley, with Venable Creek on your left. (A short side trail goes off left to Venable Falls.) Continue on the main trail, until it forks at an abandoned cabin. Take the left fork, leading to one of the Venable Lakes, and soon thereafter, to a signed fork. Take the left fork, rising southwest toward the unnamed pass, by way of a narrow shelf with steep drop-offs, known as the Phantom Terrace. At the pass, there is no sign. Leave the trail and ascend the ridge to the northwest, curving south to the summit cairn.

You may combine this hike with Hike #85, descending on the Comanche Trail, for a wonderful loop trip through the Sangre de Cristo Wilderness. Retrace your steps to the unnamed pass, then continue on the trail south for 1.0 mile, along the west flank of Spring Mountain, to another unnamed pass. Pick up the Comanche Trail here, following the directions for Hike #85 in reverse to the Rainbow Trail. Turn right (south) at the Rainbow Trail, then soon turn left (east) to return to your car.

FYI

Part of this hike utilizes the Rainbow Trail, a 85-mile route along the eastern side of the Sangre de Cristo Range. The Abbot's Lodge, passed early in the hike, was owned and operated by the Benedictine Order for many years as a summer camp, and as a support structure for the Holy Cross Abbey, a high school for boys in Canon City. Venable Pass is not traversed in this route. It lies to the west of the Venable Lakes.

Venable Peak, as viewed from Comanche Peak.

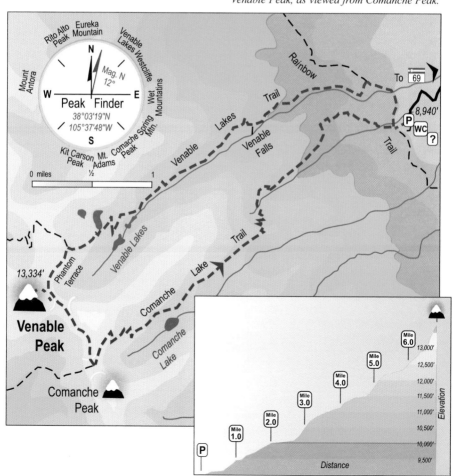

87 MOUNT LOGAN 12,871 Feet

The rolling slopes attract bighorn sheep and hikers seeking solitude in the wilderness.

Distance: 9.2 miles on ascent, 4.55 miles on descent
Hiking Time: Up in 240 minutes, down in 130 minutes
Starting Elevation: 9,320 feet
Elevation Gain: 3,795 feet
Trail: Initial 8.2 miles on ascent, final 2.0 miles on descent
Season: Mid June to early October
Jurisdiction: Pike National Forest, Mount Evans Wilderness
Maps: *USGS 7 ½'* — Harris Park, Mount Evans, and
Mount Logan; *County* — Park #2; *USFS* — Pike National Forest; *Trails Illustrated* — #104

Directions to the Trailhead

From US-285, 2.7 miles northeast of Bailey or 4.5 miles southwest of Pine Junction, drive north, then northwest, on Park County Road 43 for 8.3 miles to Deer Creek Campground. Then go 0.8 miles further to a parking area and a trail sign. Park here. (En route to this trailhead, take the left fork after 7.0 miles, then the right fork 1.3 miles further at the campground.)

The Hike

Go west a few hundred yards to some trail signs and a fork. Take the left fork, the Rosalie Trail. Follow it west and northwest, along Deer Creek and crossing it several times, for 5.8 miles to a ridge and a junction with the Threemile Creek Trail, #635. Follow the Threemile Creek Trail, as it curves south, upward between Kataka Mountain on your right (west) and subpeaks of Mount Logan on your left (east). The trail becomes rather faint. Leave the trail near treeline, going southeast up the subpeak of Mount Logan, keeping to the right of its highpoint. At the ridge, the true summit becomes visible to the south. Continue over tundra, losing 244 feet as you make directly for the highpoint. From the Threemile Creek cutoff at the Rosalie Trail, it is 3.1 miles to the top of Mount Logan, where there is a large ring of rocks, some old wooden planks and a Colorado Mountain Club register cylinder.

To descend, hike over tundra and rocks to the northeast. At the most easterly subpeak, enter the trees and bushwhack through a moderately dense forest,

FYI

Mount Logan, like the Colorado county of the same name, was named after John Alexander Logan, an Illinois politician and a Union General in the Civil War. He inaugurated the national holiday of Memorial Day.

This big peak is infrequently climbed, a condition that seems to suite a large band of bighorn sheep. Locals in the town of Grant share their backyards with them in winter, but come summer, the sheep are back up on Logan's rolling, tundra slopes.

keeping northeast to regain the Rosalie Trail. A creek becomes evident after you enter the trees. Keep this creek to your left, following it to the junction with Deer Creek. Pick up the trail here and hike two miles east to your car. (If you dislike bushwhacking, descend the same way you came up. This will add 4.65 miles to the hike.)

A cairn leads the way through willows on Mount Logan.

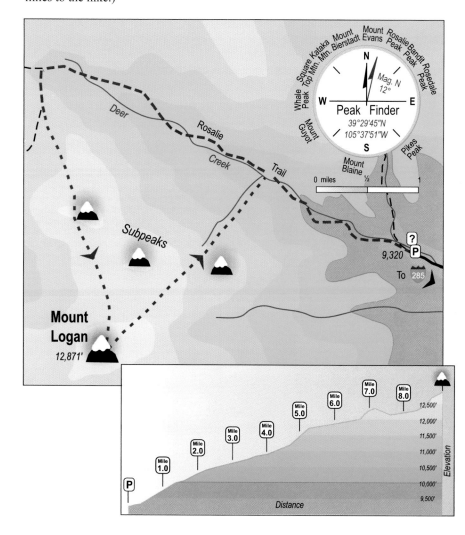

88 BUCKEYE PEAK 12,867 Feet and MOUNT ZION 12,126 Feet

Count ptarmigan and fourteeners — at least eighteen are visible — on this beautiful walk along the tundra.

Distance: 4.3 miles to Mount Zion, 3.1 miles from Mount Zion to Buckeye Peak, 7.4 miles return
Hiking Time: Up in 220 minutes, down in 180 minutes
Starting Elevation: 9,961 feet
Elevation Gain: 3,426 feet (includes 260 feet extra each way)
Trail: Initial 6.6 miles, tundra walking beyond
Season: Early June to early October
Jurisdiction: San Isabel National Forest
Maps: *USGS 7 ½'* — Leadville North; *County* — Lake;
USFS — San Isabel National Forest; *Trails Illustrated* — #109

Directions to the Trailhead

4WD option

From the north end of Leadville, at the intersection of CO-91 and US-24, drive northwest on US-24 for 1.4 miles. Turn right onto a dirt road at a sign "Mount Zion Road 5510." In 0.1 mile, this road offers three routes. Park around here. (High-clearance and four-wheel drive vehicles can traverse the entire 6.7 miles of this road to the foot of Buckeye Peak, when weather conditions permit.)

The Hike

Follow the road going left (northwest), as it rises through the trees. Take the left fork at 0.25 mile and again at mile 0.8. Pass a radio tower at mile 1.3. At mile 4.3, you will be above timberline and reach Mount Zion. The summit cairn and a jar register will be a two-minute side hike off the road to the right (east). Regain the road and continue north, with some elevation loss over the rolling tundra. The jeep trail bends northeast, rising between two unnamed peaks and ending at the foot of Buckeye Peak, with little Buckeye Lake down to the right (east). Follow the rocky ridge on the right, north toward the summit, which contains three separate USGS markers and a ring of rocks around a cairn, supporting a small metal tower. Return by way of your ascent route.

FYI

Buckeye Peak was probably named by some early miners from Ohio, the Buckeye State. There are several Mount Zions in Colorado.

Despite the modest nature of these two summits, the vistas are truly exceptional. Spread out before you is a sweeping panorama of the Sawatch Range, including Mount Elbert and Mount Massive, the two highest summits in the state. Beyond that is the Elk Range, with its own set of skyscraping fourteeners. Counting close-by Mounts Sherman, Lincoln and Democrat, there are at least eighteen fourteeners visible.

With eyes drawn to these giants, don't trip over some of the many white-tailed ptarmigan in the area.

A ptarmigan rests among rocks near the summit of Buckeye Peak. (Eric Wiseman)

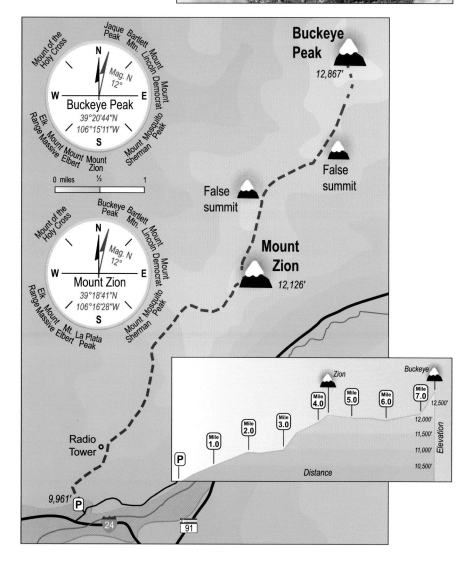

Buckeye Peak
12,867'

False summit

False summit

Mount of the Holy Cross
Jaque Peak
Bartlett Mtn.
Mount Lincoln
Mount Democrat

Mag. N 12°

N
W   E
S

Buckeye Peak
39°20'44"N
106°15'11"W

Elk Range
Mount Massive
Mount Elbert
Mount Zion
Mount Sherman
Mosquito Peak

0 miles   ½   1

Mount Zion
12,126'

Mount of the Holy Cross
Buckeye Peak
Bartlett Mtn.
Mount Lincoln
Mount Democrat

Mag. N 12°

N
W   E
S

Mount Zion
39°18'41"N
106°16'28"W

Elk Range
Mount Massive
Mount Elbert
Mt. La Plata Peak
Mount Sherman
Mosquito Peak

Radio Tower

9,961'
P

24   91

Zion   Buckeye

Mile 4.0   Mile 5.0   Mile 6.0   Mile 7.0   12,500'

Mile 1.0   Mile 2.0   Mile 3.0   12,000'
                                           11,500'
P   11,000'
                                           10,500'
                    Distance   *Elevation*

89 SOUTH TWIN CONE PEAK 12,323 Feet

*W*here fire swept through half-a-century ago, golden aspen leaves now carpet the trail.

Distance: 7.0 miles each way
Hiking Time: Up in 265 minutes, down in 183 minutes
Starting Elevation: 8,293 feet
Elevation Gain: 4,030 feet
Trail: Initial 5.5 miles, tundra walk beyond
Season: Early June to mid October
Jurisdiction: Pike National Forest
Maps: *USGS 7 ½'* — Mount Logan and Shawnee;
County — Park #2; USFS — Pike National Forest; *Trails Illustrated* — #104 & 105

Directions to the Trailhead

On US-285, either drive 2.1 miles west of the Shawnee Post Office or drive 2.7 miles east of the Camp Santa Maria entrance and park near a Ben Tyler Trail sign. There is parking on the south side of the highway.

The Hike

Proceed up the gulch to the west-southwest. In about 100 minutes, take the left fork. In about 70 more minutes, take the right fork to Rock Creek. Continue to ascend the gulch, and in 24 more minutes, reach the ridge and timberline. Then leave the trail and hike to your right (west)

Aspen leaves along Rock Creek (Terry Root)

FYI

This is one of the Platte River Mountains, visible from South Park around the town of Jefferson. Mount Blaine, one mile north, and North Twin Cone Peak, 1.3 miles northwest, can readily be reached over tundra and talus from this peak *(see Hike #68)*.

At treeline are some examples of *krummholz* (a German word meaning "crooked wood"), wind-tortured dwarf conifers that survive in this severe environment. You may also observe a few "banner trees," with branches only on the leeward

sides. The fierce, westerly prevailing winds strip any growth off the windward sides.

This is another wonderful hike in the fall season, with colorful, fallen aspen leaves blanketing the upper half of the Ben Tyler Trail. These trees are evidence of a fire that swept the gulch less than half-a-century ago. This group changes to identical shades of red and gold in unison around mid-September, evidence that they are clones, or individual tress sprouting from the same root system.

across marshy areas, willows and krummholz for about an hour. Go past a false summit, to a cairn and pole at the top. Descend by the same route.

South Twin Cone Peak, as viewed from the east.

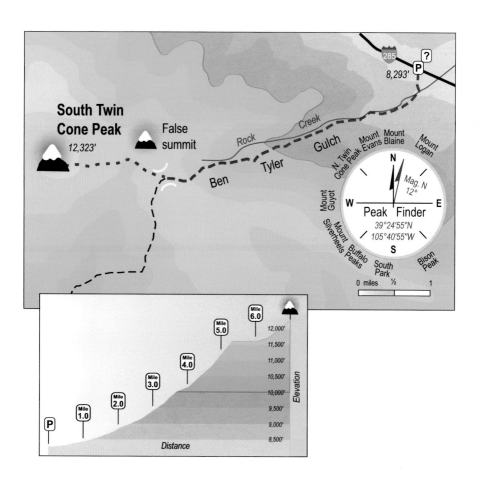

90 ANTORA PEAK 13,269 Feet

Two famous wilderness paths converge on a hike to the terminus of the Sawatch Range.

Distance: 6.5 miles each way
Hiking Time: Up in 245 minutes, down in 210 minutes
Starting Elevation: 10,886 feet
Elevation Gain: 4,423 feet (includes 1,020 feet extra each way)
Trail: Initial 5.5 miles, off-trail tundra and talus beyond
Season: Mid June to early October
Jurisdiction: San Isabel National Forest
Maps: *USGS 7 ½'* — Mount Ouray and Bonanza;
County — Saguache #2; *USFS* — San Isabel National Forest; *Trails Illustrated* — #139

Directions to the Trailhead

From west of Salida, at the junction of US-50 and US-285, drive south toward Poncha Pass for 5.2 miles. Turn right onto Chaffee County Road 200. This dirt road can be readily negotiated by regular cars all the way to Marshall Pass. Follow Chaffee County Road 200 for 2.35 miles and turn right into County Road 202. Ascend for 0.9 miles and turn right onto County Road 200 again. In 10.85 miles from US-285, Marshall Pass (10,846 feet) will be reached. Just past the sign on the pass, turn left and shortly reach a four-way intersection. Park around here. Marshall Pass can also be reached from the west, via the tiny settlement of Sargents on US-50.

The Hike

Begin south on an excellent road, part of the Colorado Trail. In about five minutes, pass through a gate, blocking the road to vehicles. Antora Peak will be visible ahead. Lose some elevation, and in about 25 minutes from the gate, take the left fork, leading upward and generally south. Within 15 minutes, you pass through a fence and encounter a trail sign. Continue south. In a mile, reach signs which indicate that you are on the Divide Trail and that the Silver Creek Trail drops down to the east. The trail continues south, and within another half hour, cuts up into trees, passing through a barbed

Sign along the Divide.
(Aaron Locander)

FYI

Marshall Pass was discovered by Army Lieutenant William L. Marshall, part of the Wheeler Survey team. The pass was first a wagon, then a railroad route between Gunnison and Salida. Antora Peak is known by climbers as the southern terminus of the mighty Sawatch Range.

A portion of this hike follows both The Colorado Trail and The Continental Divide National Scenic Trail, which are collinear in this area. Elk are numerous here — the author encountered many near timberline.

wire fence. Leave the main trail and follow this fence to the east, directly toward Antora Peak. A faint trail passes alongside this fence at times. Within another half hour, you will reach a gate through the fence and a definite trail, leading south from the gate. Follow this trail, as it curves around the western flank of Antora Peak. At a second creek crossing, reached in about twenty minutes, leave the trail and ascend to the east, along the mostly dry creek bed, into a steep talus and snow-filled gulch above timberline. Continue east, over loose rock at times, to a ridge, leading over a few false summits. Finally, reach a small cairn, an animal skull and two rock shelters at the top.

For descent, take the same general route, but instead, take the ridge to your left. This ridge runs east to west and it will enable you to descend over mostly tundra, reaching the snow-filled gulch at a lower level. Then continue back, by way of your ascent route.

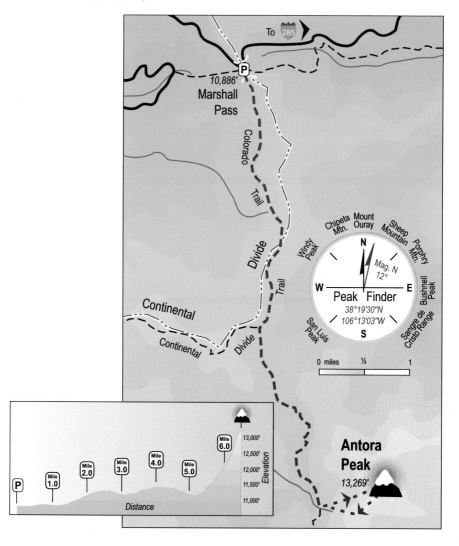

91 MOUNT SOPRIS 12,953 Ft. & WEST MT. SOPRIS 12,953 Ft.

These twin peaks are gentle giants surrounded by the rugged beauty of the Elk Range.

Distance: 6.0 miles each way
Hiking Time: Up in 285 minutes, down in 225 minutes
Starting Elevation: 8,600 feet
Elevation Gain: 5,089 feet (includes 736 ft. extra between peaks)
Trail: All the way
Season: Mid June to early October
Jurisdiction: White River National Forest
Maps: *USGS 7 ½'* — Mount Sopris and Basalt; *County* — Pitkin #1; *USFS* — White River National Forest; *Trails Illustrated* — #128

Directions to the Trailhead

Drive south on CO-133 from the junction with CO-82 at Carbondale for 2.8 miles and turn left onto a paved road with a stop sign. This is Garfield County Road 111 (changing to Pitkin County Road 5), which follows Prince Creek to the southeast. After 1.6 miles on this road, take the right fork, around where the pavement ends. Drive 4.8 miles further and again take a right fork. In 2.0 more miles, you arrive at the trailhead and parking area. All vehicular access to the trail from this point is prevented by a barrier. (The roadend is 0.4 miles further at Dinkle Lake.)

The Hike

Classics

Hike southeast, and then south, about 1.3 miles to a fork. (The left route goes to Hay Park and West Sopris Creek.) Take the right fork, going west, and then southwest, for 2.0 more miles to Thomas Lakes. From between the southeastern and the southwestern lakes, a trail leads south up a steep, vegetated ridge. Take this route, keep to the left of the talus, pass timberline and rise to the main east-west ridge. Keep on the trail, as it turns west (right) up this ridge and crosses a false, 12,453-foot summit, en route to the Mount Sopris summit cairn. West Mount Sopris lies 0.8 miles, and about 30 minutes, to the west over tundra and talus. There is a register and cairn at its summit. Follow the same trail back to the trailhead.

FYI

These two peaks are 0.8 miles apart and, interestingly, of identical height. Due to the absence of any nearby mountains of comparable height, Mount Sopris dominates the skyline, southeast from the towns of Glenwood Springs and Carbondale. It is a surprisingly gentle giant, surrounded by the rugged beauty of the Elk Range. Sitting at the far west end of the Elks (one of the few east-west trending ranges in the United States), one can see the stark contrast between the deep red, sedimentary formations of the eastern end and the almost-white, intrusive rocks of the western peaks.

The mountain is named after Captain Richard Sopris, who explored the area in 1860, discovered Glenwood Springs and later, in Denver, began City Park and became mayor.

The twin summits of Mount Sopris, as viewed from the access road. (David Hite)

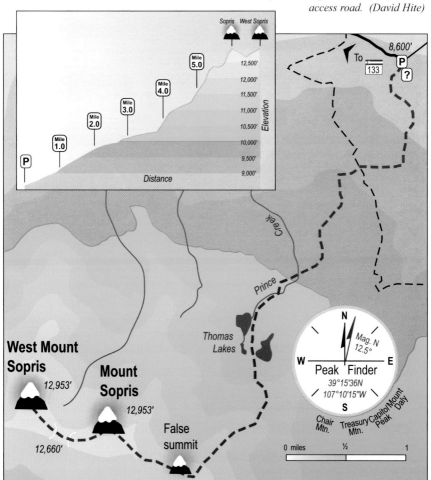

92 IOWA PEAK 13,831 Feet

*T*rek through
Missouri Basin
— a spectacular
tundra garden,
blissfully uncrowded.

Distance: 7.0 miles each way
Hiking Time: Up in 298 minutes, down in 197 minutes
Starting Elevation: 9,669 feet
Elevation Gain: 4,962 feet (includes 400 feet extra each way)
Trail: Initial 5.6 miles, off-trail tundra and talus beyond
Season: Late June to early October
Jurisdiction: San Isabel NF, Collegiate Peaks Wilderness Area
Maps: *USGS 7 ½'* — Winfield and Mount Harvard;
County — Chaffee #1; USFS — San Isabel National Forest; *Trails Illustrated* — #129

Directions to the Trailhead

Either drive south on US-24 for 19.7 miles south from Leadville or drive 15.3 miles north from the traffic light in Buena Vista. Just south of the small settlement of Granite, and north of the Clear Creek Reservoir, a clearly marked dirt road, Chaffee County Road 390, goes 7.9 miles west to the remains of Vicksburg. At Vicksburg, park in the fenced parking area on the south side of the road. Regular cars can come this far with no difficulty. (The road continues west-southwest, past Rockdale and Winfield, to an eventual dead end.)

The Hike

Follow the trail south from the parking area, cross Clear Creek on a bridge and soon, on the left, pass the grave of Baby Huffman, a miner's child who died at one month of age, many years ago. Continue steeply up into Missouri Gulch on the trail, eventually running alongside the creek. After one hour from the trailhead, reach an abandoned cabin on your left. Continue up into the basin, as two fourteeners come into view — Mount Belford on your left (east) and Missouri Mountain on your right (west). Continue on the trail

*Sunset in Missouri Basin.
(Eric Wiseman)*

FYI

The ghost town of Vicksburg was occupied from 1881 to 1885. Named after Vick Keller, an early resident, the town once had two hotels and a school. Only a small museum remains.

Nearby Emerald Peak is well-named, as Missouri Basin is a spectacular tundra garden, filled to the brim with summer wildflowers. Ringed by a dozen summits, including four fourteeners, it is one of the largest alpine basins in the Sawatch Range. But the long, arduous trail up Pine Creek keeps it blissfully uncrowded.

above timberline, and in about 130 minutes from the abandoned cabin, reach Elkhead Pass at 13,220 feet. Ahead of you lies Missouri Basin and Mount Harvard. Iowa Peak also comes into view to the southwest, with Emerald Peak on its left (south). Continue on the trail southward, down about 400 feet from Elkhead Pass. Leave the trail, whenever you see a clear, gradual route to the Iowa Peak-Missouri Mountain saddle. The saddle will be reached in about 96 minutes from the pass. Then turn left (south), ascending over easy tundra and talus in twelve minutes to the non-descript Iowa Peak summit.

Emerald Peak is an easy ridge walk to the south, if you have the time and energy. Descend by your ascent route.

93 ENGINEER MOUNTAIN 13,218 Feet

This route explores a scenic and historic byway in the heart of the San Juan Mountains.

Distance: 9.1 miles each way
Hiking Time: Up in 360 minutes, down in 240 minutes
Starting Elevation: 8,854 feet
Elevation Gain: 4,364 feet
Trail: All the way
Season: Mid June to early October
Jurisdiction: Uncompahgre National Forest
Maps: *USGS 7 ½'* — Handies Peak; *County* — Ouray #2 and San Juan; *USFS* — Uncompahgre National Forest; *Trails Illustrated* — #141

Directions to the Trailhead

4WD option

Drive south from Ouray on US-550 (the *Million Dollar Highway*) for 3.4 miles to a cutoff to the east, marked with a stop sign, an Ouray County Road 18 sign, and an Engineer Mountain Road sign, with recommendations for four-wheel drive. Park here at the start of this road. (If you are able to drive your vehicle up this rough road, it will decrease the distance, time and elevation gain listed for this hike accordingly. High clearance is essential and four-wheel drive will be needed on occasion.)

The Hike

Proceed up the road, taking the left fork at 2.3 miles. (The right fork leads into Poughkeepsie Gulch.) After 2.7 more miles, again take the left fork. (The right fork goes to Mineral Point.) In 1.9 miles further, continue again on the left fork. (The right fork leads south to Animas Forks and Cinnamon Pass.) By a series of switchbacks, you will reach the high point of this road in 1.9 miles from the last fork. At this highest point, leave the main road and ascend to the east-southeast via an old mining road for 0.3 miles to the summit, marked by a metal rod embedded in a rock. Return as you ascended. (The main road continues north for 0.4 miles to Engineer Pass and a large sign. The road then drops down into Henson Gulch, ending at Lake City.)

 FYI

Engineer Mountain is a name also given to other Colorado peaks. This peak lies just south of the Engineer Pass route, built in 1877 by Otto Mears to carry stage coaches and wagons between Lake City on the east and Ouray and Silverton on the west. The original Engineer Pass was located closer to the Engineer Mountain summit and was steeper.

The road can be a dusty affair on weekends, when it is popular with four-wheel drive enthusiasts. Shorten your return by heading due west off the summit of Engineer Mountain. Follow the ridge down for a mile, then pick up an old road that switchbacks south into a gulley, past old mines and prospects, to intercept the Engineer Mountain Road.

The Engineer Mountain Road passes close to the summit.

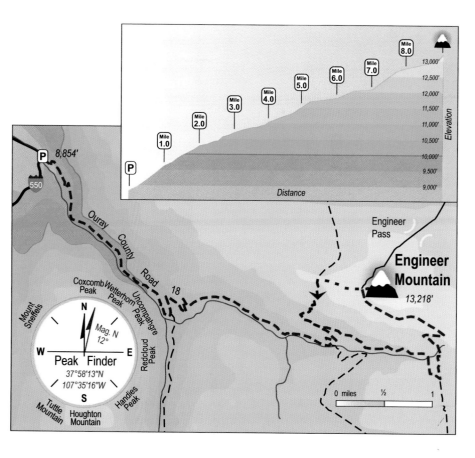

94 PAGODA MOUNTAIN 13,497 Feet

*E*njoy this fine summit in wonderful Wild Basin all to yourself, as the masses toil up nearby Longs Peak.

Distance: 6.2 miles each way
Hiking Time: Up in 375 minutes, down in 278 minutes
Starting Elevation: 8,380 feet
Elevation Gain: 5,117 feet
Trail: Initial 3.0 miles, only intermittent and faint trail beyond
Season: Late June to early October
Jurisdiction: Roosevelt NF and Rocky Mountain National Park
Maps: *USGS 7 ½'* — Longs Peak, McHenrys Peak, Allens Park & Isolation Peak; *County* — Boulder; *USFS* — Roosevelt NF; *Trails Illustrated* — #200, Rocky Mountain National Park map

Directions to the Trailhead

Drive 2.2 miles north of Allenspark or 1.1 miles south of Meeker Park on CO-7. Take the paved road going southwest for 0.4 miles and make a right turn onto a dirt road that leads to Copeland Lake and the Wild Basin Ranger Station. Park in the designated area within 100 yards on your right. This is the Sandbeach Lake Trailhead, your starting point.

The Hike

Proceed northwest, to the right of Copeland Lake, for 100 yards to a sign and the Sandbeach Lake Trailhead. The trail begins steeply to the northwest, and then curves west for about 3.0 miles to a point where Hunters Creek, flowing from the northwest, crosses the trail . This junction will be reached in about 90 minutes. Leave the Sandbeach Lake Trail and angle obliquely to the northwest, following Hunters Creek, keeping it on your left. After about 1.3 miles along Hunters Creek, reach a junction of two branches of the creek. Cross this junction, continue northwest and leave the creeks.

Stay close to the base of Mount Meeker, lying to the right. Pagoda Mountain will now be visible. Continue eventually in a more northerly direction, often over rocks, and up into a couloir with talus, scree and some loose footing. Ascend this to the saddle which lies between Pagoda Mountain

Pagoda Mountain is named after the prominent configuration of its summit, seen on clear days from the Boulder and Denver areas as the peak to the left of Longs Peak. Although this mountain, and most of the described hike, lie within Rocky Mountain National Park, no park fee is required for access to this trail.

From the summit, there are panoramic views into aptly-named Wild Basin, as well as a front row seat for watching the masses toil up the "Homestretch" on Longs Peak. In contrast, you are likely to enjoy Pagoda's fine summit all to yourself!

to the west (left) and Longs Peak to the east (right). From the saddle, turn west and ascend steeply over boulders to a summit cairn and a register cylinder. Some easy hand work is necessary between the

Lunch on Pagoda Peak with a view of Longs Peak. (Nelson Chenkin)

saddle and the top, but the footing is quite solid. Return the same way you ascended.

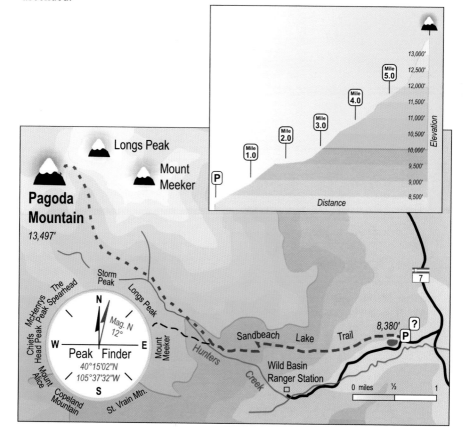

95 CAPITOL PEAK 14,130 Feet

This challenging fourteener is considered by most climbers as one of the best in the state.

Distance: 8.12 miles each way
Hiking Time: Day 1: 197 minutes to base camp, Day 2: up in 218 minutes, down to base camp in 188 minutes, base camp to trailhead in 162 minutes.
Starting Elevation: 9,420 feet
Elevation Gain: Day 1: 2,660 feet, Day 2: 3,000 feet (includes 475 feet extra each way), Total: 5,660 feet.
Trail: All the way, but with moderate/difficult scrambling near top
Season: Early July to late September
Jurisdiction: White River NF, Maroon Bells-Snowmass WA
Maps: *USGS 7 ½'* — Capitol Peak; *County* — Pitkin #1; *USFS* — White River National Forest; *Trails Illustrated* — #128

Directions to the Trailhead

May be needed for last mile.

Drive north from the Castle Creek bridge in Aspen on CO-82 for 13.8 miles or drive south from Glenwood Springs on CO-82 for 23 miles. At the Snowmass Post Office and a service station on the south side of the road, turn south along Snowmass Creek for 1.8 miles to a "T". Turn right and drive southwest. After 4.9 miles from the "T", the road paving ends. Continue on the dirt road for 3.4 more miles to the road end, in a grove of aspen trees. A sign marks the trail on your left. Park here. The road is steep and rough in spots over the last mile. A high-clearance vehicle or four-wheel drive may be required in certain years or after a storm.

The Hike

Classics

From the trailhead, there is a lovely view of Capitol Peak at the end of the basin. Hike down and south on the excellent trail. You will lose 380 feet en route to a crossing of Capitol Creek, over a large tree trunk. (The crossing may be difficult in June due to high water.) The trail then rises, crossing Capitol Creek a few more times. The trail is not steadily upward; occasionally it loses altitude. After more than six miles, arrive at a flat, tree covered area, just at timberline, to the right of the trail. This makes a good camp site. Several hundred yards further south lies Capitol Lake, often frozen well into July.

FYI

This is the most strenuous hike in this guide, but also the most spectacular. Climbers consider this classic fourteener to be one of the more challenging peaks, famous for its exposed ridge. While it has been done in a day, you will want to take two or three days with an idyllic camp beneath Capitol Lake. Capitol Peak and nearby Snowmass Mountain were called "The Twins" or the "Capitol" and the "Whitehouse" by earlier residents of the area.

The next morning, continue south on the trail which soon forks. Continue steeply up and east to the saddle between Mount Daly on the left and Capitol Peak on the right. From this saddle, the trail proceeds south, high along the eastern flanks of Capitol Peak's north ridge. The trail at this point is marked by cairns and follows a series of ledges. Some use of hands may be necessary, but the exposure is usually slight. Eventually a talus slope is reached. Cross this to gain the summit of a subpeak at 13,664 feet, called K-2. The Capitol Peak summit will now be visible to the southwest across a rocky ridge. Descend from K-2 toward this ridge, to a narrow section known as the "Knife Edge." This famous spot, about 60 feet long, is best traversed by straddling. The rock is solid enough, but the drop-offs on both sides are quite abrupt and lengthy. In good weather, this crossing can readily be made, although with care. (This is not a good place to be if lightning is approaching!) Once beyond the Knife Edge, continue scrambling north along the ridge for 150 yards, then traverse left out onto the main face. The trail then continues by way of cairn-marked ledges in a clockwise direction to the summit cairn and a Colorado Mountain Club register cylinder.

After returning back across the Knife Edge, you may avoid the rocky ledges between K-2 and the Mount Daly—K-2 saddle by dropping more easterly from the K-2 summit onto snowfields, traversing around the ridge, then rising north to reach the Mount Daly—K-2 saddle. An ice axe will be needed here. This snowfield route is an easier, less-exposed route, despite the need to lose and regain some altitude. From the saddle, return by your ascent trail to camp.

*Capitol Peak from
just below K-2.
(Eric Wiseman)*

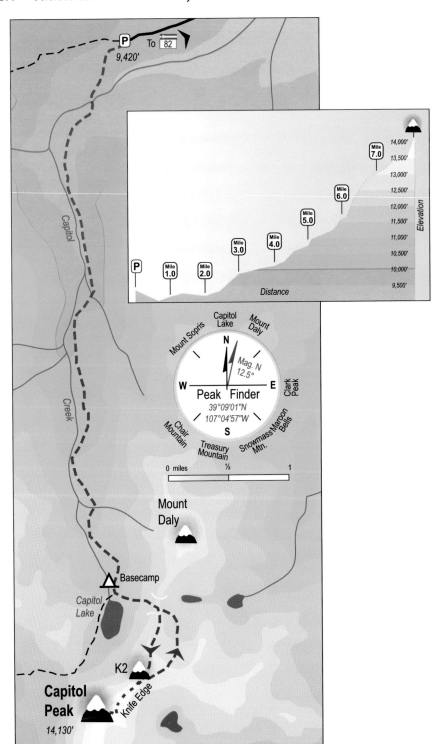

To 82

P
9,420'

Capitol

Creek

14,000'
13,500'
13,000'
12,500'
12,000'
11,500'
11,000'
10,500'
10,000'
9,500'

Elevation

Mile 7.0
Mile 6.0
Mile 5.0
Mile 4.0
Mile 3.0
Mile 2.0
Mile 1.0

P

Distance

Capitol Lake
Mount Sopris
Mount Daly

N

Mag. N
12.5°

W   E

Peak   Finder
39°09'01"N
107°04'57"W

Clark Peak

Chair Mountain

S

Treasury Mountain

Snowmass Mtn.

Maroon Bells

0 miles   ½   1

Mount Daly

Basecamp

Capitol Lake

K2

Capitol Peak
14,130'

Knife Edge

RESOURCE GUIDE

Relevant Organizations 216
Land Management Agencies 217
Further Reading 218
Index 219

Enjoying the Colorado Rockies. (Nelson Chenkin)

RELEVANT ORGANIZATIONS

American Alpine Club
710 10th Street #100
Golden, CO 80401
(303) 384-0110
(303) 384-0111 Fax
www.americanalpineclub.org
A climbers' organization devoted to exploration of high mountain elevations, dissemination of information about mountaineering, conservation and preservation of mountain regions.

American Hiking Society
1422 Fenwick Lane
Silver Spring, MD 20910
(301) 565-6704
(301) 565-6714 Fax
www.americanhiking.org
A national organization dedicated to promoting hiking and to establishing, protecting and maintaining foot trails throughout the United States.

The Colorado Fourteeners Initiative
710 Tenth Street, Suite 220
Golden, Colorado 80401
(303) 278-7525
(303) 279-9690 Fax
www.coloradofourteeners.org
An organization to protect and preserve the natural integrity of Colorado's Fourteeners and the quality of the recreational opportunities they provide.

Colorado Mountain Club
710 10th Street #200
Golden, CO 80401
(303) 279-3080
(303) 279-9690 Fax
www.cmc.org
The largest hiking/climbing club in the Rocky Mountain Region. The club organizes over 2,000 hikes, ski trips, backpacking trips, bike trips, and other outdoor activities annually, and offers numerous classes in mountain-related activities.

Colorado Outward Bound School
910 Jackson Street
Golden, CO 80401
(720) 497-2400
(720) 497-2401 Fax
www.cobs.org
An educational institution dedicated to teaching wilderness-oriented skills and leadership, including backpacking and mountaineering courses.

Appalachian Mountain Club
AMC Main Office, 5 Joy Street
Boston, MA 02108
(617) 523-0636
(617) 523-0722 Fax
www.outdoors.org
The largest organization of its kind in the U.S., the AMC promotes the protection, enjoyment, and wise use of the mountains, rivers, and trails of the Northeast.

Leave No Trace, Inc.
P.O. Box 997
Boulder, CO 80306
(800) 332-4100
(303) 442-8217 Fax
www.lnt.org
An organization whose mission is to promote and inspire responsible outdoor recreation through education and partnerships.

The Mountaineers
300 Third Ave West
Seattle, Wa 98119
(206) 284-6310
(206) 284-4977 Fax
www.mountaineers.org
The largest outdoor recreation and conservation club in the Puget Sound region with an extensive outing and outdoor education program.

National Outdoor Leadership School
284 Lincoln Street
Lander, WY 82520-2848
(307) 332-5300
(307) 332-1220 Fax
www.nols.edu
An educational institution dedicated to teaching wilderness-oriented skills and leadership, including backpacking and mountaineering courses.

LAND MANAGEMENT AGENCIES

Arapaho & Roosevelt National Forests
www.fs.fed.us/r2/arnf]
Boulder Ranger District
2140 Yarmouth Avenue
Boulder, CO 80301
303-444-6600

Canyon Lakes Ranger District
1311 South College
Ft. Collins, CO 80524
970-498-2770

Clear Creek Ranger District
101 Chicago Creek
P.O. Box 3307
Idaho Springs, CO 80452
303-567-3000

**Uncompahgre & Gunnison National
Forests**
www.fs.fed.us/r2/gmug/
Gunnison Ranger District
216 North Colorado
Gunnison, CO 81230
970-641-0471

Ouray Ranger District
2505 South Townsend
Montrose, CO 81401
970-240-5400

Pike & San Isabel National Forests
www.fs.fed us/r2/psicc/
Leadville District
2015 North Poplar
Leadville, CO 80461
719-486-0749

Pikes Peak Ranger District
601 South Weber
Colorado Springs, CO 80903
719-636-1602

Salida District
325 West Rainbow Blvd.
Salida, CO 81201
719-539-3591

South Park Ranger District
320 Highway 285
P.O. Box 219
Fairplay, CO 80440
719-836-2031

South Platte District
19316 Goddard Ranch Court
Morrison, CO 80465
303-697-0414

White River National Forest
www.fs.fed. us/r2/whiteriver/
Aspen District
806 West Hallam
Aspen, CO 81611
970-925-3445

Dillon Ranger District
680 Blue River Parkway
P.O. Box 620
Silverthorne, CO 80498
970-468-5400

Holy Cross District
24747 U.S. Highway 24
P.O. Box 190
Minturn, CO 81645
970-827-5715

Rocky Mountain National Park
1000 Highway 36
Estes Park, CO 80517-8397
970-586-1206
www.nps .gov/romo/

Golden Gate Canyon State Park
3873 Highway 46
Golden, CO 80403
303-582-3707
www.parks.state.co.us/default.asp

**Colorado Springs Parks and Recreation
Department**
1401 Recreation Way
Colorado Springs, CO 80905-1975
(719) 385-5940
www.springsgov.com

Jefferson County Open Space Parks
700 Jefferson County Parkway
Golden, CO 80401
(303) 271-5925

Denver Mountain Parks
P.O. Box 1007
Morrison, CO 80465
(303) 697-4545

FURTHER READING

Aldrich, John K. *Ghosts of Park County: A Guide To The Ghost Towns and Mining Camps of Park County.* Lakewood, Colorado; Centennial Graphics, 1984.

Borneman, Walter R. and Lampert, Lyndon L A *Climbing Guide To Colorado's Fourteeners.* Boulder, Colorado; Pruett Publishing Company, 1978.

Borneman, Walter R. *Colorado's Other Mountains.* Evergreen, Colorado; Cordillera Press, Inc. 1984.

Brown, Robert L *Uphill Both Ways.* Caldwell, Idaho; Caxton Printers, Ltd. 1976.

Bueler, William M. *Roof of the Rockies: A History of Colorado Mountaineering.* Golden, Colorado; Colorado Mountain Club Press, 2001.

Dallas, Sandra. *Colorado Ghost Towns and Mining Camps.* Norman, Oklahoma; University of Oklahoma Press, 1985.

Dannen, Kent and Dannen, Donna. *Rocky Mountain National Park Hiking Trails.* Charlotte, North Carolina; East Woods Press Books, 1978.

Dawson, J. Frank. *Place Names in Colorado.* Denver, Colorado; The J. Frank Dawson Publishing Company, 1954.

Eichler, George R. *Colorado Place Names.* Boulder, Colorado; Johnson Publishing Co., 1977.

Ellis, Erl and Ellis, Carrie S. *The Saga Of Upper Clear Creek.* Frederick, Colorado; Jende-Hagan Book Corporation, 1983.

Garratt, Mike and Martin, Bob. *Colorado's High Thirteeners.* Evergreen, Colorado; Cordillera Press, Inc. 1984.

Gilliland, Mary E. *The Summit Hiker.* Silverthorne, Colorado; Alpenrose Press,1983.

Hagen, Mary. *Hiking Trails of Northern Colorado.* Boulder, Colorado; Pruett Publishing Company, 1979.

Hill, Alice Polk. *Colorado Pioneers In Picture And Story.* Denver, Colorado; Brock-Haffner Press, 1915.

Jacobs, Randy and Ormes, Robert M. *Guide To The Colorado Mountains.* Golden, Colorado; Colorado Mountain Club Press, Tenth Edition, 2000.

Koch, Don. *The Colorado Pass Book.* Boulder, Colorado; Pruett Publishing Company, 1980.

Kramarsic, Joseph D. *Bibliography of Colorado Mountain Ascents 1863-1976.* Dillon, Colorado; Self Published, 1979.

LaBaw, Wallace L *God, Gold, Girls and Glory.* Broomfield Colorado; Ingersoll Publications, 1966.

Lowe, Don and Lowe, Roberta. *80 Northern Colorado Hiking Trails.* Beaverton, Oregon; The Touchstone Press, 1973.

Mahoney, Stanley. *Mount Evans Above Timberline.* Westminster, Colorado; Self Published, 1970.

Mahoney, Stan and Mahoney, Martha. *Roads and Trails and Timberline Snails.* Boulder, Colorado; Johnson Publishing Company, 1972.

Martin, Bob. *Hiking Trails of Central Colorado.* Boulder, Colorado; Pruett Publishing Company, 1983.

Martin, Bob. *Hiking the Highest Passes.* Boulder, Colorado; Pruett Publishing Company, 1984.

Ringrose, Linda W. and Rathbun, Linda M. *Foothills To Mount Evans.* Evergreen, Colorado; The Wordsmiths, 1980.

A
abandoned mines 20
Alderfer-Three Sisters Park 42
alpine lifezone 12
Alps Mountain 46-47
altitude sickness 20
American Alpine Club 216
American Hiking Society 216
Antora Peak 202-203
Appalachian Mountain Club 216
Arapaho Glacier 114, 182
Arapaho National Forest 217
Arapaho Pass 182
Arapaho Peaks 182
aspen 82, 144, 158, 190, 200
Audobon, Mount 162
avalanche awareness 20

B
Bakerville 100
Bald Mountain 128-129
Baldy Peak 48-49
Bandit Peak 188-189
banner trees 200
Bard Peak 96
Barr Trail 146
Barr, Fred 146
Bartlet Mountain 36
Belford, Mount 206
Bell, W.A. 192
Bergen Peak 122-123
Bergen, Thomas C. 122
Berthoud Pass 52, 108, 112, 170
Berthoud Pass Ski Area 52
Berthoud, Edward Louis 52
Bethel, Ellsworth 120, 162
Bethel, Mount 120-121
Bierstadt, Mount 78, 142, 160, 190
Big Blue Wilderness Area 152
bighorn sheep 160, 174, 188, 196
Bills Peak 154-155
Birthday Peak 156-157
Bison Peak 174-175
Black Hawk 44, 90
Blaine, Mount 158-159, 200
Blue Lake 162
Boreas Mountain 128-129
Boreas Pass 82, 98, 128
Boreas Pass Road 82, 98, 128
Bottle Pass 102
Bottle Peak 102-103
Breakneck Pass 84
Breckinridge Peak 170-171

Breckinridge, John Cabell 150, 170
Brittle Silver Mountain 94
Brother, The 42-43
Buckeye Peak 198-199
Buckhorn Valley 76
Buckskin, Mount 184-185
Buckskin Pass 185
buffalo 24
Buffalo Bill Museum 63
Buffalo Creek fire 124, 178
Buffalo Mountain 148-149

C
Cameron Pass 72
Cameron, R. A. 72
Camp Hale 126, 176
Camp St. Malo 106
Capitol Lake 212
Capitol Peak 212-214
Caribou (townsite)114
Caribou Pass 182
Caribou Peak 114-115
Central City 44, 114
Chalk Mountain 36-37
Cheesman Mountain 40-41
Cheesman, Walter S. 40
Chessman Lake 40
Chief Mountain 64-65
Climax Mine 36
clothing and equipment 22
Collegiate Peaks 156
Colorado Mines Peak 52-53
Colorado Mountain Club 216, 223
Colorado Outward Bound School 216
Colorado School of Mines 52, 62
Colorado Trail, The 80, 124, 134, 136,
    176, 202
colors; hike ratings (defined) 13
Columbia, Mount 156
Comanche Lake 192
Comanche Peak 192-193
Como 82, 98, 128
Continental Divide 30, 36, 52, 58, 70,
    74, 90, 100, 112, 116, 118, 132, 144,
    156, 166, 180, 182, 202
Continental Divide Trail, The 52, 112,
    132, 166, 202
Coon Hill 70-71
Corbett Peak 176-177
Corona Pass 88
Crater Lake 184
Cutler, Henry 32
Cutler, Mount 32-33

D
Daly, Mount 213
Decatur Mountain 94
Democrat, Mount 198
Denver Mountain Park system 24
Devils Head 50-51
Diamond Lake 183
Diamond Peaks 72-73

E
Eagles Nest Wilderness Area 186
East White Pine Mountain 76
Eisenhower-Johnson Memorial Tunnel
    70, 116, 120, 148
Elbert, Mount 36, 136, 198
elevation gain (defined) 13
Elk Range 184, 198, 204, 212
Elkhead Pass 206
Emerald Peak 206
Emma Burr Mountain 58-59
Engelmann, George 172
Engineer Mountain 208-209
Engineer Pass 208
Englemann Peak 172-173
Epworth, Mount 88-89
equipment list 23
Estes Cone 110-111
Estes Park 66, 110
Estes, Joel 110
Eugenia Mine 110
Evans, Mount 44, 122, 142, 160, 188, 190

F
Fairburn Mountain 44-45
Falcon, Mount 28-29
fault-block mountains 192
fire lookout tower 34, 50
Fitzpatrick Peak 60-61
Flora, Mount 170
foothills lifezone 12
Fox Mountain 30-31, 86
Fraser Experimental Forest 102
Frazier, Reuben 102
Fremont Pass 36
Fremont, John C. 36
French Pass 180
FYI box (defined) 18

G
Ganley Mountain 164-165
Ganley, John W. 164
Gaskill, Gudy 124
Genesee Mountain 24-25
Geneva Mountain 78-79
Georgetown 104
Georgia Pass 180
Gibson Lake 144
Glacier Peak 80-81

Glacier Ridge 80
Gold Camp Road 38
Golden Gate Canyon State Park 90
Gore Range 134, 186
Gore, Sir St. George 186
Gray Wolf Mountain 142
Gray, Asa 166
Grays Peak 100, 160, 164, 166-167
Green Mountain 68-69
Green Mountain conglomerate 68
Gregory Gulch 44
Griffith Mountain 104-105
Griffith, David 104
Griffith, George 104
Grizzly Peak 118-119
Guanella Pass 78, 138, 190
Guanella, Byron 78
Guyot, Arnold Henry 180
Guyot, Mount 180-181

H
Hall, William Jairus 144
Harr, Neal 52
Harvard, Mount 156, 206
Hayden Green Mountain Park 68
Hayman fire 40
Henderson Mine 96
hiking time (defined) 13
Holy Cross, Mount of the 36, 130, 176
Hope, Mount 136
Hornsilver Mountain 130-131
Horseshoe Lake 154
Horseshoe Mountain 140-141
Horsetooth Peak 106-107
hypothermia 21

I
Indian Peaks 162
Indian Peaks Wilderness Area 162, 182
Iowa Peak 206-207

J
Jackson, George 46
Jackson, W.H. 130
Jaque Peak 134-135
Jaque, J.C. 134
Jefferson 80, 200
Jefferson County Open Space Park system
    62, 122
Jefferson, Thomas 80
jurisdiction (defined) 15

K
K2 213
Kataka Mountain 190-191, 196
Keller, Vick 206
Kelso Mountain 100-101
Kelso, William Fletcher 100

Kenosha Pass 158
Kingston Peak 86-87
Knife Edge 213
Kokomo Pass 176
krummholz 200

L
Lake Dillon 56, 150
Lake Dorothy 182
Lake Edith 142
Lariat Loop Road 62
Leave No Trace, Inc. 19, 216
lightning 21
Lily Mountain 66-67
Lincoln, Mount 198
Little Baldy Mountain 98-99
lodgepole pine 66
Logan, John Alexander 196
Logan, Mount 196-197
Long Scraggy Peak 178-179
Longs Peak 66, 110, 210
Lookout Mountain 62-63
Lookout Mountain Conference and Nature
    Center 63
Lost Creek Wilderness Area 174, 200
Loveland Pass 74, 118

M
Manitou, Mount 146-147
maps (defined) 15
Maroon Bells 184
Maroon Bells/Snowmass Wilderness Area
    184, 212
Maroon Lake 184
Marshall, William L. 202
Mason, James R. 76
Massive, Mount 36, 198
Matterhorn Peak 152-153
McClellan, Mount 138
McCurdy Mountain 174
Mears, Otto 208
Medicine Bow Mountains 72
Meeker, Mount 106, 110, 210
Million Dollar Highway, The 208
Mirror Lake 58, 60
Missouri Basin 206
Missouri Mountain 206
Mitchell Lake 162
molybdenum 36, 108
Mount Evans Wilderness Area 78, 142,
    168, 188, 190, 196
Mount Falcon Park 28
mountain climate and weather 10-11
mountain geography 9-10
mountain geology 11
mountain goat 74, 142, 148, 166
mountain lifezones 12

N
Napoleon Mountain 60
Napoleon Pass 60
National Outdoor Leadership School 216
Neva, Mount 182-183
North Cheyenne Cañon Park 32
North Twin Cone Peak 158-159

O
Ormes Peak 26-27
Ormes, Manley 26
Ormes, Robert M. 26
Otter Mountain 138-139
Ouray 208

P
Pagoda Mountain 210-211
Paiute Peak 162-163
Papoose Mountain 64
Parnassus, Mount 96
Parry, Charles C. 166, 170
Patterson, E.H.N. 74, 170
Peak 8 150-151
Peerless Mountain 92, 140
pegmatite 168
Pegmatite Point 168
Pendleton Mountain 164-165
Pendleton, George H. 164
Phantom Terrace 194
Pike National Forest 217
Pike, Zebulon M. 48
Pikes Peak 26, 146
Pikes Peak granite 48, 174
Platte River Mountains 200
Pope John Paul II 106
Princeton, Mount 156
ptarmigan 78, 198
Ptarmigan Peak 102
Pumphouse Lake 88

Q
Quail Mountain 136-137

R
Rainbow Trail 193-194
Raleigh Peak 124-125
Rampart Range Road 26, 50
Rawah Range 72
Red Mountain 108-109
Red Rocks Park 28
Republican Mountain 160-161
Resolution Mountain 126-127, 130
Revenue Mountain 94-95
Rio Grande National Forest 217
Robeson Peak 172-173
Robeson, Solomon 172
rock fall 21
Rocky Mountain 146-147

Rocky Mountain National Park 66, 106, 110, 210
Rollins Pass 88
Rollins, John Quincy Adams 88
Roosevelt National Forest 217
Roosevelt, Theodore 38
Rosalie Peak 188
Rosedale Peak 168-169
Round Hill 84-85
Royal Mountain 56-57

S
Saint Elmo 58, 60
San Isabel National Forest 217
San Juan Mountains 152
Sangre de Cristo Mountains 192, 194
Sangre de Cristo Wilderness Area 193-194
Satanta Peak 182-183
Sawatch Range 60, 136, 156, 198, 202, 206
Sawtooth Ridge 78
Searle Pass 134
season (defined) 14
Seven Falls 32
Sheridan, Mount 92-93
Sherman, Mount 92, 198
Shrine Pass 130
Silver Mountain 94
Sniktau, Mount 74-75
Snowmass Mountain 212
Sopris, Mount 204-205
Sopris, Richard 204
Sopris, West Mount 204-205
South Park 82, 84, 98, 190, 200
South Park City Museum 84
South Peak 54-55
South Twin Cone Peak 200-201
Spring Mountain 193, 194
Squaw Mountain 34-35, 64
St. Marys Glacier 30, 86
St. Marys Lake 30, 86
St. Peters Dome 38-39
starting elevation (defined) 13
staying found 22
subalpine lifezone 12
Sugarloaf Peak 142-143
Summit Huts Association 128
sun exposure 21
symbols; access roads 15
symbols; special hikes 17

T
Tarryall Range 174
Tenmile Range 56, 134, 150, 186
Tenth Mountain Division 126
The Colorado Fourteeners Initiative 216
The Mountaineers 216
Three Sisters, The 42

Tincup Pass 58, 60
Torrey, John 166
Torreys Peak 100, 160, 164, 166-167
trail (defined) 14
Trelease, Mount 116-117
Tremont Mountain 90-91
turkey vulture 42
Twin Cones 132-133

U
Uncompahgre National Forest 217
Uncompahgre Peak 152
Uneva Lake 186
Uneva Mountain 186-187
Urad Mine 108

V
Vasquez Peak 112-113
Vasquez Peak Wilderness Area 112
Vasquez, Louis 112
Venable Lakes 194
Venable Peak 194-195
Vicksburg 206
Volz, Mount 82-83

W
Waldorf (townsite) 138, 164
Walker, John Brisben 28
water 22
West White Pine Mountain 76-77
Westcliffe 192, 194
Weston Pass 54, 84
Weston, Algeron S. 54
Weston, Phuo M. 54
Wetterhorn Peak 152
Whale Peak 144-145
Wheeler Lakes 186
Wheeler, John C. 186
White National Forest 217
Wilcox, Edward John 138
Wilcox, Mount 138-139
wildlife encounters 22
Windy Saddle 62
Windy Saddle Park 62
Woods Mountain 96-97

Y
Yale, Mount 156

Z
Zinn, Ralph Theodore 50
Zion, Mount 62 (Jefferson County), 198 (Lake County)

THE
COLORADO
MOUNTAIN CLUB

The Colorado Mountain Club is a non-profit outdoor recreation, education and conservation organization founded in 1912. Today with over 10,000 members, 14 branches in-state, and one branch for out-of-state members, the CMC is the largest organization of its kind in the Rocky Mountains. *Membership opens the door to:*

Outdoor Recreation: *Over 3100 trips and outings led annually.* Hike, ski, climb, backpack, snowshoe, bicycle, ice skate, travel the world and build firendships that will last a lifetime.

Conservation: *Supporting a mission which treasures our natural environment.* Committed to environmental education, a strong voice on public lands management, trail building and rehabilitation projects.

Outdoor Education: *Schools, seminars, and courses that teach outdoor skills through hands-on activities.* Wilderness trekking, rock climbing, high altitude mountaineering, telemark skiing, backpacking and much more — plus our Youth Education Program *(YEP!)* designed to inspire lifelong stewardship in children and young adults.

Publications: *A wide range of outdoor publications to benefit and inform members.* Trail and Timberline Magazine, twice-a-year Activity Schedule, monthly group newsletters, and 20% discount on titles from CMC Press.

The American Mountaineering Center: *A world-class facility in Golden, Colorado.* Featuring the largest mountaineering library in the western hemisphere, a mountaineering museum, a 300-seat, state-of-the-art auditorium, a conference center, free monthly program nights and a technical climbing wall.

Visit the beautiful American Mountaineering Center!

JOINING IS EASY!

Membership opens the door to:
ADVENTURE!

The Colorado Mountain Club
710 10th St. #200 Golden, CO 80401
(303) 279-3080 1(800) 633-4417
FAX (303) 279-9690
Email: cmcoffice@cmc.org
Website: www.cmc.org

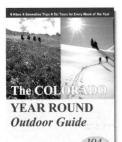